Betty Crocker's
PIE and PASTRY Cookbook

DRAWINGS BY **Bill Goldsmith**
COVER ART BY **Wilson McLean**

Golden Press • New York
Western Publishing Company, Inc.
Racine, Wisconsin

Copyright © 1968, 1972 by General Mills, Inc., Minneapolis, Minn.

All rights reserved. No portion of this book may be reprinted or reproduced in any form or in any manner without the written permission of the publishers, except by a reviewer who wishes to quote brief passages in connection with a review.

Produced in the U.S.A. by Western Publishing Company, Inc.

Library of Congress Catalog Card Number: 68-9287.

SECOND PRINTING, 1972

Table of Contents

What Makes a Pie? 5
    Equipment Notes 7
    Standard Pastry 8
    Oil Pastry 13
    Other Crusts 18
    Freezing Information 20
    Toppings and Glazes 23

Pie as a Preliminary 28

Pie as the Main Event 38

Pie for the Grand Finale 54
    Fruit Pies 56
    Custard, Cream and Meringue Pies 74
    Chiffon Pies 83
    Refrigerated and Frozen Pies 90

Pies from Coast to Coast 98
    South 100
    East 103
    Midwest 108
    West 109

Pie in the Sky 112
    Holiday Pies 115
    Spectaculars 127

Pies in Disguise 140

Index 155

Dear Friend,

According to a fine old American tradition, the mark of a good cook is her ability to turn out a delicious pie—the kind of pie that walks off with honors at every county fair, sells five minutes after any church bake sale opens, or disappears to the last flaky crumb each time it appears on the family dinner table. And that's the kind of pie this book is all about. In the pages that follow you'll find every variety—big pies, little pies; warm pies, chilled pies; production-number pies designed for leisure-time baking and made-in-jigtime pies for practically instant hospitality.

Moreover, these are pies that any cook, novice or near-professional can make to perfection. For the beginner, the rudiments of fine pastry-making are so clearly and completely detailed that even a very first pie is assured of success. For the already proficient cook, there are some brand-new ideas for speeding up tedious procedures (a notable case in point is our streamlined puff pastry). And the step-by-step directions take the touch-and-go aspects out of even the most delicate operations.

We've included dozens and dozens of pies proper, but also added many other members of the pastry family—from tortes, tarts and turnovers to canapés, cobblers and cream puffs.

Homemakers all over the country have tried all of our recipes and given them hearty approval. (They tell us their families and guests have approved the results heartily, too!) So why wait till tomorrow—why not leaf through these pages, pick out a recipe and surprise your family with a gala pie this very evening.

Betty Crocker

What Makes a Pie?

More than any other kind of baking, pie-making is a precision operation. Certain rules apply to it and certain techniques must be well learned and faithfully followed, whether you're making your first pie or your five hundredth. If you're a novice this chapter will initiate you in the time-honored fundamentals and get you off to a banner beginning in your pie-making career. And even if your pies have been winning blue ribbons for years, you'll find some brand-new refinements that will add luster to your reputation.

It goes without saying that the all-important basis of a good pie is tender, flaky pastry. And the open secret of making pastry lies in the way you handle the dough. Pastry must be put together knowledgeably and handled with the deftest of touches. Our step-by-step directions for making pastry are not difficult—but they should be followed meticulously if you want to be assured of a flaky, delicate crust. Our basic recipe is used throughout the book, and you'll be returning to it over and over until it's indelibly etched on your memory. You'll find detailed directions for other standard pastry recipes, too; if you prefer Oil Pastry, for example, turn to page 13.

After a few go-arounds you may want to branch out a bit—try varying the flavor of the pastry with cinnamon or cheese or orange peel or nuts (we've listed eleven piquant alternatives). Or perhaps you'll elect to substitute a Crumb or Cookie Crust or Egg Pastry for Standard Pastry (the directions are all here). Or maybe you'll add artistry to the finished product with fancy fluting, latticework or pastry cutouts. (We show you how—see pages 14–16).

If you have a freezer—you're in clover. You can take advantage of harvest-time fruits and bake pies to enjoy all winter; or you can make several pies at a time and enjoy one on a half hour's notice any time the spirit moves you. Be sure to note our up-to-the-minute information and special instructions for freezing different kinds of pies. We detail the pre-freeze preparation and packaging and the post-freeze thawing and warming—information that will bring your frozen pies to the table exactly as handsome and delicious as if they had been freshly baked only an hour ago.

As a bonus in this chapter, we've assembled a marvelous collection of toppings that add another delicious dimension to pie.

Equipment Notes

Pie Pans: For well-baked, golden brown bottom crusts, use pans made of heat-resistant glass, dull anodized aluminum, enamel or darkened metal. They absorb heat, insuring that crusts brown perfectly. Shiny metal pans reflect heat so bottom crusts are soggy.

Our recipes call for 8-, 9- or 10-inch pans. Check the size printed on the pan or measure across the tops from rim to rim. Depending on the richness of the filling, you can plan on 4 to 6 servings from an 8-inch pie, 6 to 8 servings from a 9-inch pie and 8 to 10 servings from a 10-inch pie.

Pastry Blender: Best way to cut shortening evenly into flour for Standard Pastry unless following new electric mixer method. You can also use 2 table knives in a cutting motion.

Pastry Cloth and Stockinet: These two items are essentials for rolling pastry successfully. Pastry is rolled on the cloth; the stockinet covers the rolling pin. Rub flour well into the cloth, then roll covered rolling pin across cloth to coat it lightly with flour. Both cloth and stockinet add to the ease of rolling and keep the pastry from sticking without picking up excess flour. Available as a set in department stores.

Rolling Pin: Find one that feels right to you—good pie bakers are as particular about their rolling pins as artists are with their brushes. Ball bearings in the pin make rolling much easier.

Pastry Wheel: Cuts pretty, fluted edges for lattice tops, appetizers, tarts and cutouts.

Standard Pastry

Here is our basic pastry recipe, which you will refer to again and again in using this book. (We've also included a condensed version of Standard Pastry on page 12 for the experienced pie-maker.) If you prefer Oil Pastry (page 13), you can substitute it in any recipe that calls for Standard Pastry.

One-crust Pie

8- OR 9-INCH

1 cup all-purpose flour*
½ teaspoon salt
⅓ cup plus 1 tablespoon shortening
  or ⅓ cup lard
2 to 3 tablespoons cold water

10-INCH

1⅓ cups all-purpose flour*
½ teaspoon salt
½ cup shortening or ¼ cup plus
  3 tablespoons lard
3 to 4 tablespoons cold water

Two-crust Pie

8- OR 9-INCH

2 cups all-purpose flour*
1 teaspoon salt
⅔ cup plus 2 tablespoons shortening
  or ⅔ cup lard
4 to 5 tablespoons cold water

10-INCH

2⅔ cups all-purpose flour*
1 teaspoon salt
1 cup shortening or ¾ cup plus
  2 tablespoons lard
7 to 8 tablespoons cold water

*If using self-rising flour, omit salt. Pie crusts made with self-rising flour differ in flavor and texture from those made with plain flour.

Standard Method

Measure flour and salt into mixing bowl. With pastry blender, using an up-and-down chopping motion, thoroughly cut in shortening until particles are size of tiny peas.

Sprinkle in water, *1 tablespoon* at a time, tossing with a fork after each addition. Mix lightly until all flour is moistened and dough almost cleans side of bowl (1 to 2 teaspoons water can be added if needed).

Gather dough together with hands; press firmly into a ball—handle like a snowball.

Electric Mixer Method

Measure flour, salt and shortening into large mixer bowl. Mix at low speed 1 minute, scraping bowl constantly with rubber scraper.

Add water and continue mixing, scraping bowl constantly, until flour is moistened and dough *begins* to gather into beaters—about 10 seconds for regular flour, 1 minute for quick-mixing flour.

Gather dough together with hands; press firmly into a ball.

10 STANDARD PASTRY

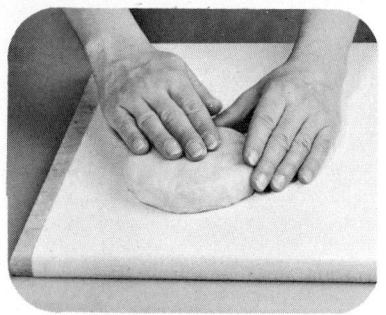 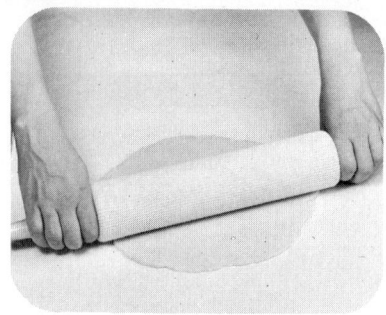 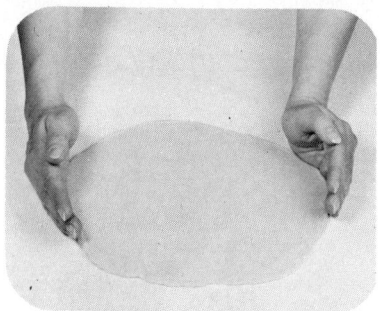

For one-crust pie, shape dough into flattened round on lightly floured cloth-covered board. For two-crust pie, divide dough in half; place each half cut side down and flatten into a round.

With floured stockinet-covered rolling pin, roll dough from center to outside evenly in all directions. Lift rolling pin at edge of dough to prevent outer edge from becoming too thin.

Keep circular by pushing edge in gently with slightly cupped hands. If edge begins to break or crack, pinch together immediately.

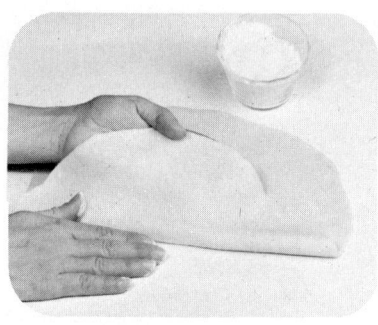 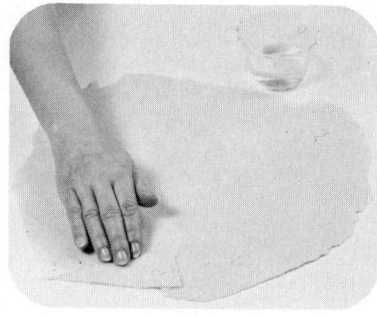 

Lift dough occasionally to make sure it is not sticking. If it does stick, carefully lift dough and rub a little extra flour into cloth.

If patching is necessary, cut a piece of pastry from edge to fit hole. Moisten edge of area to be patched and press piece of pastry into place.

Roll dough 2 inches larger all around than inverted pie pan. (Dough should be about 1/8 inch thick.) If necessary, trim uneven edge.

 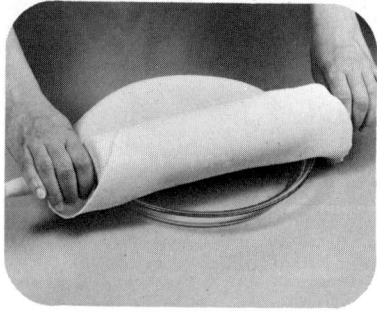 

Lift circle carefully to pan by *either* of the following methods:
(a) Fold pastry in quarters and place in pan with point in center; unfold.

(b) Roll pastry around rolling pin and unroll into pan.

Ease dough gently into pie pan and toward center by pressing with fingertips. This helps prevent stretching, which causes shrinkage of pastry.

STANDARD PASTRY 11

For One-crust Pie

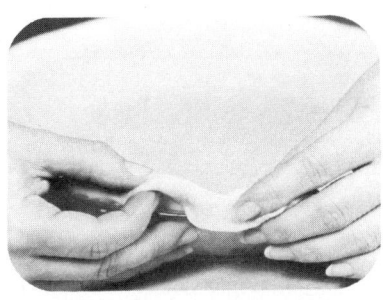

If necessary, trim overhanging edge of pastry so it is 1 inch from rim of pan. Make edge even with pan by folding and rolling pastry under. Flute (page 14).

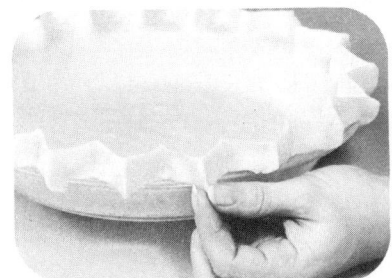

To help prevent shrinkage, hook fluting points under pan rim. Fill and bake as directed in recipe.

For Baked Pie Shell

Follow directions for one-crust pie (left) except—prick bottom and side thoroughly with fork to prevent puffing while shell bakes. Bake at 475° for 8 to 10 minutes. Cool before filling.

For Two-crust Pie

Turn desired filling into pastry-lined pan. If necessary, trim overhanging edge of pastry so it is ½ inch from rim of pan.

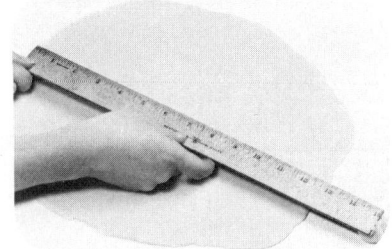

Roll second half of dough 2 inches larger all around than inverted pie pan. (Dough should be about ⅛ inch thick.) If necessary, trim uneven edge. Lift circle carefully to pan by *either* of the following methods:

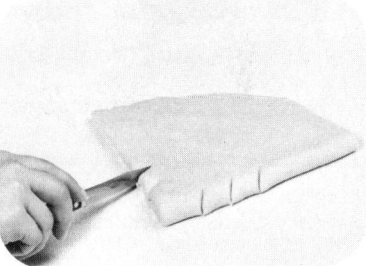

(a) Fold in quarters; cut slits so steam can escape. (Or cut special design in pastry before folding—see page 16.) Carefully place folded pastry over filling and unfold.

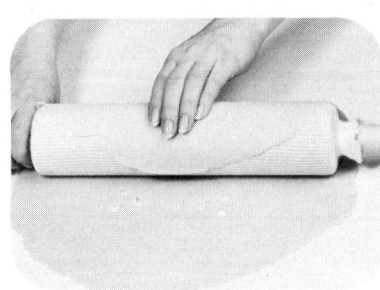

(b) Cut slits or special design in pastry; roll around rolling pin and unroll over filling.

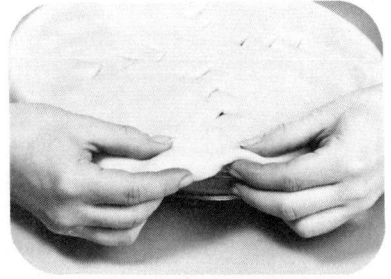

If necessary, trim overhanging edge of pastry 1 inch from rim of pan. Fold and roll edge of top pastry under edge of lower pastry on rim. Press edge with fingers so it is thoroughly sealed. Flute (page 14).

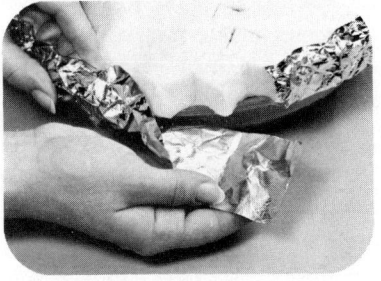

Cover edge with a 2- to 3-inch strip of aluminum foil to prevent excessive browning. Bake as directed in recipe. Remove foil last 15 minutes of baking.

Standard Pastry—Condensed Method

One-crust Pie

8- OR 9-INCH

1 cup all-purpose flour*
½ teaspoon salt
⅓ cup plus 1 tablespoon shortening or ⅓ cup lard
2 to 3 tablespoons cold water

10-INCH

1⅓ cups all-purpose flour*
½ teaspoon salt
½ cup shortening or ¼ cup plus 3 tablespoons lard
3 to 4 tablespoons cold water

Two-crust Pie

8- OR 9-INCH

2 cups all-purpose flour*
1 teaspoon salt
⅔ cup plus 2 tablespoons shortening or ⅔ cup lard
4 to 5 tablespoons cold water

10-INCH

2⅔ cups all-purpose flour*
1 teaspoon salt
1 cup shortening or ¾ cup plus 2 tablespoons lard
7 to 8 tablespoons cold water

Measure flour and salt into mixing bowl. Cut in shortening thoroughly. Sprinkle in water, 1 tablespoon at a time, mixing with fork until all flour is moistened and dough almost cleans side of bowl (1 to 2 teaspoons water can be added if needed). Gather dough into ball; shape into flattened round on lightly floured cloth-covered board. (For Two-crust Pie, divide in half and shape into 2 flattened rounds.) With floured stockinet-covered rolling pin, roll dough 2 inches larger than inverted pie pan. Fold pastry into quarters; unfold and ease into pan.

For One-crust Pie, trim overhanging edge of pastry 1 inch from rim of pan. Fold and roll pastry under, even with pan, and flute. Fill and bake as directed in recipe. For Baked Pie Shell, prick bottom and side thoroughly with fork. Bake at 475° for 8 to 10 minutes.

For Two-crust Pie, turn desired filling into pastry-lined pie pan. Trim overhanging edge of pastry ½ inch from rim of pan. Roll second round of dough. Fold into quarters; cut slits so steam can escape. Place over filling and unfold. Trim overhanging edge of pastry 1 inch from rim of pan. Fold and roll top edge under lower edge, pressing on rim to seal. Flute. Cover edge with 2- to 3-inch strip of aluminum foil to prevent excessive browning. Bake as directed in recipe. Remove foil last 15 minutes of baking.

If using self-rising flour, omit salt. Pie crusts made with self-rising flour differ in flavor and texture from those made with plain flour.

Oil Pastry

8- OR 9-INCH ONE-CRUST PIE
1 cup plus 2 tablespoons
 all-purpose flour*
½ teaspoon salt
⅓ cup salad oil
2 to 3 tablespoons cold
 water

**10-INCH ONE-CRUST PIE OR
8- OR 9-INCH TWO-CRUST PIE**
1¾ cups all-purpose flour*
1 teaspoon salt
½ cup salad oil
3 to 4 tablespoons cold
 water

10-INCH TWO-CRUST PIE
2⅔ cups all-purpose flour*
1½ teaspoons salt
¾ cup salad oil
4 to 5 tablespoons cold
 water

Measure flour and salt into mixing bowl. Add oil; mix with fork until particles are size of small peas.

Sprinkle in water, *1 tablespoon* at a time, mixing with fork until flour is moistened and dough almost cleans side of bowl (1 to 2 tablespoons oil can be added if needed). Gather dough together with hands; press firmly into a ball.

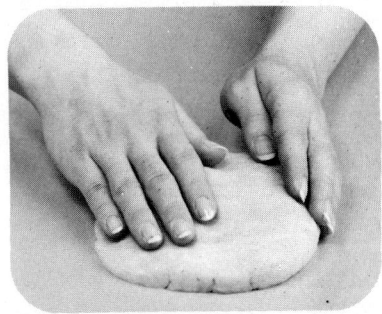

For one-crust pie, shape dough into flattened round. For two-crust pie, divide dough in half; place each half cut side down and flatten into a round.

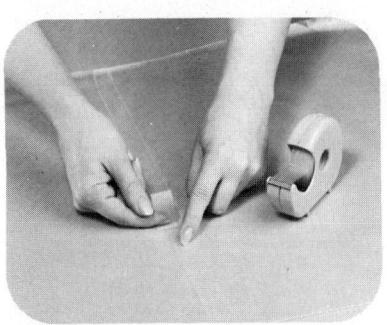

Place flattened round between two 15-inch strips of waxed paper (for 9- and 10-inch pies, tape two pieces of paper together to make wider strips).

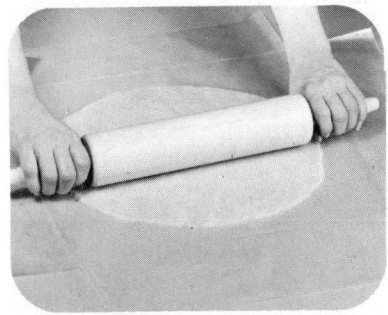

Wipe table with damp cloth to prevent paper from slipping. Roll pastry 2 inches larger than inverted pie pan. Peel off top paper.

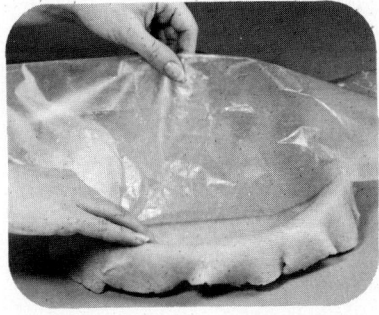

Place pastry paper side up in pan. Peel off paper. Ease pastry loosely into pan. Trim and complete as for Standard Pastry (pages 10–11) except— Baked Pie Shell requires 12 to 15 minutes of baking at 475°. Roll top crust in same way as bottom crust. Cut slits after peeling off top paper; place over filling in pan. Trim and complete as indicated on page 11.

For best results, use only regular all-purpose flour. If using self-rising flour, omit salt. Pie crusts made with self-rising flour differ in flavor and texture from those made with plain flour.

Edges

Make pies picture pretty with an unusual fluted edge. Unless recipe notes otherwise for a specific edge, always fold and roll edges of pastry under to seal and build up the rim before fluting.

Fork: Flatten pastry on rim of pan or trim overhang even with edge of pan. Press around edge with tines of fork. Dip fork in flour to prevent sticking. For variety, use teaspoon, curved side down, to mark edge.

Pinch: Place right index finger on inside of rim, left thumb and index finger on outside of pastry. Pinch pastry into V-shape; sharpen points by pinching firmly.

Rope: Place thumb on edge at an angle. Pinch dough between index finger and thumb by pressing and twisting index finger knuckle toward thumb. Repeat at same angle around pie. To sharpen edges, go around a second time.

Ruffle: Place left thumb and index finger ½ inch apart on pastry rim. With right index finger pull pastry between fingers and toward the outside of pie.

Spoon Scallop: Trim overhanging edge of pastry so it is ¼ inch from rim of pan. Cut a scalloped edge with tip of teaspoon. If desired, mark scallops with fork.

Cutouts: For one-crust pie, trim overhang even with pan; on two-crust pie, flatten pastry on rim of pan. With tiny cookie cutter, thimble or bottlecap, cut ¾-inch circles, leaves, stars, hearts, etc., from pastry scraps. Moisten rim and place cutouts on rim, slightly overlapping. Press into place.

Lattice Top

Prepare pastry as directed for Two-crust Pie (page 11) except—leave 1-inch overhang on lower crust. After rolling circle for top crust, cut circle into strips, about ½ inch wide. A pastry wheel can be used for more decorative strips.

Place 5 to 7 strips (depending on size of pie) across filling in pie pan.

Weave a cross strip through center by first folding back every other strip going the other way. Continue weaving until lattice is complete, folding back alternate strips each time a cross strip is added. (To save time, do not weave strips. Simply lay second half of strips across first strips.) Trim ends of strips.

Fold trimmed edge of lower crust over ends of strips, building up a high edge. (A juicy fruit pie is more likely to bubble over when topped by lattice than when the juices are held in by a top crust. Be sure to build up a high pastry edge.) Seal and flute.

Lattice Variations

Diamond: Follow directions for Lattice Top (above) except—weave second half of the strips diagonally across first strips.

Twister: Follow directions for Lattice Top (above) or Diamond variation (left) except—twist strips as they are placed on the filling.

Spiral: Follow directions for Lattice Top (above) except—beginning with one strip and from center of pie, twist strip and place in a spiral on pie, adding strips as needed by moistening ends and pinching together. Moisten trimmed edge of lower crust; place tightly twisted pastry strip around edge, pressing to seal.

PASTRY CUTOUTS

Leftover pastry makes a pie topper that's an eye stopper. Try it with your next pie.

Press leftover pastry into a ball. (If extensive designs are desired, make additional pastry as directed for 8- or 9-inch One-crust Pie, page 8.) Roll 1/8 inch thick. Cut out designs, using cookie cutters or by cutting around a pattern.

Place designs on ungreased baking sheet. Insert a wooden pick in each cutout or leave plain. If desired, paint cutouts with Egg Yolk Paint (below). Bake at 425° for 6 to 8 minutes or until very lightly browned. Place on or insert in top of finished pie.

Egg Yolk Paint

Beat one egg yolk; divide among several small custard cups and mix desired food coloring into each cup. Use a small paintbrush to apply each color.

PASTRY SILHOUETTES

Roll pastry for top crust of a Two-crust Pie as directed except—do not cut slits. Cut top crust in one of the following ways:
1. With cookie cutter or pattern, cut out design from center of crust.
2. Cut slits to form an initial, 2 to 3 inches high, to represent the flavor of the pie.
3. Cut out a fruit shape to represent the flavor of the pie.

Place pastry over filling in pie pan; seal and flute. Bake as directed in recipe.

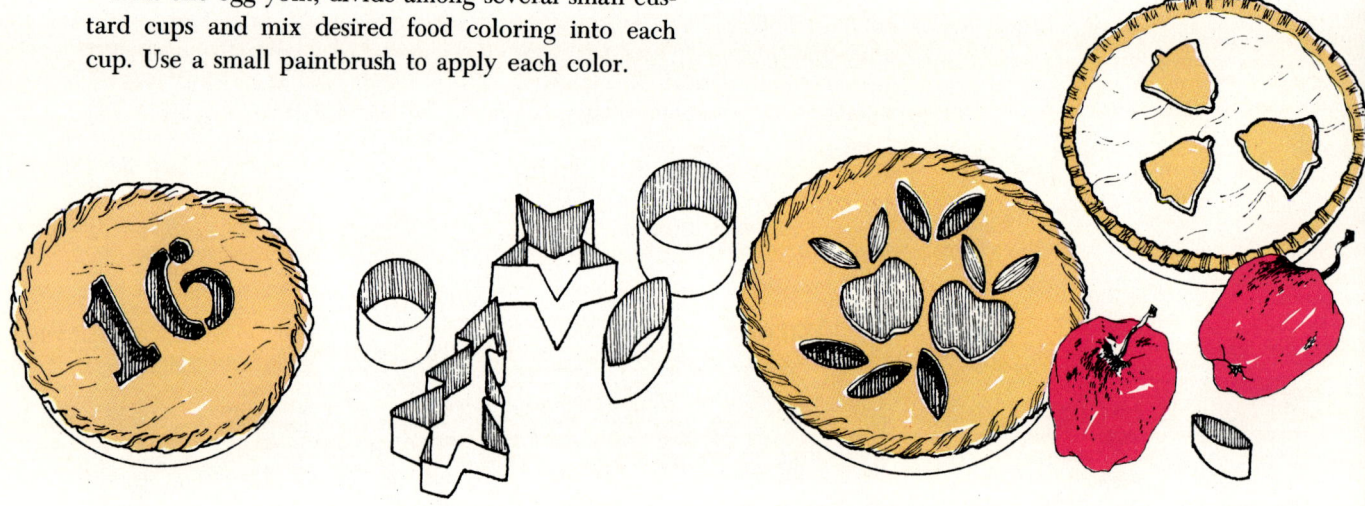

LEFTOVER PASTRY SNACKS

Turn pastry scraps into snacks; it's as easy as pie.

Heat oven to 475°. Gather leftover pastry into a ball; shape into a flattened round. Roll 1/8 inch thick. Complete as directed below or at right. Place on ungreased baking sheet; bake 8 to 10 minutes.

Perky Pastries: Cut pastry into desired shapes. Prick each and sprinkle with sesame or poppy seed, seasoned or garlic salt, cinnamon and sugar, or grated cheese and paprika. Bake as directed above.

Jelly Gems: Cut pastry into rounds. Place a small amount of jelly on center of half the circles. Top each with a remaining circle which has a hole cut in the center. Seal edges of rounds together. Bake as directed at left.

Snack Stacks: Cut pastry into desired shapes. Prick each and bake as directed at left. Cool. Fill each two shapes with any flavor canned frosting.

Pastry Variations

Prepare Pastry for 8- or 9-inch One-crust Pie (page 8) or as directed on a pie crust mix package except—stir into flour or dry mix one of the following. Double the amount for an 8- or 9-inch Two-crust Pie (page 8).

NAME	ADDITION	SUGGESTED USES
Celery Seed	1 teaspoon celery seed	Yankee Doodle Pie (page 41)
Cheese	½ cup shredded Cheddar cheese	Appetizers (pages 30, 31) Apple Pie (page 68) Pear Pie (page 61) Old-fashioned Mince Pie (page 122)
Cinnamon	1 teaspoon cinnamon	Apple Pie (page 68) Pear Pie (page 61) Blueberry Pie (page 56)
Colored	3 drops food coloring added to the water	Baked Alaska Spumoni Pie (page 131)
Cornmeal	¼ cup cornmeal (increase water to 3 tablespoons)	Sombrero Pie (page 51)
Dill	1 teaspoon dill weed	Homespun Sausage Pie (page 42)
Lemon	1½ teaspoons finely shredded peel	Lemon Meringue Pie (pages 80–81)
Nut	2 tablespoons finely chopped nuts	Frosty Pumpkin Pie (page 117)
Orange	1½ teaspoons finely shredded peel	Orange-glazed Cherry Pie (page 58)
Poppy Seed	1 teaspoon poppy seed	Tuna Pie (page 40) Ham Stacks (page 41)
Sesame Seed	1 tablespoon toasted sesame seed	Chicken Dinner Pie (page 46) Homespun Sausage Pie (page 42)

Other Crusts

EGG PASTRY

A beautiful golden color and especially easy to handle!

2 cups all-purpose flour*
1 teaspoon salt
⅔ cup plus 2 tablespoons shortening
1 egg
2 to 3 tablespoons cold water

Stir flour and salt together in mixing bowl. Cut in shortening thoroughly. Beat egg slightly; beat in water and pour into flour mixture. Mix with fork until flour is moistened. Gather into a ball. Roll and finish as for Standard Pastry (pages 10–11). Bake pie shells at 475° for 12 to 15 minutes. Bake two-crust pie as directed in recipe. *Enough for one 9-inch Two-crust Pie or two 9-inch One-crust Pies.*

°If using self-rising flour, omit salt.

TOASTED COCONUT CRUST

An elegant crust for chiffon or ice-cream fillings.

Heat oven to 325°. Spread 3 tablespoons soft butter or margarine on bottom and side of 9-inch pie pan. With fingers, press 1½ cups (3½-ounce can) flaked coconut firmly and evenly against bottom and side of pie pan. Bake 15 to 20 minutes or until golden brown. Cool.

SHORT PIE CRUST

A rich cookie-like crust; superexcellent when filled with ice cream and fresh fruit.

Heat oven to 450°. In small mixing bowl or 9-inch pie pan, combine 1 cup buttermilk baking mix and ¼ cup soft butter or margarine. Add 3 tablespoons boiling water; stir vigorously until dough forms a ball and cleans the bowl. Dough will be puffy and soft. With floured hands, pat dough evenly against bottom and side of pie pan. Flute edge if desired. Bake 8 to 10 minutes. Cool.

COOKIE CRUST

A crisp buttery crust, good with refrigerated, chiffon or cream fillings. If using with ice cream, fill just before serving.

¾ cup all-purpose flour*
6 tablespoons soft butter or margarine
3 tablespoons confectioners' sugar
¼ teaspoon vanilla

Heat oven to 400°. With hands mix all ingredients until crumbly. Press mixture firmly and evenly against bottom and side of 8- or 9-inch pie pan. Bake 10 to 15 minutes or until lightly browned. Cool.

°If using quick-mixing flour, add 1 tablespoon milk. Do not use self-rising flour in this recipe.

Variations

Nut Crust: Follow recipe for Cookie Crust (above) except—add ¼ cup finely chopped nuts.

Butter-crunch Crust: Follow recipe for Cookie Crust (above) except—substitute 3 tablespoons brown sugar for the confectioners' sugar; omit the vanilla and add ¼ cup finely chopped nuts.

CHOCOLATE COCONUT CRUST

2 squares (1 ounce each) unsweetened chocolate
2 tablespoons butter or margarine
2 tablespoons milk
⅔ cup confectioners' sugar
1½ cups (3½-ounce can) flaked coconut

Butter 9-inch pie pan. In small saucepan melt chocolate and butter over low heat. Add milk, sugar and coconut; mix thoroughly. Press mixture firmly and evenly against bottom and side of pie pan. Refrigerate 2 hours. (When you are ready to serve pie, place it on a damp, hot cloth. This releases crust from the pan, and cutting is easier.)

CRUNCHY NUT CRUST

Use your favorite kind of nuts to make this delightful crunch crust. It's especially good with an ice-cream filling as a contrasting texture.

Heat oven to 450°. Butter 9-inch pie pan. Mix 1½ cups ground nuts, 3 tablespoons sugar and 2 tablespoons soft butter or margarine. Press mixture firmly and evenly against bottom and side of pie pan. Bake 6 to 8 minutes. Cool.

MERINGUE PIE SHELL

Heat oven to 275°. Generously butter 9-inch pie pan. In small mixer bowl, beat 2 egg whites (¼ to ⅓ cup) and ¼ teaspoon cream of tartar until frothy. Beat in ½ cup sugar, 1 tablespoon at a time; continue beating until stiff and glossy. *Do not underbeat.* Pile into prepared pan, pressing meringue up against side of pan. Bake 45 minutes. Turn off oven; leave meringue in oven with door closed 45 minutes. Remove from oven; finish cooling away from draft.

Crumb Crusts

For praiseworthy pies every time, pair a crunchy crumb crust with a fluffy chiffon or velvety cream or ice-cream filling.

NAME	CRUMBS	SUGAR	BUTTER OR MARGARINE	BAKING TEMPERATURE AND TIME
GRAHAM CRACKER 8-inch pie	1¼ cups (about 16 crackers)	2 tablespoons	¼ cup, melted	350° 10 minutes
9-inch pie	1½ cups (about 20 crackers)	3 tablespoons	⅓ cup, melted	350° 10 minutes
10-inch pie	1¾ cups (about 24 crackers)	¼ cup	½ cup, melted	350° 15 minutes
COOKIE (vanilla or chocolate wafers or gingersnaps) 9-inch pie	1½ cups		¼ cup, melted	350° 10 minutes
PEANUT BUTTER 9-inch pie	1½ cups graham cracker crumbs (about 20 crackers)	3 tablespoons	¼ cup, melted with ¼ cup creamy peanut butter	350° 10 minutes

Heat oven to 350°. Mix crumbs, sugar and butter. If desired, reserve 2 to 3 tablespoons crumb mixture for topping. Press remaining mixture firmly and evenly against bottom and side of pie pan. Bake as directed in the chart above. Cool.

Freezing Information

Pie dough, pie shells, fruit and chiffon pies all freeze well. And what a joy this is to a homemaker who wishes to capitalize on fresh fruit in season or to bake party pies ahead of time.

Packaging and wrapping materials are all-important for freezing success. This means using plastic wrap, heavy-duty (or freezer style) aluminum foil or polyethylene bags, any of which are moisture-vapor-proof and will protect the product from the drying air in the freezer. Seal each package securely. Use either freezer tape or a tight double fold (for foil) or wire ties (for bags). Packages should be labeled with the contents and the date.

Always arrange your freezer so pies frozen first are the ones to be used first. Chiffon pies are delicate even when frozen so give them plenty of room in the freezer.

If your supply of pie pans is limited, use aluminum foil pie pans. Foil pans are shiny and reflect heat, so these pies should be baked on a baking sheet for proper browning of bottom crusts.

Fruit pies can be frozen either baked or unbaked—but we recommend that they be baked. A baked fruit pie that has been frozen needs only to be "freshened" by heating in the oven. However, an unbaked frozen pie needs special care. Excessive juice will develop during freezing and thawing of the pie; to compensate for this, the thickener should be increased in the filling. A longer baking time is needed because of the frozen fruit filling and added thickener. Unfortunately, this frequently results in an overbrowned top crust.

The following information is a guide to the successful freezing—and thawing—of pastry and pies.

PIE SHELLS

General Information: Can be frozen baked or unbaked (if baked, cool first); wrap and freeze.

Defrosting: *Baked*—Remove wrap; thaw at room temperature about 15 minutes *or* in 350° oven 6 to 10 minutes. *Unbaked*—Remove wrap. Place directly in 475° oven; bake 8 to 10 minutes.

Storage Time: *Baked*—4 to 6 months. *Unbaked*—2 to 3 months.

PIE DOUGH

General Information: Form into ball; wrap and freeze. *Or* roll pastry into desired size circle; place on sheet of freezer paper (several circles can be stacked with a layer of paper between each). Wrap and freeze.

Defrosting: Thaw. Ball of dough will take 2 to 4 hours, depending on size; rolled circles will thaw in 10 to 15 minutes. Complete as directed in recipe.

Storage Time: 2 to 3 months.

PUMPKIN PIES

General Information: Freezing after baking is the preferred method to prevent a soggy bottom crust.

Defrosting: Thaw as for baked Two-crust Fruit Pies (page 21).

Storage Time: 4 to 6 months.

CHIFFON PIES

General Information: Prepare as directed in recipe. Freeze and then wrap.

Defrosting: Remove wrap; thaw 2 to 4 hours or overnight in refrigerator.

Storage Time: 1 month.

BAKED ALASKA PIES

General Information: Meringue can be placed on ice cream anytime within 24 hours before serving; freeze but do not wrap.

Defrosting: Bake as directed in recipe.

Storage Time: 1 day.

TWO-CRUST FRUIT PIES

General Information: Freezing after baking is preferred because pies frozen unbaked tend to have soggy bottom crusts. If pies are frozen before baking, however, increase thickener by 1 to 3 tablespoons. Use cornstarch or tapioca for thickening brightly colored fruit pies.° (Flour sometimes gives a gray color to the frozen fruit.) Fresh apples and peaches should be treated to prevent discoloration.°°

°*2 tablespoons flour is the equivalent of 1 tablespoon cornstarch.*

°°*Slice peeled apples (up to ½ bushel) directly into mixture of 1 teaspoon sodium bisulfite dissolved in 1 gallon cold water. Let stand 5 minutes; drain. For peaches, combine ½ teaspoon ascorbic acid with the sugar before adding to fruit. Or use a commercial preparation as directed on package.*

Defrosting: *Baked*—Let stand wrapped at room temperature 30 minutes. Remove wrap. (Place on baking sheet if using aluminum foil pans.) Heat in 350° oven 30 minutes. Remove from oven; let stand at least 15 minutes before serving. *Unbaked*—Remove from wrap. (Place on baking sheet if using aluminum foil pans.) Bake as directed in recipe except—increase baking time 10 to 20 minutes. (Fruit pies should bubble in center when done.)

Storage Time: *Baked*—4 to 6 months. *Unbaked*—2 to 3 months.

DUMPLINGS

General Information: Not recommended because freezing often results in a very soggy product.

CREAM AND CUSTARD PIES

General Information: Tend to weep and separate, so freezing is not recommended.

PIE FILLINGS

General Information: Frozen pies are bulky, so if freezer space is limited, the fillings can be frozen without the crust.
Fruit—Combine fruit and other ingredients as directed in recipe (1 to 3 tablespoons additional thickener may be needed). Fresh apples and peaches should be treated to prevent discoloration.° Pour filling into rigid container; freeze. *Or* use a foil-lined pie pan: Line pie pan with heavy-duty aluminum foil so it extends 5 to 6 inches beyond rim; pour in filling. Loosely cover filling with foil liner; freeze. When filling has frozen, seal foil liner and remove from pie pan.
Pumpkin—Combine ingredients as directed in recipe; pour into rigid container and freeze.

°*Slice peeled apples (up to ½ bushel) directly into mixture of 1 teaspoon sodium bisulfite dissolved in 1 gallon cold water. Let stand 5 minutes; drain. For peaches, combine ½ teaspoon ascorbic acid with the sugar before adding to fruit. Or use a commercial preparation as directed on package.*

Defrosting: Thaw or partially thaw; place in pastry-lined pie pan and finish as directed in recipe.

Storage Time: *Fruit*—10 to 12 months. *Pumpkin*—4 to 6 months.

CREAM PUFFS OR STREAMLINED PUFF PASTRY

General Information: Freeze after baking, but do not fill, frost or glaze. Pack in rigid containers to prevent breaking.

Defrosting: Thaw wrapped at room temperature 20 to 30 minutes *or* heat unwrapped in 325° oven 3 to 5 minutes.

Storage Time: 4 to 6 months.

MAIN DISH PIES

General Information: Can be frozen baked or unbaked with the exception of those having a bottom crust. These are best when frozen baked (this prevents a soggy bottom crust). Also, biscuit toppings are best when frozen baked.

Undercook filling ingredients slightly so they will not overcook when reheated or baked later. Cut potatoes into small cubes. Use shallow baking dishes to insure thorough reheating.

To prevent contamination, food should be cooled quickly, wrapped and frozen. If freezing only a few pies at one time, cool slightly on wire rack at room temperature. Place in freezer uncovered, freeze and then wrap. (Don't put too many warm pies in the freezer at one time; they will raise the temperature of the freezer.)

Defrosting: *Baked*—To reduce baking time of large dishes, partially thaw in refrigerator. Bake in 350° oven until center bubbles—time will vary with the type of food and container. *Unbaked*—Follow directions for thawing unbaked fruit pies (page 21).

Storage Time: *Baked*—3 to 6 months. *Unbaked*—2 to 3 months.

COBBLERS

General Information: Can be frozen baked or unbaked. If freezing unbaked, fresh apples and peaches should be treated to prevent discoloration.° Biscuit toppings are best when frozen baked.

°*Slice peeled apples (up to ½ bushel) directly into mixture of 1 teaspoon sodium bisulfite dissolved in 1 gallon cold water. Let stand 5 minutes; drain. For peaches, combine ½ teaspoon ascorbic acid with the sugar before adding to fruit. Or use a commercial preparation as directed on package.*

Defrosting: *Baked*—Let stand wrapped at room temperature 30 to 45 minutes. (Use the longer time for larger pans.) Remove wrap. Heat in 375° oven 30 to 45 minutes. Remove from oven; let stand 15 minutes before serving. *Unbaked*—Remove from wrap. Bake as directed in recipe except—increase baking time 10 to 20 minutes. (Fruit will bubble in center when done.)

Storage Time: *Baked*—4 to 6 months. *Unbaked*—2 to 3 months.

Shortcuts To Pie Making With A Mix

Many homemakers prefer the convenience and simplicity of a pie crust mix.

The mixes contain quality ingredients specially selected for flaky, tender pastry. The pastry is easy to make because the ingredients are already accurately measured and blended for you. For perfect results, follow the directions on the package carefully. Roll out the pastry as you do Standard Pastry, using a stockinet-covered rolling pin and a lightly floured pastry cloth.

Toppings and Glazes

If pie unadorned is a treat in itself, pie plus a topping or glaze is twice as nice. So don't always stop at the crustline—occasionally consider a bit of superstructure. Of course you're familiar with the delights of a foamy topping of swirled meringue or great dollops of whipped cream. But for a change of pace, why not a jewellike covering of fresh fruit, or a ravishingly rich frosting of fudge sauce, or great spoonfuls of brandy-flavored hard sauce? Why not gild the lily with Spicy Sour Cream Topping, melting marvelously over warm apple pie; or Heavenly Topping, whipped cream flavored with crème de cacao, heaped on banana cream. And even if there's a weight watcher at your table he or she needn't forego the treat. Our Low-calorie Whipped Topping "costs" just seven calories per tablespoon.

STRAWBERRY SAUCE

Now that strawberries are available almost year 'round in supermarkets, this sauce can be enjoyed anytime; it's great on ice-cream pies.

Crush 2 cups washed hulled strawberries; stir in 3 tablespoons sugar. *Makes about 2 cups.*

OLD-FASHIONED LEMON SAUCE

Make this tangy sauce in minutes—especially good with blueberry and mincemeat pies.

1 cup sugar
½ cup butter or margarine
¼ cup water
1 egg, well beaten
¾ teaspoon grated lemon peel
3 tablespoons lemon juice

In saucepan combine all ingredients. Heat to boiling over medium heat, stirring constantly. Serve warm or cool. Store sauce in covered container in refrigerator. *Makes 1⅓ cups.*

DARK SWEET CHERRY SAUCE

Drain 1 can (1 pound) pitted dark sweet cherries, reserving syrup. Mix 1 tablespoon sugar and 1 tablespoon cornstarch in saucepan. Stir in ½ cup reserved syrup. Cook, stirring constantly, until mixture thickens and boils. Boil and stir 1 minute. Cool; stir in 1½ teaspoons rum flavoring and the cherries.

FLAMING ORANGE SAUCE

¼ cup butter
⅓ cup brown sugar (packed)
1 teaspoon grated orange peel
2 cans (11 ounces each) mandarin orange segments, drained
¼ cup white rum*

In chafing dish or small skillet, heat butter, sugar and orange peel over medium heat, stirring constantly, until mixture is bubbly. Add orange segments; cook about 2 minutes or until heated through. Heat rum *just* until warm; pour over orange segments, but *do not stir*. Flame immediately; stir and serve. *Makes 2 cups.*

*If desired, omit rum; do not flame sauce.

CINNAMON BLUEBERRY SAUCE

Serve warm over peach pie à la mode . . . a marvelous combination of flavors.

1 cup fresh or frozen blueberries
2 tablespoons water
2 tablespoons sugar
1 tablespoon lemon juice
1 teaspoon cornstarch
¼ teaspoon cinnamon

In saucepan combine all ingredients. Heat to boiling, stirring constantly. Reduce heat; simmer 5 minutes, stirring occasionally. Serve warm or cool. *Makes about ⅔ cup.*

BROWNED BUTTER-RUM SAUCE

The delicate flavor of this buttery sauce is especially complementary to chocolate- or coffee-flavored pies.

¼ cup butter
½ cup confectioners' sugar
2 tablespoons maple syrup
¼ cup water
1 teaspoon rum or ½ teaspoon rum flavoring
½ cup chopped nuts

In small saucepan brown butter over medium heat. Cool. Add sugar gradually, mixing until smooth. Stir in syrup and water. Heat to boiling; boil and stir 1 minute. Cool slightly. (Sauce will become thicker when cool.) Stir in rum and nuts.

Makes about 1 cup.

BUTTERSCOTCH SAUCE

Try this favorite ice-cream topper on apple or banana cream pie.

1½ cups brown sugar (packed)
½ cup light corn syrup
¼ cup butter or margarine
½ cup whipping cream
1 teaspoon vanilla

In saucepan heat sugar, syrup and butter to boiling over low heat, stirring constantly. Remove from heat; stir in cream and vanilla. Serve warm or cool; stir with fork before serving. *Makes 1 cup.*

TANGY MINCEMEAT SAUCE

Enhance your favorite apple or pumpkin pie with this tasty topper.

Heat 1 cup prepared mincemeat and ½ cup port or ½ cup cranberry cocktail. Serve warm. Store sauce in covered container in refrigerator.

Makes about 1½ cups.

HARD SAUCE

This rich topping smoothly complements any warm fruit pie, but it's almost a "must" for mince or raisin.

Beat ½ cup soft butter in small mixer bowl at high speed until very creamy, fluffy and light in color, about 5 minutes. Gradually beat in 1 cup confectioners' sugar. Stir in 2 teaspoons vanilla or ½ teaspoon rum flavoring. Chill about 1 hour. *Makes 1 cup.*

Variations

Fluffy Hard Sauce: Follow recipe for Hard Sauce (above) except—beat in 1 egg white with the sugar. Sprinkle with nutmeg; chill.

Orange Hard Sauce: Follow recipe for Hard Sauce (above) except—omit vanilla and stir in 1 teaspoon grated orange peel and 1 tablespoon orange juice.

Brandied Hard Sauce: Follow recipe for Hard Sauce (above) except—omit vanilla and stir in 1 tablespoon brandy.

FUDGE SAUCE

Probably the most popular of all sauces. Our rich and thick version is perfect for ice-cream pies.

1 can (14½ ounces) evaporated milk
2 cups sugar
4 squares (1 ounce each) unsweetened chocolate or 4 envelopes (1 ounce each) premelted unsweetened chocolate
¼ cup butter or margarine
1 teaspoon vanilla
½ teaspoon salt

In saucepan heat milk and sugar to a rolling boil, stirring constantly; boil and stir 1 minute. Reduce heat to medium. Add chocolate, stirring until melted. Keep over heat and beat with spoon until smooth. Remove from heat; stir in butter, vanilla and salt. Serve warm or cool. Store sauce in covered container in refrigerator; to serve, reheat over low heat, stirring constantly. *Makes 3 cups.*

LEMON GLAZE

Created especially for mince pie; try it on blueberry, too.

Mix 1 cup confectioners' sugar, 2 teaspoons grated lemon peel and 2 tablespoons lemon juice until smooth. Spread over top of warm pie.

ORANGE GLAZE

Try this tangy glaze on any tart fruit pie with a top crust—especially recommended for cherry.

Blend ½ cup confectioners' sugar, 2 teaspoons finely shredded orange peel and 1 tablespoon orange juice. Spread over top of warm pie.

CRUNCHY PECAN GLAZE

Spread this golden glaze over an apple, peach or pineapple pie.

In small saucepan combine ¼ cup brown sugar (packed), ⅓ cup chopped pecans and 2 tablespoons light cream. Cook over low heat, stirring constantly, until of glaze consistency. Spread over top of warm pie.

VANILLA GLAZE

Add the cool, special look of a vanilla glaze to your favorite two-crust pie.

Mix 1 cup confectioners' sugar and about 2 tablespoons light cream until smooth. Spread over top of warm pie.

WHIPPED CREAM CHEESE

Use this to garnish your favorite fruit glacé pie.

With fork beat 1 package (3 ounces) cream cheese, softened, and 1 tablespoon milk until fluffy.

LOW-CALORIE WHIPPED TOPPING

A dream come true for weight watchers . . . only 7 calories per tablespoon.

½ cup nonfat dry milk
½ cup iced water
1 egg white
1 tablespoon lemon juice
¼ cup sugar
½ teaspoon vanilla

In small mixer bowl whip nonfat dry milk, iced water and egg white 3 minutes on high speed. Add lemon juice; whip 1 minute longer on high speed. Gradually add sugar and vanilla; blend on low speed 1 minute. Serve immediately. Leftover topping can be frozen for later use as a frozen dessert.

Makes 4 cups.

SPICY SOUR CREAM TOPPING

Serve on a warm fruit pie; subtly sparks the flavor of apple, cherry or blueberry.

In small bowl blend 1 cup dairy sour cream, 2 tablespoons sugar, ½ teaspoon cinnamon and ⅛ teaspoon nutmeg. *Makes 1 cup.*

SPICED ORANGE CREAM TOPPING

A new topper for that old favorite, pumpkin pie. Good, too, on other custard-type pies.

½ cup chilled whipping cream
1 tablespoon confectioners' sugar
¼ cup dairy sour cream
½ teaspoon cinnamon
⅛ teaspoon nutmeg
¼ cup orange marmalade

In chilled bowl whip cream and sugar until stiff. Stir together sour cream, cinnamon, nutmeg and marmalade. Fold marmalade mixture into whipped cream. Chill until serving time. *Makes about 1 cup.*

Whipped Cream Favorites

Whipped cream is always a proper topper. Serve it plain
(to add a festive touch to almost any pie) or select one of the fancy fix-ups below.

SWEETENED WHIPPED CREAM

In chilled bowl whip 1 cup chilled whipping cream and ¼ cup confectioners' sugar. Spoon on pie; garnish with chopped nuts, shaved chocolate, toasted slivered almonds, toasted coconut, shredded orange peel or crushed candy. *Makes 2 cups.*

HONEY-GINGER CREAM TOPPING

In chilled bowl whip 1 cup chilled whipping cream, gradually adding 2 tablespoons honey and ¼ teaspoon ginger. Serve with pumpkin pie.
Makes 2 cups.

CHOCOLATE TOFFEE WHIPPED TOPPING

Chill 2 bars (¾ ounce each) chocolate-covered toffee candy. Crush bars. In chilled bowl whip 1 cup chilled whipping cream and ¼ cup confectioners' sugar; fold in crushed candy. Serve with chocolate or coffee chiffon pie. *Makes 2 cups.*

PINK PEPPERMINT FLUFF

In chilled bowl whip 1 cup chilled whipping cream, ¼ cup confectioners' sugar, ⅛ teaspoon peppermint extract and 2 or 3 drops red food coloring. Serve with chocolate cream pie. Garnish with shaved chocolate.
Makes 2 cups.

CANDY FLUFF TOPPING

In chilled bowl whip ½ cup chilled whipping cream. Fold in ¼ cup finely crushed peppermint stick candy. Serve with chocolate or vanilla cream pie.
Makes 1¼ cups.

HEAVENLY TOPPING

In chilled bowl whip 1 cup chilled whipping cream. Gently fold in ¼ cup crème de cacao. (If desired, omit crème de cacao and gradually add ¼ cup dry instant sweetened chocolate drink mix while beating cream.) Serve with vanilla or banana cream pie. Garnish each serving with toasted diced almonds.
Makes 2 cups.

MINT TOPPING

In chilled bowl whip 1 cup chilled whipping cream. Fold in 3 tablespoons green crème de menthe. (If desired, omit crème de menthe and before whipping the cream, add ¼ teaspoon mint extract, 5 drops green food coloring and 2 tablespoons sugar.) Serve with chocolate cream or chocolate chiffon pie. Garnish each serving with sprig of mint and a maraschino cherry. *Makes 2 cups.*

CARAMEL FLUFF

In chilled bowl whip 1 cup chilled whipping cream, ¼ cup brown sugar (packed) and ½ teaspoon vanilla. Serve with custard or pumpkin pie. *Makes 2 cups.*

PEANUT CRUNCH TOPPING

In chilled bowl whip ½ cup chilled whipping cream. Fold in ¼ cup finely crushed peanut brittle. Serve with butterscotch cream pie or pumpkin pie.
Makes 1¼ cups.

Picture-perfect Garnishes

LEMON ROSES

Cut a thin slice from stem end of a lemon to form base. Starting just above base, cut around lemon without removing knife to form spiral of peel. Curl peel onto base to resemble a rose. Lime Roses can also be made. Perfect for a lemon or lime chiffon pie.

CHEESE CUTOUTS

Cut thin slices of cheese into wedge shapes or, using small cookie cutters, cut designs from each slice. Place on top of warm pie. Especially nice for fruit pies.

FROZEN WHIPPED CREAM

Cover baking sheet with waxed paper. Place cookie cutters open side up on baking sheet; fill with whipped cream. Place in freezer about 1 hour or until firm. With heated knife, remove cream from cutter and, if desired, cut frozen cream horizontally into several slices. For added color, dip frozen cream into decorators' sugar.

ORANGE OR LEMON WINDMILLS

Cut unpeeled orange or lemon into ⅛-inch slices. Cut out a few sections so slice looks like a windmill. With sharp knife, cut small V-shaped notches around edge.

CHEESE PUMPKINS

Allow process cheese to come to room temperature. Form cheese into balls, using about 1 teaspoonful for each. Score side of each with wooden pick to resemble lines in pumpkin; top each with a small slice of olive for stem. Perfect for an apple pie.

TOASTED MARSHMALLOW TREAT

Set oven control at broil and/or 550°. Cover top of baked pie with miniature marshmallows. Broil pie 3 inches from heat 1 minute. Attractive and tasty on a pumpkin pie.

CHOCOLATE CURLS

With a vegetable parer or thin, sharp knife, slice across bar of sweet milk chocolate with long, thin strokes. Semisweet or unsweetened chocolate can be used, but curls will be smaller.

GUMDROP CAT

For each cat, slice a 1-inch black gumdrop horizontally into 3 pieces. Use small rounded end slice for head and largest slice for body; cut tail and ears from third slice. Great for a Halloween pie (page 117).

ALMOND DAISY

On a custard, cream or chiffon pie, arrange sliced toasted almonds in the shape of a flower; add slice of a small gumdrop for center.

Pie as a Preliminary

Though most people think of dessert when they think of pastry, keep in mind that flaky bite-size bits of pastry with cheese or shrimp or meat make delicious appetizers or snacks. So when it's party time, remember that it's time to explore the possibilities of the recipes in this chapter. Serve them in the living room with mugs of hot or cold soup before dinner, as a substitute for a first course at the table. Or make them the mainstay of a cocktail party menu. Or mix them sweet and non-sweet for a gala high tea or a morning coffee party (you'll find recipes for the former in the last chapter). On any of these occasions your company will find them far more imaginative than the ubiquitous cracker.

When they're part of a prelude to dinner you'll probably want to have just one kind and couple it with a raw vegetable for contrast—perhaps Cocktail Kabobs with mushroom caps or our Crabmeat Puffs with crisp carrot sticks and juicy little cherry tomatoes. For an open house or cocktail party extend yourself a bit. Make up a big batch of Cornucopia dough and then shape it into Circles, Sandwiches, Pocketbooks and Twists as well as the tiny horns of plenty. For a change of flavor, brush mustard on some, catsup on others. Or fill half a baking of Streamlined Cheese Puff Pastry rounds with a mixture of bacon, onion and sour cream; the other half with cream cheese, garlic salt and chopped shrimp. Take a look at the picture on page 32–33 for an interesting way to serve these at a party.

If you're in the mood for a party with a foreign flavor, these little tidbits will fit in perfectly. For instance, you can create a south-of-the-border atmosphere with Mexican background music and big bouquets of larger-than-life-size paper flowers; then serve a sangria-type punch and Mexicali Puffs with rich spicy Guacamole or Empanaditas filled with chili-flavored Chicken.

If you want to go Gallic, use a French tricolor scheme with red wine and baskets of blue and white grapes. The *pièce de resistance:* Quick Lorraine Tarts.

In a Roman holiday mood attend the latest, artiest Italian movie; then invite the crowd back to your house for espresso and pint-size pizzas called Bambinos or prosciutto-flecked Italian Cheese Puffs.

And don't imagine that these demi-pastries are for parties only or that they are for adults only. All pair happily with fruit juice or punch, iced tea or iced coffee for little between-meals meals.

And although some may be a bit sophisticated for young palates, many—such as Cheese Pennies, Cheese Straws and some of the versions of Savory Surprises—delight children as much for their miniature size as for their taste.

MEXICALI PUFFS

Dip these crisp, tostada-like puffs in spicy Guacamole for real south-of-the-border flavor.

1 cup all-purpose flour
¾ cup yellow cornmeal
2 teaspoons salt
¾ teaspoon chili powder
½ cup water
Guacamole (below)

Mix flour, cornmeal, salt and chili powder in bowl. Adding water gradually, stir until flour mixture is moistened. Turn out onto lightly floured cloth-covered board; knead until smooth. Cover dough with plastic wrap and set aside for 30 minutes. In heavy kettle or deep-fat fryer, heat fat (1 inch deep) to 400°. Roll dough into large paper-thin circle; cut into 1½-inch rounds. Fry rounds until golden brown, turning once, about 1½ minutes on each side. Drain on paper towels. Serve warm or cool with Guacamole.

Makes about 5 dozen puffs.

Guacamole

2 ripe avocados, peeled and pitted
1 medium onion, finely chopped
2 green chili peppers, finely chopped
1 tablespoon lemon juice
1 teaspoon salt
½ teaspoon coarsely ground pepper
1 medium tomato, peeled and finely chopped
Mayonnaise or salad dressing

Mash avocados; add onion, peppers, lemon juice, salt and pepper and beat until creamy. Fold in tomato. Spoon into serving dish; spread top with thin layer of mayonnaise. Stir gently just before serving.

COCKTAIL KABOBS

For that very special occasion, arrange these tiny kabobs, Cornucopias and variations (pages 32–33), Italian Cheese Puffs (page 31), Bambinos (page 36) and Streamlined Cheese Puff Pastry Appetizers (page 37) on your most elegant tray. Pictured on pages 32–33.

Cheese Pastry for 8- or 9-inch One-crust
    Pie (page 17)
16 half-inch cubes sausage (Vienna, salami,
    bologna)
16 pimiento-stuffed small olives

Heat oven to 475°. Prepare pastry except—roll ⅛ inch thick. Cut into forty-eight 1-inch rounds. On each of 16 wooden picks, alternate 3 pastry rounds, 1 sausage cube and 1 olive. Lay kabobs horizontally on ungreased baking sheet. Bake 6 to 8 minutes. Serve warm.

Makes 16 kabobs.

CHEESE STRAWS

Crisp cheese appetizer snacks that do double duty as accompaniments for soups and salads. As an interesting change, make the Cheese Pastry with shredded Swiss cheese instead of the Cheddar.

Cheese Pastry for 8- or 9-inch One-crust
    Pie (page 17)
Caraway or poppy seed
Paprika

Heat oven to 450°. Prepare pastry except—divide dough in half. On lightly floured cloth-covered board, roll each half of dough into rectangle, 13x10 inches. Place on ungreased baking sheet. With sharp knife, cut rectangles lengthwise into thirds. Cut each third crosswise to make 15 strips. (Do not separate strips; they will bake apart.) Sprinkle with caraway seed and paprika. Bake 8 to 10 minutes or until lightly browned. Serve warm or cool.

Makes about 90 straws.

CRABMEAT PUFFS

Bake and broil these seafood delicacies on foil for easy post-party cleanup.

Pastry for 8- or 9-inch Two-crust Pie (page 8)
1 egg white
1 cup mayonnaise or salad dressing
1 can (6½ ounces) crabmeat, drained and cartilage removed
Salt and pepper
Paprika

Heat oven to 475°. Cover baking sheet with aluminum foil. Prepare pastry except—roll each half 3/16 inch thick and cut into 2-inch rounds. Place on foil-covered baking sheet; prick rounds 2 or 3 times with fork. Bake 8 to 10 minutes or until lightly browned.

Just before serving set oven control at broil and/or 550°. Beat egg white until stiff. Fold in mayonnaise and crabmeat. Season with salt and pepper. Spoon mixture onto rounds; sprinkle with paprika. Broil rounds 3 inches from heat about 3 minutes or until puffy and lightly browned.

Makes about 7 dozen puffs.

ITALIAN CHEESE PUFFS

Tiny cream puffs that are fun and flavorful. Pictured on pages 32–33.

½ cup water
¼ cup butter or margarine
½ cup all-purpose flour
2 eggs
⅓ cup grated Parmesan cheese
¼ cup finely chopped cooked ham, dried beef or prosciutto

Heat oven to 400°. Heat water and butter to a rolling boil in saucepan. Stir in flour all at once. Stir vigorously over low heat until mixture leaves side of pan and forms a ball, about 1 minute. Remove from heat. Beat in eggs thoroughly. Beat mixture until smooth and velvety. Mix in cheese and ham. Drop dough by teaspoonfuls onto ungreased baking sheet. Bake 25 minutes or until puffed and golden brown.

Makes about 30 puffs.

OLIVE-CHEESE BALLS

2 cups shredded sharp natural Cheddar cheese (8 ounces)
1¼ cups all-purpose flour*
½ cup butter or margarine, melted
About 36 pimiento-stuffed small olives, drained

Work cheese and flour together until crumbly. Add butter and mix well with fork. (If dough seems dry, work with hands.) Mold 1 teaspoon dough around each olive; shape into ball. Place 2 inches apart on ungreased baking sheet. Cover and chill 1 hour or longer.

Heat oven to 400°. Bake 15 to 20 minutes. Serve hot.

Makes about 3 dozen balls.

*Do not use self-rising flour in this recipe.

SAVORY SURPRISES

Versatile Cheese Pastry wrapped around a variety of savory fillings—be a people-pleaser by making some of each.

Cheese Pastry for 8- or 9-inch Two-crust Pie (page 17)
Fillings: Rolled anchovy fillets
         Cocktail wieners, cut in thirds
         Small cubes salami or smoked sausage
         Cream cheese balls wrapped in dried beef
         Stuffed olives (with pimiento, onion or almond)
         Salted peanuts

Heat oven to 450°. Prepare pastry except—with hands pat dough, about 1 teaspoonful at a time, into thin rounds. Wrap each around one of the Fillings. Place filled rounds on ungreased baking sheet. Bake 10 to 15 minutes. Serve warm.

Makes about 40 surprises.

CORNUCOPIAS

Sour cream is the magic ingredient in this elegant, rich pastry. To save time on party-day, make dough ahead of time. Wrap it tightly in aluminum foil or waxed paper and refrigerate. Soften to room temperature before rolling.

2 cups all-purpose flour*
1 teaspoon salt
¾ cup soft butter
½ cup dairy sour cream
Cooked ham or luncheon meat

Heat oven to 475°. Mix flour and salt in bowl. Cut in butter thoroughly. Mix in sour cream. Gather dough into firm ball; divide in half. On floured cloth-covered board roll each half 1/8 to 1/16 inch thick. Cut pastry into 2-inch circles. Cut cooked ham into small strips. Place meat strip in center of each pastry circle. Fold pastry over to form small cornucopia and seal edges. Place on ungreased baking sheet. Bake 8 to 10 minutes or until golden brown.

Makes about 8 dozen cornucopias.

*Do not use self-rising flour in this recipe.

Cornucopias; Cocktail Kabobs (page 30); Italian Cheese Puffs (page 31); Bambinos (page 36)

Variations

Circles: Follow recipe for Cornucopias (page 32) except—on each of the pastry circles, place a thin slice of cooked ham or luncheon meat cut to fit. After baking, brush tops with prepared mustard; if desired, garnish each with parsley sprig or pimiento strip.

Makes about 8 dozen circles.

Sandwiches: Follow recipe for Cornucopias (page 32) except—on each of half of the pastry circles, place a thin slice of cooked ham or luncheon meat cut to fit. Top with remaining circles.

Makes about 4 dozen sandwiches.

Pocketbooks: Follow recipe for Cornucopias (page 32) except—brush pastry circles with prepared mustard or catsup. Place small square of cooked ham or luncheon meat on half of each circle. Fold pastry over and seal edges.

Makes about 8 dozen pocketbooks.

Twists: Follow recipe for Cornucopias (page 32) except—divide dough into fourths. Roll each fourth into a square, 8x8 inches; cut into strips ¼ inch wide. Cut ¼-inch slices cooked ham or luncheon meat into strips, 3¼x¼ inch. Wrap a pastry strip in a spiral around each meat strip.

Makes about 10 dozen twists.

Circles; Sandwiches; Pocketbooks; Twists; Streamlined Cheese Puff Pastry Appetizers (page 37)

TRIPLE-CHEESE APPETIZER WHEEL

Say cheese, cheese and cheese again for a gourmet appetizer with triple goodness.

1 cup all-purpose flour*
½ cup shredded natural Swiss cheese
½ teaspoon salt
⅓ cup plus 1 tablespoon shortening
2 to 3 tablespoons cold water
Cheese Filling (right)

Heat oven to 475°. Stir flour, cheese and salt together. Cut in shortening thoroughly. Sprinkle water over mixture, 1 tablespoon at a time, mixing with fork until flour is moistened. Gather into a ball; divide dough in half. On lightly floured cloth-covered board, roll half of dough into 9-inch circle. Place on ungreased baking sheet; turn under ½ inch all around. Crimp edge; prick circle with fork. Bake 8 to 10 minutes or until lightly browned.

*If using self-rising flour, omit salt.

Roll other half of pastry into 7-inch circle; place on baking sheet. Score into 16 sections, cutting only part way through pastry. Cut around rim of each section to form scalloped edge. Cut out a 1-inch circle from center. Bake about 10 minutes or until lightly browned. Cool. Just before serving, spread Cheese Filling evenly to edge of 9-inch circle; place scored circle on top. If desired, garnish with parsley and olives. To serve, cut into wedges.   *16 servings.*

Cheese Filling

Soften 4 ounces cream cheese; beat with 2 ounces blue cheese and 1 tablespoon horseradish until fluffy. Add 1 tablespoon milk; beat until fluffy. Fold in ¼ cup sliced pimiento-stuffed olives.

CHEESE PENNIES

Try these crunchy, easy-to-do pastries with a variety of pasteurized process cheese spreads—bacon, garlic or hickory smoke flavored could be used.

1 jar (5 ounces) pasteurized process sharp
　　American cheese spread
¼ cup shortening
⅔ cup all-purpose flour

In small mixer bowl, mix all ingredients at medium speed 20 to 30 seconds. On lightly floured cloth-covered board, mold dough into two 8-inch rolls, each about 1 inch in diameter. (Dough will be soft but not sticky.) Wrap in waxed paper or plastic wrap; refrigerate 2 hours or overnight.

Heat oven to 375°. Cut rolls into ¼-inch slices; place on ungreased baking sheet. Bake 10 to 12 minutes or until slightly browned.

Makes about 5 dozen appetizers.

Variations

Penny Surprises: Follow recipe for Cheese Pennies (above) except—divide dough into fourths. Roll each fourth into an oblong, about 8x2 inches. Place a row of small pimiento-stuffed olives, anchovies, cocktail wieners or ¼-inch salami strips lengthwise in center of oblong. Mold edges of dough together to form a roll. Wrap, refrigerate and bake as directed except—cut rolls into ⅜-inch slices or into diagonal slices.

Makes about 7 dozen appetizers.

Cheese Sticks: Follow recipe for Cheese Pennies (above) except—after mixing dough, place in cookie press with star plate. *Heat oven to 350°.* Form sticks on ungreased baking sheet; cut into 3-inch lengths. Bake 10 minutes or until lightly browned. Immediately remove sticks to cooling rack.

Makes about 4 dozen sticks.

EMPANADITAS

Mexican turnovers done in miniature with a chili-chicken filling.

¾ cup chopped cooked chicken
3 tablespoons chili sauce
Pinch of chili powder
2 cups all-purpose flour*
2 tablespoons sugar
½ teaspoon salt
2 tablespoons butter or margarine
1 tablespoon shortening
1 egg yolk
½ cup water

Mix the chicken, chili sauce and chili powder; set aside. Combine flour, sugar and salt in bowl. Cut in butter and shortening thoroughly. Mix in egg yolk. Adding water gradually, mix until dough forms a ball. Turn out on floured cloth-covered board; knead until springy, 2 to 3 minutes. Divide in half. Roll dough 1/8 to 1/16 inch thick (it may be a little hard to roll, similar to yeast dough). Cut into 2½-inch rounds.

Place 1 teaspoon chicken mixture on half of each round; fold pastry over and press firmly with tines of fork to seal. In large skillet heat fat (½ inch deep) to 350°. Fry filled rounds, turning once, until lightly browned, about 2 minutes per side. Drain on paper towels. Serve hot.　　*Makes about 36 empanaditas.*

*If using self-rising flour, omit salt.

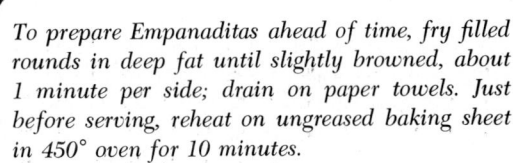

To prepare Empanaditas ahead of time, fry filled rounds in deep fat until slightly browned, about 1 minute per side; drain on paper towels. Just before serving, reheat on ungreased baking sheet in 450° oven for 10 minutes.

QUICK LORRAINE TARTS

A delightful appetizer adaptation of Quiche Lorraine. For party-time ease, bake in advance, cool and wrap in aluminum foil. Just before serving heat in 350° oven for 10 minutes.

1 package pie crust mix
1 tablespoon poppy seed
1⅓ cups coarsely shredded natural Swiss cheese
⅔ cup chopped salami
⅓ cup sliced green onions
4 eggs, slightly beaten
1⅓ cups dairy sour cream
1 teaspoon salt
1 teaspoon Worcestershire sauce

Heat oven to 375°. Prepare pastry for Two-crust Pie as directed on package except—stir in poppy seed before mixing. Roll pastry 1/16 inch thick on lightly floured cloth-covered board; cut into 3-inch rounds. Fit rounds into 2½-inch ungreased muffin cups. Combine cheese, salami and onions; spoon into pastry-lined muffin cups. Stir together eggs, sour cream, salt and Worcestershire sauce; pour about 1 tablespoon sour cream mixture into each muffin cup. Bake 20 to 25 minutes or until lightly browned. Cool in pans 5 minutes. *Makes 36 tarts.*

BAMBINOS

Petite pizzas that mean happy hostessing because the rounds can be baked ahead of time. Pictured on pages 32–33.

Pastry for 8- or 9-inch Two-crust Pie (page 8)
1 can (6 ounces) tomato paste
1 teaspoon garlic salt
¼ teaspoon ground oregano
⅛ pound sliced pepperoni or salami
¼ pound mozzarella or process American cheese, shredded

Heat oven to 475°. Cover baking sheet with aluminum foil. Prepare pastry except—roll each half 3/16 inch thick and cut into 2-inch rounds. Place on foil-covered baking sheet; prick rounds 2 or 3 times with fork. Bake 8 to 10 minutes or until lightly browned.

Reduce oven temperature to 400°. Mix tomato paste, garlic salt and oregano. Spoon small amount of tomato mixture on each baked pastry round. Top with meat and sprinkle with cheese. If desired, sprinkle with oregano. Bake 3 to 5 minutes or until cheese melts. Serve hot. *Makes about 7 dozen bambinos.*

LIVER PATE CANAPES

Pastry for 8- or 9-inch One-crust Pie (page 8)
1 can (3 ounces) liver pâté
2 tablespoons finely chopped pimiento-stuffed olives

Heat oven to 450°. Prepare pastry except—roll into a rectangle, 14x10 inches. Place on ungreased baking sheet. Mix liver pâté and olives; spread over half of rectangle. Fold pastry over filled half. With ruler as guide, make cuts ¾ to 1 inch apart across filled pastry. Make cuts diagonally across straight cuts to form diamond shapes. Bake about 15 minutes or until lightly browned. Serve warm. *Makes about 45 canapés.*

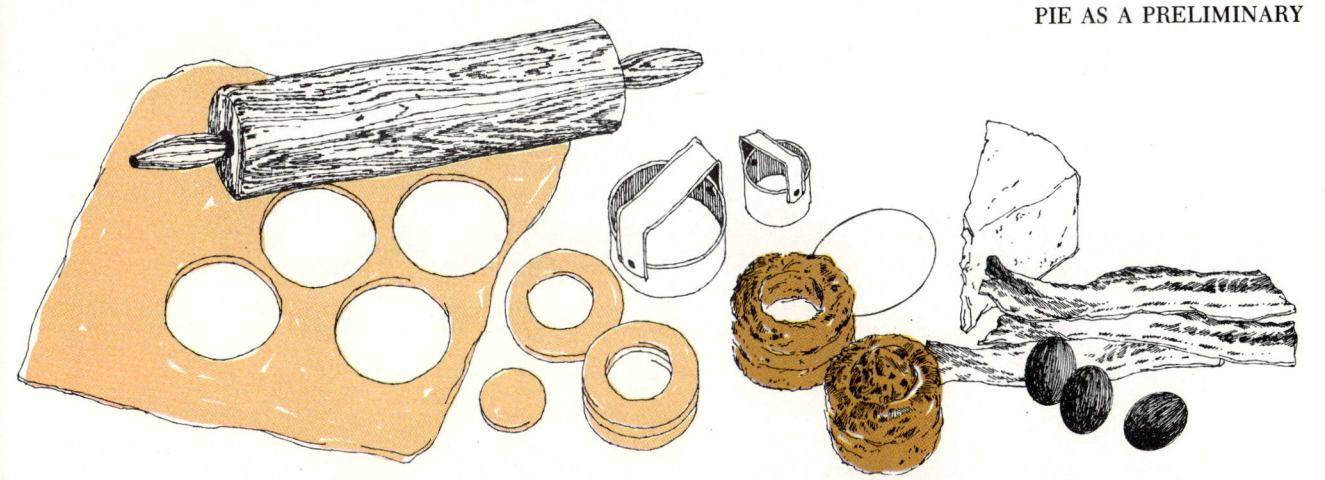

STREAMLINED CHEESE PUFF PASTRY APPETIZERS

Flaky, melt-in-your-mouth appetizers . . . so easy even novices can make them. Pictured on pages 32–33.

1 cup butter
1½ cups all-purpose flour*
½ cup dairy sour cream
½ cup shredded sharp natural Cheddar cheese
1 egg
Bacon Bit, Shrimp or Harlequin Dip (right)

Cut butter into flour with pastry blender until completely mixed. With fork stir in sour cream and cheese until thoroughly blended. Divide dough into two equal parts; wrap each and refrigerate 8 hours or overnight.

Heat oven to 350°. On *well-floured* cloth-covered board roll one part of pastry to 1/16 inch; cut into 2-inch rounds with a plain or scalloped cutter. In ⅔ of the rounds, cut out 1-inch circles. (Refrigerate scraps of dough before rerolling.)

Place plain rounds on ungreased baking sheet; brush with slightly beaten egg. Top each with a round with center removed. Brush with egg and top with another round with center removed (you will have 3 layers—one plain, 2 with centers removed). Repeat for second half of pastry. Bake 20 to 25 minutes. Cool. Fill with Bacon Bit, Shrimp or Harlequin Dip or with 1½ cups of your favorite thick dip.

Makes about 3 dozen appetizers.

*Self-rising flour can be used in this recipe. Baking time may be shorter.

Bacon Bit Dip

Fry 10 slices bacon until crisp. Drain on paper towels; crumble. Mix 1½ teaspoons instant minced onion and 1½ teaspoons water; let stand 5 minutes. Mix bacon and onion with 1½ cups dairy sour cream. Chill several hours. *Makes 1½ cups.*

Shrimp Dip

Soften 1 package (8 ounces) cream cheese in small mixing bowl; gradually beat in ¼ cup milk. Add 1 teaspoon lemon juice, 1 teaspoon Worcestershire sauce, ½ teaspoon garlic salt and ¼ teaspoon dill weed; mix thoroughly. Fold in ½ cup (half of 4½-ounce can) shrimp, drained and chopped. Cover and chill. The remaining shrimp can be used for garnishing tops of appetizers. *Makes 1½ cups.*

Harlequin Dip

In small mixer bowl, blend ½ cup dairy sour cream and ½ cup mayonnaise. Stir in ½ cup chopped pitted ripe olives, 2 tablespoons chopped chives, 1 teaspoon Worcestershire sauce, ½ teaspoon prepared mustard and ½ teaspoon curry powder. Cover and chill at least 1 hour. *Makes 1½ cups.*

Pie as the Main Event

Throughout Europe, pie is and has always been primarily a main dish, a delicious solution devised by frugal housewives for using up every edible bit of meat, fowl, vegetables and gravy left over from a Sunday dinner. Originally an economy measure, these entrée pies long ago acquired a gourmet status of their own and are now part of the culinary national treasure of their countries of origin. British Steak and Kidney Pie, with its wonderful contrasting textures, is a man-pleaser from the word go. French Quiche Lorraine, a pie shell filled with creamy cheese-flavored custard, rates raves at any luncheon or after-the-theatre party. Italian Pizza with cheese, meat, sausage, shellfish, anchovies, mushrooms or any combination thereof, is every teenager's dream of ambrosia; the less familiar Spanish version made with cornmeal offers a new taste treat for the high school set *and* their parents. Then there are rarebit-ish Cheddar Cheese Pie; semi-circular Cornish Pasties filled with meat, potatoes and vegetables; and Spanish Meatball Pie, spiced with olives and topped with cheese pastry.

Taking up where their old-country forebears left off, American cooks have concocted their own classics such as Chicken Dinner Pie and Cheeseburger Pie, and then gone on to invent artful new ways of putting fish, sausage or cheese in crusts.

There are even pies that are "non-pies"—meat loaf topped with a meringue-like cover of mashed potatoes for a favorite family dinner; ham and eggs aboard pastry squares for a gala Sunday breakfast; a pie with tender cream cheese pastry that comes out in pinwheel-patterned slices; or little tart shells filled with shrimp in a creamy dill-flavored sauce. When time is of the essence, serve one of the several made-in-minutes pies or pielets in this section with simple salad and fruit accompaniments. But when a production number is in order, you'll find a choice of genuine fourteen-carat partyworthies in the recipes that follow in this chapter.

TUNA PIE

Pastry for 9-inch Two-crust Pie (page 8)
2 eggs
½ cup milk
1 tablespoon butter or margarine, melted
¼ cup chopped onion
2 tablespoons minced parsley
¾ teaspoon basil leaves
¼ teaspoon salt
2 cans (6½ ounces each) tuna, drained and flaked
Egg Sauce or Easy Mushroom Sauce (below)

Heat oven to 425°. Prepare pastry. In mixing bowl beat eggs; stir in remaining ingredients except Egg Sauce. Pour tuna mixture into pastry-lined pie pan. Cover with top crust which has slits cut in it. Seal and flute. Cover edge with 2- to 3-inch strip of aluminum foil to prevent excessive browning; remove foil last 15 minutes of baking. Bake 35 to 40 minutes or until crust is nicely browned. Serve with Egg Sauce.
6 servings.

Egg Sauce

Melt ¼ cup butter or margarine over low heat in saucepan. Blend in ¼ cup all-purpose flour, ½ teaspoon salt and ¼ teaspoon pepper. Cook over low heat, stirring until mixture is smooth and bubbly. Remove from heat. Stir in 2 cups milk. Heat to boiling, stirring constantly. Boil and stir 1 minute. Carefully stir in 4 diced hard-cooked eggs. Season to taste.

Easy Mushroom Sauce

Drain 1 can (2 ounces) sliced mushrooms; reserve liquid. Cook and stir mushrooms and 1 tablespoon minced onion in 1 tablespoon butter until onion is tender. Add 1 can (10½ ounces) cream of mushroom soup, reserved mushroom liquid and a few drops Worcestershire sauce. Cook over medium heat, stirring occasionally, until heated through.

SHRIMP SUPREME

Luscious dill-flavored shrimp in individual tart shells—rich and dainty for that special luncheon.

Baked Tart Shells (page 146)
1 can (10¾ ounces) frozen cream of shrimp soup
½ cup milk
1 cup cleaned cooked or canned shrimp
1 package (10 ounces) frozen peas and onions, cooked and drained
2 teaspoons lemon juice
½ teaspoon dill weed
Lemon wedges

Bake tart shells. In saucepan heat soup and milk over low heat, stirring constantly, until heated through. Stir in shrimp, peas and onions, lemon juice and dill weed; heat through. Serve in tart shells; garnish with lemon wedges.
Makes 8 tarts.

CRAB REMOULADE PIE

An unforgettable seafood pie from an unforgettable dining capital, New Orleans.

Cheese Pastry for 9-inch Two-crust Pie (page 17)
1 cup mayonnaise or salad dressing
¼ cup chili sauce
¼ cup finely chopped dill pickles
1 tablespoon finely chopped drained capers
1½ teaspoons prepared mustard
1½ teaspoons each chopped parsley, tarragon and chervil
2 cans (7¾ ounces each) crabmeat, drained and cartilage removed

Heat oven to 425°. Prepare pastry. Combine remaining ingredients and mix well. Pour into pastry-lined pie pan. Cover with top crust which has slits cut in it. Seal and flute. Cover edge with 2- to 3-inch strip of aluminum foil to prevent excessive browning; remove foil last 15 minutes of baking. Bake 30 minutes or until brown.
6 to 8 servings.

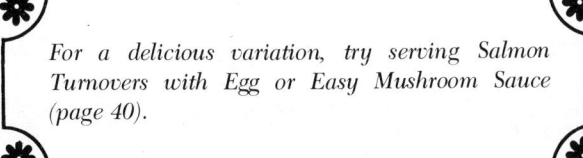

For a delicious variation, try serving Salmon Turnovers with Egg or Easy Mushroom Sauce (page 40).

SALMON TURNOVERS

1 package pie crust mix
1 can (7¾ ounces) salmon, drained
1 tablespoon mayonnaise or salad dressing
1 teaspoon lemon juice
Cucumber Sauce (below)
Paprika

Heat oven to 425°. Prepare pastry for Two-crust Pie as directed on package except—roll dough into rectangle, 16x12 inches. Cut rectangle into twelve 4-inch squares with pastry wheel or knife. Remove bones and skin from salmon; break fish into pieces. Fold mayonnaise and lemon juice into salmon. Place about 1 tablespoon salmon filling on each square of pastry. Moisten edges of each square with water. Fold pastry over to make triangles; press edges together with tines of fork to seal. Prick tops of triangles with fork. Bake on ungreased baking sheet 15 to 20 minutes or until golden brown. Serve hot with Cucumber Sauce; sprinkle with paprika. *4 to 6 servings.*

Cucumber Sauce

¼ cup butter or margarine
¼ cup all-purpose flour
½ teaspoon salt
⅛ teaspoon pepper
2 cups milk
1 cup diced pared cucumber
1 teaspoon instant minced onion
1 tablespoon horseradish

In saucepan melt butter over low heat; blend in flour, salt and pepper. Cook over low heat, stirring constantly, until mixture is smooth and bubbly. Remove from heat. Stir in milk. Heat to boiling, stirring constantly. Boil and stir 1 minute. Stir in cucumber, onion and horseradish; simmer 10 minutes.

YANKEE DOODLE PIE

For a meal-in-minutes try flavorful macaroni and cheese in a crisp celery seed crust.

9-inch Baked Celery Seed Pie Shell
 (page 17)
1 package (8 ounces) macaroni and
 Cheddar dinner
1 can (6½ ounces) tuna, drained and flaked
1 medium tomato
Snipped parsley

Bake pie shell. *Heat oven to 375°.* Prepare macaroni and Cheddar as directed on package for saucepan method except—when sauce is heated *just* to boiling, remove from heat; stir in tuna. Pour mixture into baked pie shell. If desired, peel tomato; cut tomato into thin wedges. Arrange wedges around edge of pie. Bake 10 minutes. Garnish with snipped parsley.
4 to 6 servings.

HAM STACKS

Pastry for 8- or 9-inch One-crust Pie
 (page 8)
2 tablespoons butter or margarine
¼ cup chopped onion
2 tablespoons chopped green pepper
1 cup cubed cooked ham
⅓ cup milk
1 can (10½ ounces) condensed cream of
 mushroom soup
1 cup shredded sharp natural Cheddar
 cheese (about 4 ounces)
½ teaspoon Worcestershire sauce
2 hard-cooked eggs, sliced

Heat oven to 475°. Prepare pastry except—roll into rectangle, 12x9 inches. Cut into twelve 3-inch squares. Prick with fork. Place on ungreased baking sheet. Bake 8 to 10 minutes or until lightly browned.

Melt butter in skillet; cook and stir onion and green pepper in butter until onion is tender. Stir in ham, milk, soup, cheese, Worcestershire sauce and eggs; heat through. Arrange half of squares on plates. Spoon half of ham mixture over squares. Top each with a remaining square. Spoon remaining ham mixture over tops. If desired, garnish with parsley. *6 servings.*

CHEESEBURGER PIE

All America's favorite—now baked in a pie shell and served with a spicy tomato sauce.

Pastry for 9-inch One-crust Pie (page 8)
1 pound ground beef
1 teaspoon salt
½ teaspoon ground oregano
¼ teaspoon pepper
½ cup fine dry bread crumbs
1 can (8 ounces) tomato sauce
¼ cup chopped onion
¼ cup chopped green pepper, if desired
Cheese Topping (below)
½ cup chili sauce

Heat oven to 425°. Prepare pastry. In skillet cook and stir ground beef until brown. Drain fat from skillet. Stir in salt, oregano, pepper, crumbs, ½ cup of the tomato sauce, the onion and green pepper. Pour into pastry-lined pie pan. Spread Cheese Topping evenly over filling. Cover edge with 2- to 3-inch strip of aluminum foil to prevent excessive browning; remove foil last 15 minutes of baking. Bake about 30 minutes. Cut into wedges. Stir together remaining tomato sauce and the chili sauce; heat if desired. Serve with pie.
6 to 8 servings.

Cheese Topping

1 egg
¼ cup milk
½ teaspoon each salt, dry mustard and
    Worcestershire sauce
2 cups shredded mellow natural Cheddar
    cheese (about 8 ounces)

Beat egg and milk in bowl. Stir in seasonings and cheese.

MEAT LOAF PIE

Have fun with meat loaf by topping it with a "meringue" of fluffy mashed potatoes.

1 pound ground beef
2 slices soft bread, torn into pieces
⅔ cup milk
1 egg, slightly beaten
¼ cup chopped onion
1 tablespoon Worcestershire sauce
1¼ teaspoons salt
Instant mashed potato puffs (enough for
    4 servings)
½ cup shredded sharp natural Cheddar
    cheese

Heat oven to 350°. Lightly mix ground beef, bread, milk, egg, onion, Worcestershire sauce and salt. Spread mixture evenly in 9-inch pie pan. Bake 35 to 40 minutes. Prepare mashed potato puffs as directed on package. Drain fat from meat loaf. Pile mashed potatoes on meat loaf as for a meringue on a pie. Sprinkle cheese over potatoes. Bake 3 to 4 minutes longer or until cheese melts. *4 or 5 servings.*

HOMESPUN SAUSAGE PIE

1½ pounds bulk pork sausage
½ cup chopped onion
1 medium cabbage (1¾ pounds), cut into
    large chunks and cored
1 can (1 pound) tomatoes
1 tablespoon sugar
1½ teaspoons salt
Pastry for 8- or 9-inch One-crust
    Pie (page 8)
2 tablespoons flour
¼ cup cold water

In Dutch oven cook and stir sausage and onion until meat is cooked thoroughly. Drain fat from pan. Add cabbage, tomatoes (with liquid), sugar and salt; cover and simmer 10 minutes.

Heat oven to 400°. Prepare pastry except—roll dough to fit top of 2-quart casserole. Mix flour and water; stir into hot meat mixture and pour into casserole. Cover with pastry which has slits cut in it. Seal pastry to edge of casserole. Bake 25 to 30 minutes or until crust is brown. *6 servings.*

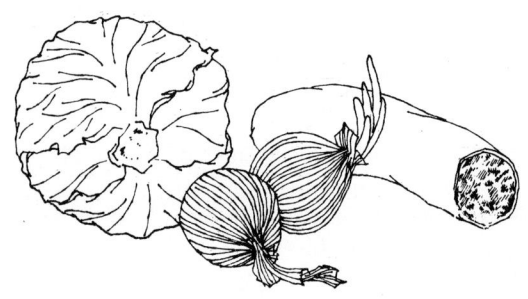

Cheeseburger Pie

Plantation Ham 'n Chicken Pie

PLANTATION HAM 'N CHICKEN PIE

2 tablespoons butter or margarine
3 cups cubed cooked ham
½ cup chopped green pepper
1 medium onion, sliced
2 cans (10½ ounces each) condensed
    cream of chicken soup
1 cup milk
Parsley Pinwheels (below)

Heat oven to 425°. Melt butter in large skillet. Cook and stir ham, green pepper and onion in butter until ham is golden and onion is tender. Stir in soup and milk. Heat, stirring frequently, *just* to boiling. Pour mixture into square baking dish, 8x8x2 inches; place in oven to keep hot. Prepare Parsley Pinwheels and place cut side up on *hot* mixture. Bake 20 to 25 minutes. *6 to 9 servings.*

Parsley Pinwheels

Prepare biscuit dough as directed on package of buttermilk baking mix except—roll into rectangle, 12x7 inches. Sprinkle ½ cup chopped parsley over dough. Beginning at wide side, roll up tightly. Seal well by pinching edge of dough into roll. Cut into 9 equal slices.

CHICKEN PARTY PIE

9-inch Baked Cheese Pie Shell (page 17)
1½ cups diced cooked chicken
1 can (8¾ ounces) pineapple tidbits, drained
⅓ cup sliced pitted ripe olives
¾ to 1 cup toasted slivered almonds
½ cup sliced celery
1 teaspoon salt
1 cup dairy sour cream
⅔ cup mayonnaise or salad dressing
3 tablespoons shredded sharp natural
    Cheddar cheese
6 pitted ripe olives

Bake pie shell. Combine chicken, pineapple, ⅓ cup sliced olives, the almonds, celery and salt in bowl. Blend sour cream and mayonnaise. Mix ⅔ cup of the sour cream mixture into chicken mixture. Pour into baked pie shell; top with remaining sour cream mixture. Sprinkle with cheese; refrigerate 4 hours. Garnish with 6 pitted olives. *6 servings.*

HENNY PENNY CASS-A-ROLLS

Cream Cheese Pastry rolled pinwheel-style with a colorful chicken filling.

Cream Cheese Pastry (below)
2 cups chopped cooked chicken or turkey
¼ cup chopped ripe olives
1 tablespoon chopped pimiento
½ teaspoon instant minced onion
½ teaspoon salt
¼ teaspoon paprika
2 tablespoons butter or margarine, melted
1 can (10½ ounces) condensed cream of
    mushroom soup
⅓ cup milk

Prepare pastry. *Heat oven to 450°.* Stir together chicken, olives, pimiento, onion, salt, paprika and butter. On lightly floured cloth-covered board, roll each ball of pastry into rectangle, 11x9 inches. Spread each with half of the chicken mixture. Fold in ends; beginning at long side, roll as for jelly roll. Seal edges; place rolls on ungreased baking sheet. Bake 15 to 20 minutes. In small saucepan, heat soup and milk *just* to boiling, stirring constantly. Cut each hot roll into 4 servings; pour soup mixture over each serving. *8 servings.*

Cream Cheese Pastry

1 cup all-purpose flour*
½ teaspoon salt
¼ cup shortening
1 package (3 ounces) cream cheese
3 tablespoons cold water

Measure flour and salt into mixing bowl. Cut in shortening and cheese thoroughly. Sprinkle with water, 1 tablespoon at a time, mixing with fork until flour is moistened. Form into 2 balls; wrap in plastic wrap or waxed paper. Chill 15 to 20 minutes.

*If using self-rising flour, omit salt.

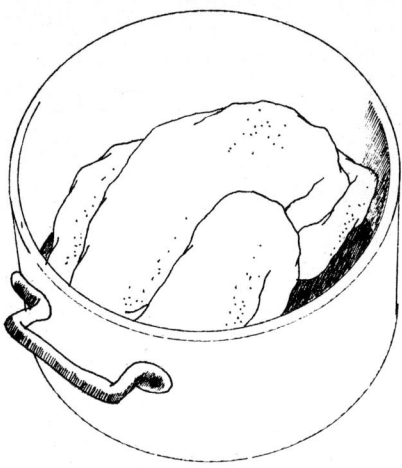

CHICKEN DINNER PIE

Colorful peas and carrots peek through the lattice crust on this all-time favorite chicken pie.

Pastry for 9-inch Two-crust Pie (page 8)
2 tablespoons butter or margarine
2 tablespoons flour
1 teaspoon salt
⅛ teaspoon pepper
⅛ teaspoon ground thyme
½ cup chicken broth*
½ cup light cream
2 cups cubed cooked chicken
1 can (1 pound) peas and carrots, drained, or 1 package (10 ounces) frozen peas and carrots, cooked and drained
1 can (8 ounces) small whole onions, drained

Heat oven to 425°. Prepare pastry except—cut pastry for top crust into twelve ½-inch lattice strips (page 15). Melt butter in large skillet over low heat; stir in flour, salt, pepper and thyme. Cook, stirring until mixture is smooth and bubbly. Remove from heat. Stir in chicken broth and cream. Heat to boiling, stirring constantly. Boil and stir 1 minute. Stir in chicken and vegetables. Pour into pastry-lined pie pan.

Cover with Lattice Top (page 15). Cover edge with 2- to 3-inch strip of aluminum foil to prevent excessive browning; remove foil last 15 minutes of baking. Bake 35 to 40 minutes or until crust is brown.

6 servings.

*Chicken broth can be made by dissolving 1 chicken bouillon cube in ½ cup boiling water, or use canned chicken broth.

SCRAMBLED EGGS IN PUFFY BOWL

½ cup water
¼ cup butter or margarine
½ cup all-purpose flour
⅛ teaspoon salt
11 eggs
1 cup cottage cheese with chives
¼ teaspoon salt
3 tablespoons butter or margarine

Heat oven to 400°. Grease 9-inch glass pie pan. Heat water and ¼ cup butter to a rolling boil in saucepan. Stir in flour and ⅛ teaspoon salt. Stir vigorously over low heat until mixture leaves side of pan and forms a ball, about 1 minute. Remove from heat; cool slightly, about 10 minutes. Add 2 of the eggs, beating until mixture is smooth and velvety. Spread batter evenly in prepared pie pan (have batter touching side of pie pan, but do not spread up side). Bake 45 to 50 minutes.

During the last 10 minutes bowl bakes, prepare scrambled eggs: Beat the remaining 9 eggs thoroughly; stir in cottage cheese and ¼ teaspoon salt. Heat 3 tablespoons butter in large skillet over medium heat until just hot enough to sizzle drop of water. Pour egg mixture into skillet. When mixture starts to set at bottom and side, lift cooked portions with spatula and turn gently to cook evenly. Avoid constant stirring. Cook until eggs are thickened throughout, but still moist. Mound eggs into puffy bowl. If desired, garnish with chives and pimiento. Cut into wedges to serve.

6 servings.

When you're planning a spectacular brunch, try the Scrambled Eggs in Puffy Bowl. Start with wedges of cool melon; accompany the creamy cheese-scrambled eggs with slices of crisp bacon and plenty of coffee.

Scrambled Eggs in Puffy Bowl

CORNISH PASTIES

One of these large he-man-size turnovers would be a complete meal for the hungriest miner in Cornwall; for less hearty appetites cut each pasty in two. Cornishmen traditionally mark their initials on each pasty before baking and serve pasties with tart relishes.

1 package (22 ounces) pie crust mix
2 cups diced pared potato
1 pound beef chuck or top round steak, cut into ¼-inch pieces
2 teaspoons salt
2 cups diced carrot
1 cup diced onion
1 cup diced turnip or rutabaga
Pepper
4 tablespoons butter or margarine
4 tablespoons water
Milk or light cream
Corn relish, pickled beets, chili sauce and pickles

Heat oven to 350°. Prepare pastry for 2 Two-crust Pies as directed on package. Divide dough into 4 parts. Roll each part into 12-inch circle. Using 2 baking sheets, place a circle on each end of each baking sheet. On one half of each circle, spread ¼ each of the potato and the meat; sprinkle with ¼ teaspoon of the salt. On top of meat arrange in layers ¼ each of the carrot, onion and turnip. Sprinkle with ¼ teaspoon of the salt and a dash of pepper. Dot each with 1 tablespoon butter and sprinkle 1 tablespoon water over filling of each circle.

Moisten edges of pastry with water. Fold pastry over filling, turning edge of bottom pastry over edge of top pastry. Seal and flute. Prick tops with fork; brush with milk. Bake 1 hour. Serve with corn relish, pickled beets, chili sauce and pickles.   *4 large servings.*

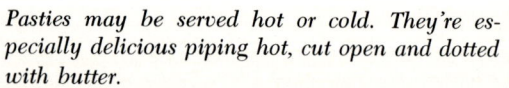

Pasties may be served hot or cold. They're especially delicious piping hot, cut open and dotted with butter.

DOUBLE MEAT PIE

Golden Egg Pastry filled with pork and beef—a meat pie that is all meat.

Egg Pastry for 9-inch Two-crust Pie (page 18)
½ pound bulk pork sausage
1 pound ground beef
1 medium onion, coarsely chopped
1 egg, slightly beaten
¼ cup water
½ teaspoon salt
Tomato Sauce (below)

Heat oven to 400°. Prepare pastry. Brown sausage in skillet; add ground beef and onion. Cook and stir until beef is brown and onion is tender. Drain fat from skillet. Combine egg, water and salt; stir into meat mixture. Fill pastry-lined pie pan with meat mixture. Cover with top pastry. Seal and flute edge; prick top pastry with fork. Cover edge of pastry with 2- to 3-inch strip of aluminum foil to prevent excessive browning; remove foil last 15 minutes of baking. Bake 30 minutes or until brown. Serve with Tomato Sauce.   *6 servings.*

Tomato Sauce

1 tablespoon butter or margarine
2 tablespoons chopped onion
2 tablespoons chopped green pepper
1 can (8 ounces) tomato sauce
¼ teaspoon salt
⅛ teaspoon pepper

Melt butter in small skillet; cook and stir onion and green pepper in butter until onion is tender. Stir in tomato sauce, salt and pepper; heat over low heat.

STEAK AND KIDNEY PIE

The most famous of all English pies, this was a favorite of Dr. Johnson's over 200 years ago.

¾ pound beef kidney
1 teaspoon salt
¾ pound round steak
⅓ cup all-purpose flour
½ teaspoon salt
¼ teaspoon pepper
¼ cup shortening
1 cup chopped onion
½ cup sherry or, if desired, ½ cup water
 and 1 beef bouillon cube
¾ cup water
½ pound fresh mushrooms, washed,
 trimmed and sliced, or 1 can (3 ounces)
 sliced mushrooms (undrained)
¼ cup minced parsley
¼ cup chopped celery
1 bay leaf
1 teaspoon salt
¼ teaspoon ground thyme
¼ teaspoon ground marjoram
Dash pepper
Pastry Topping (right)
⅓ cup water
1 tablespoon flour

Remove skin and membrane from kidney; split in half and remove white veins and fat with kitchen scissors. Cut into 1-inch cubes. Place in saucepan with water to cover. Add 1 teaspoon salt; simmer 30 minutes. Rinse with hot water and drain thoroughly.

Cut steak into 1-inch cubes. Mix ⅓ cup flour, ½ teaspoon salt and ¼ teaspoon pepper; roll kidney and steak cubes in flour mixture. Melt shortening in large skillet; cook and stir meat and onion in shortening until meat is brown and onion is tender. Add sherry, ¾ cup water, the mushrooms, parsley, celery, bay leaf, 1 teaspoon salt, the thyme, marjoram and dash pepper. Cover tightly and simmer 1 hour.

Heat oven to 400°. Prepare Pastry Topping. Mix ⅓ cup water and 1 tablespoon flour; stir into meat mixture. Heat to boiling, stirring constantly. Boil and stir 1 minute. Remove bay leaf; pour hot mixture into 1½-quart casserole. Top with Pastry Topping; seal pastry to edge of dish. Bake 30 to 35 minutes.

4 to 6 servings.

Pastry Topping

Combine 1¼ cups all-purpose flour° and ½ teaspoon salt in bowl. Cut in ½ cup shortening thoroughly. Sprinkle with 3 tablespoons cold water, 1 tablespoon at a time, mixing with fork until flour is moistened (1 to 2 teaspoons water may be added if needed). Gather into a ball. Shape into flattened circle on lightly floured cloth-covered board. Roll to fit top of casserole, about 8½ inches in diameter. Fold pastry in half; cut slits along folded edge. Place on top of hot meat mixture; unfold. (This will be a thick topping.)

°*If using self-rising flour, omit salt in Pastry Topping.*

CHEDDAR CHEESE PIE

England's answer to France's Quiche Lorraine. Serve with a crisp green salad and fresh fruit for dessert.

9-inch Baked Pie Shell (page 11)
3 cups shredded sharp natural Cheddar
 cheese (about ¾ pound)
1 teaspoon instant minced onion
½ teaspoon each salt, dry mustard and
 Worcestershire sauce
3 eggs
6 medium tomatoes, peeled
Salt and pepper
1 to 2 tablespoons chopped green pepper

Bake pie shell. *Heat oven to 325°.* In top of double boiler heat cheese, onion, salt, mustard and Worcestershire sauce over boiling water, stirring until cheese melts. Remove from heat. In mixing bowl beat eggs until frothy. Adding cheese mixture gradually to eggs, continue beating until smooth. Pour into baked pie shell. Bake 25 minutes or until filling is *just* set. Remove pie from oven. Cut tomatoes into thin slices. Overlap slices around edge of pie to form a wreath; sprinkle with salt and pepper. Garnish center of wreath with green pepper. Bake 15 minutes longer.

6 to 8 servings.

SHEPHERDS' PIE

Traditionally made by the thrifty English with Sunday's leftover roast and potatoes.

Instant mashed potato puffs (enough for 8 servings)
2 tablespoons parsley flakes
2 cups cubed cooked lamb, beef or veal
¼ cup chopped onion
2 cups cooked vegetables (peas, carrots or corn)
2 cups gravy*
½ teaspoon salt

Heat oven to 350°. Prepare potato puffs as directed on package except—stir in parsley flakes; set aside. In 2½-quart casserole stir together remaining ingredients. Mound potatoes on meat mixture. Bake 30 minutes or until potatoes brown slightly.

4 to 6 servings.

*2 cans (10¾ ounces each) gravy can be used or use leftover gravy and enough canned mushroom gravy to measure 2 cups.

QUICHE LORRAINE

Originally claimed by Alsace-Lorraine, this cheese-custard classic is a perfect luncheon main dish.

Pastry for 9-inch One-crust Pie (page 8)
12 slices (½ pound) bacon, crisply fried and crumbled
1 cup shredded natural Swiss cheese (about 4 ounces)
⅓ cup minced onion
4 eggs
2 cups whipping cream or, if desired, light cream
¾ teaspoon salt
¼ teaspoon sugar
⅛ teaspoon cayenne pepper

Heat oven to 425°. Prepare pastry. Sprinkle bacon, cheese and onion in pastry-lined pie pan. With rotary beater, blend remaining ingredients; pour over bacon mixture. Bake 15 minutes.

Reduce oven temperature to 300°. Bake 30 minutes longer or until knife inserted 1 inch from edge comes out clean. Let stand 10 minutes before cutting.

6 servings.

BEEF BURGUNDY PIE

1 tablespoon butter or margarine
1 small onion, sliced
1 pound beef or veal stew meat, cut into 2-inch cubes
1 cup red Burgundy or, if desired, 1 cup hot water and 1 beef bouillon cube
2 cups hot water
2 teaspoons salt
¼ teaspoon pepper
2 medium onions, coarsely chopped
1 cup sliced carrots
1 cup diced pared potatoes
½ cup diced celery
1 tablespoon flour
¼ cup cold water
Dill Pastry for 8- or 9-inch One-crust Pie (page 17)

Melt butter in large skillet. Cook and stir sliced onion and the meat in butter until meat is brown and onion is tender. Stir in wine, 2 cups hot water, the salt and pepper. Cover and simmer over low heat until meat is tender, 2 to 3 hours. Add vegetables during last half hour of cooking time. Mix flour and ¼ cup cold water; stir into meat and vegetable mixture. Cook, stirring constantly, until mixture thickens and boils. Boil and stir 1 minute. Keep warm over low heat.

Heat oven to 450°. Prepare pastry except—roll into 10-inch square. Cut slits in pastry. Pour hot meat mixture into square baking dish, 8x8x2 inches. Place pastry over filling and flute edge. Bake 20 minutes or until brown.

4 or 5 servings.

PIZZA

To Pizza People everywhere, with love—Italy's delectable contribution to the world of pie and pastry.

2 cups all-purpose flour*
2 teaspoons baking powder
1 teaspoon salt
⅔ cup milk
6 tablespoons salad oil
Pizza Topping (below)

Heat oven to 425°. Measure flour, baking powder and salt into mixing bowl. Add milk and 4 tablespoons salad oil to dry ingredients in bowl. Stir vigorously with fork until mixture leaves side of bowl. Gather dough together and press into ball. Knead dough in bowl 10 times to make smooth. Divide dough in half.

On lightly floured cloth-covered board, roll each half into 13-inch circle. Place on pizza pan or baking sheet. Turn up edge ½ inch and pinch or pleat. Brush each circle with 1 tablespoon oil. Divide Pizza Topping and place on each circle in order listed. Bake 20 to 25 minutes. Cut into wedges to serve.
8 to 10 servings.

*If using self-rising flour, omit baking powder and salt.

Pizza Topping

½ cup grated Parmesan cheese
1 can (8 ounces) tomato sauce
1 tablespoon chopped onion
½ teaspoon salt
½ teaspoon ground oregano
¼ teaspoon pepper
½ pound shredded mozzarella cheese

Variations

Pepperoni Pizza: Follow recipe for Pizza (above) except—before adding mozzarella cheese, sprinkle ½ cup thinly sliced pepperoni on circles.

Ground Beef Pizza: Follow recipe for Pizza (above) except—before adding mozzarella cheese, sprinkle 1 pound ground beef, browned, on circles.

Sausage Pizza: Follow recipe for Pizza (left) except—before adding mozzarella cheese, sprinkle 2 cups cut-up brown and serve sausage links on circles.

Shrimp Pizza: Follow recipe for Pizza (left) except—before adding mozzarella cheese, sprinkle 2 cans (4½ ounces each) deveined shrimp, rinsed and drained, on circles.

Mushroom Pizza: Follow recipe for Pizza (left) except—before adding mozzarella cheese, sprinkle ½ cup sliced mushrooms, ¼ cup sliced pitted ripe olives and ¼ cup chopped green pepper on circles.

Anchovy Pizza: Follow recipe for Pizza (left) except—before adding mozzarella cheese, place 1 can (2 ounces) anchovies, drained, in spoke fashion on circles.

SOMBRERO PIE

Translated from the Mexican tamale pie.

½ pound ground beef
½ pound ground lean pork
1 large onion, sliced
2½ cups tomato juice
1 can (12 ounces) whole kernel corn,
    drained, or 1 package (10 ounces)
    frozen corn
1 to 2 tablespoons chili powder
1 teaspoon salt
¼ teaspoon pepper
Cornmeal Pastry for One-crust Pie
    (page 17)

In large skillet cook and stir meat and onion until meat is brown and onion is tender. Drain fat from skillet. Stir in tomato juice, corn, chili powder, salt and pepper. Heat to boiling; simmer 10 minutes.

Heat oven to 400°. Prepare pastry. Pour hot meat mixture into oblong baking dish, 11½x7½x1½ inches. Cover with Cornmeal Pastry which has slits cut in it. Seal pastry to edge of baking dish. Bake 30 to 35 minutes.
4 to 6 servings.

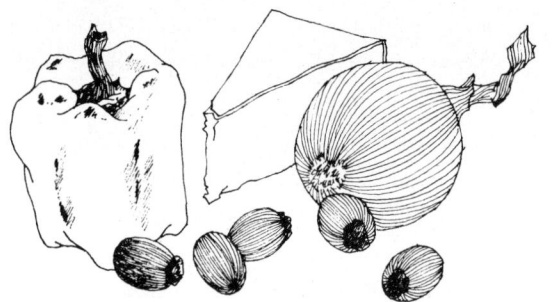

SPANISH MEATBALL PIE

In Spain these zesty meatballs are called albóndigas and are served with rice; our Americanized version tops them with cheese pastry and they become a pie.

1 pound ground beef
¼ cup fine dry bread crumbs
⅔ cup chopped onion
2 teaspoons salt
Dash pepper
½ cup milk
2 tablespoons butter or margarine
⅓ cup chopped onion
¼ cup chopped green pepper
1 can (1 pound) tomatoes
½ cup sliced pimiento-stuffed olives
¼ teaspoon pepper
¼ teaspoon garlic salt
⅛ teaspoon crushed red pepper or pinch cayenne pepper
1 can (6 ounces) tomato paste
Cheese Pastry for One-crust Pie (page 17)

Mix ground beef, crumbs, ⅔ cup onion, the salt, dash pepper and the milk. Using a slightly rounded tablespoon of meat for each ball, shape into 20 meatballs. Melt butter in large skillet; brown meatballs in butter. Push meatballs to side of skillet; add ⅓ cup onion and the green pepper. Cook and stir until vegetables are tender. Stir in tomatoes, olives, ¼ teaspoon pepper, the garlic salt, red pepper and tomato paste. Heat to boiling over medium heat. Keep hot over low heat.

Heat oven to 425°. Prepare pastry except—roll into 10-inch square. Pour hot meat mixture into square baking dish, 8x8x2 inches. Cut slits in pastry; place over meat mixture and flute edge. Bake 30 minutes or until brown.

6 servings.

SPANISH PIZZA

Cornmeal dough is the base of this unusual pizza. It's topped with a hot, hot sauce, but mellows under a lattice of cream cheese as it bakes.

1 envelope (2¼ ounces) spaghetti sauce mix
1 can (1 pound 12 ounces) tomatoes, drained
1 can (8 ounces) tomato sauce
½ cup chopped green pepper
1 teaspoon red pepper sauce
Spanish Pizza Dough (below)
1 package (10 ounces) brown 'n serve beef sausages*
2 packages (8 ounces each) cream cheese, chilled

In bowl stir together sauce mix, tomatoes, tomato sauce, green pepper and pepper sauce; set aside. *Heat oven to 400°.* Prepare Spanish Pizza Dough. Spread half of tomato mixture over each circle. Cut sausages into thin slices; place on tomato mixture. Cut cream cheese lengthwise into thin strips; place strips lattice-fashion over each pizza. Bake 15 minutes.

8 to 10 servings.

*1 package (8 ounces) fully cooked pork sausages can be substituted for the beef sausages.

Spanish Pizza Dough

1 package active dry yeast
2 tablespoons warm water (105 to 115°)
1 teaspoon salt
2 tablespoons salad oil
1 egg, well beaten
2 cups all-purpose flour*
1 cup cornmeal
1 cup cold water

Dissolve yeast in warm water; mix in salt, oil, egg, flour, cornmeal and cold water. Do not let dough rise. Turn onto well-floured cloth-covered board; knead 2 to 3 minutes. Divide dough in half. Roll each half into 12-inch circle; place each on ungreased baking sheet. Pinch up edges of circles.

*For best results, use only regular all-purpose flour. If using self-rising flour, omit salt.

Spanish Pizza

Pie for the Grand Finale

There are no two ways about it, pie for dessert makes even the most ordinary meal special. Men love it. Teenagers love it. Children love it. So any time you want to boost your popularity rating with family or guests, it's as easy as pie. Furthermore the variety is so wide that with no trouble at all you can find a pie that exactly complements whatever dinner you're serving. If the main course is on the hearty side, say pot roast or a rich lamb stew, counterpoint it with a fluffy meringue or chiffon pie. Follow a dinner of filet of sole or broiled chicken with something more robust—Pecan (page 100), or Cherry Banana or Pear Mincemeat Pie. Play pork off against any one of our twelve apple pie recipes or serve Lime Meringue Pie after roast lamb. Celebrate the berry season with Fresh Raspberry Pie and while they last, use blackberries, loganberries, boysenberries or strawberries.

Be inventive with garnishes too. Frost a clockface or a four-leaf clover or any simple outline on the top of a two-cruster to entertain the children. Sprinkle heart-shaped cinnamon candies or little silver dragées on a cream topping. Rim a pumpkin pie with a tiny picket fence of corn candies. Serve little clusters of white grapes with Fresh Peach Pie or two or three unhulled sugared strawberries with Creamy Cheesecake Pie.

Try big scoops of new or favorite ice-cream flavors on wedges of warm fruit pies for surprise taste combinations—maybe cinnamon ice cream on blueberry pie, peach ice cream on pineapple pie or butterscotch revel ice cream on plum pie; suit yourself with unusual combinations.

Go utterly elegant with candied violets wreathing a whipped cream topping. Taking these little liberties with your pies guarantees that everyone will consider them a happy ending.

Fruit Pies

There is no fruit we can think of (with the possible exception of the avocado) that can't be made into a delicious pie filling. So use whatever's fresh and abundant in your area at any particular season; between harvests substitute frozen or canned fruits for fresh. We've developed our apple, blueberry, cherry, peach and rhubarb pies in 8-, 9-, and 10-inch sizes; one will surely suit your family's size and appetite. And we especially urge you to try some of our unusual fruit combinations—such as Grape and Raspberry, Peach-Green Apple, Rhubarb-Pear, Cherry-Pineapple or Cherry Banana.

BLUEBERRY PIE

8-INCH PIE

Pastry for 8-inch Two-crust Pie (page 8)
⅓ cup sugar
¼ cup all-purpose flour
½ teaspoon cinnamon, if desired
3 cups fresh blueberries
1 teaspoon lemon juice
1 tablespoon butter or margarine

9-INCH PIE

Pastry for 9-inch Two-crust Pie (page 8)
½ cup sugar
⅓ cup all-purpose flour
½ teaspoon cinnamon, if desired
4 cups fresh blueberries
1 tablespoon lemon juice
2 tablespoons butter or margarine

10-INCH PIE

Pastry for 10-inch Two-crust Pie (page 8)
⅔ cup sugar
¼ cup plus 2 tablespoons all-purpose flour
½ teaspoon cinnamon, if desired
5 cups fresh blueberries
2 tablespoons lemon juice
3 tablespoons butter or margarine

Heat oven to 425°. Prepare pastry. Stir together sugar, flour and cinnamon; mix lightly with berries. Turn into pastry-lined pie pan; sprinkle fruit with lemon juice and dot with butter. Cover with top crust which has slits cut in it; seal and flute. Cover edge with 2- to 3-inch strip of aluminum foil to prevent excessive browning; remove foil last 15 minutes of baking. Bake 8- and 9-inch pies 35 to 45 minutes, 10-inch pie 45 to 50 minutes or until crust is nicely browned and juice bubbles through slits. Serve warm.

Variations

Canned Blueberry Pie: Follow recipe for 9-inch Blueberry Pie (above) except—substitute 3 cans (14 ounces each) blueberries, drained, for the fresh blueberries.

Frozen Blueberry Pie: Follow recipe for Blueberry Pie (above) except—substitute unsweetened frozen blueberries, partially thawed, for the fresh blueberries.

GOOSEBERRY PIE

Pastry for 9-inch Two-crust Pie (page 8)
1¾ cups sugar
½ cup all-purpose flour
4 cups fresh gooseberries
2 tablespoons butter or margarine

Heat oven to 425°. Prepare pastry. Stir together sugar and flour. Turn half of berries into pastry-lined pie pan; sprinkle with half of sugar mixture. Repeat with remaining berries and sugar; dot with butter. Cover with top crust which has slits cut in it; seal and flute. Cover edge with 2- to 3-inch strip of aluminum foil to prevent excessive browning; remove foil last 15 minutes of baking. Bake 35 to 45 minutes or until crust is nicely browned and juice begins to bubble through slits in crust. Cool.

FRESH RASPBERRY PIE

Pastry for 9-inch Two-crust Pie (page 8)
1 cup sugar
⅓ cup all-purpose flour
4 cups fresh raspberries
2 tablespoons butter or margarine

Heat oven to 425°. Prepare pastry. Stir together sugar and flour; mix lightly with berries. Turn into pastry-lined pie pan; dot with butter. Cover with top crust which has slits cut in it; seal and flute. Cover edge with 2- to 3-inch strip of aluminum foil to prevent excessive browning; remove foil last 15 minutes of baking. Bake 35 to 45 minutes or until crust is nicely browned. Serve slightly warm.

Variations

Fresh Berry Pie: Follow recipe for Fresh Raspberry Pie (above) except—substitute 4 cups fresh blackberries, loganberries or boysenberries for the raspberries.

Strawberry Pie: Follow recipe for Fresh Raspberry Pie (above) except—decrease sugar to ½ cup and substitute 4 cups sliced fresh strawberries for the raspberries. Sprinkle fruit in pastry-lined pan with 1 tablespoon lemon juice.

GRAPE JAM PIE

Pastry for 9-inch Two-crust Pie (page 8)
¼ cup water
¼ cup lemon juice
¼ cup cornstarch
1 jar (20 ounces) whole grape preserves
2 tablespoons butter or margarine

Heat oven to 425°. Prepare pastry. In bowl blend water, lemon juice and cornstarch. Stir in preserves. Turn into pastry-lined pie pan; dot with butter. Cover with top crust which has slits cut in it; seal and flute. Cover edge with 2- to 3-inch strip of aluminum foil to prevent excessive browning; remove foil last 15 minutes of baking. Bake 35 to 45 minutes or until crust is nicely browned. Serve slightly warm and, if desired, top with ice cream.

GRAPE AND RASPBERRY PIE

A unique summer pie—these two fruits in combination taste very much like rhubarb!

Pastry for 9-inch Two-crust Pie (page 8)
¾ cup sugar
¼ cup all-purpose flour
½ teaspoon salt
1½ cups fresh raspberries
1½ cups seedless green grapes
2 tablespoons butter or margarine

Heat oven to 425°. Prepare pastry. Stir together sugar, flour and salt; mix lightly with berries and grapes. Turn into pastry-lined pie pan; dot with butter. Cover with top crust which has slits cut in it; seal and flute. Cover edge with 2- to 3-inch strip of aluminum foil to prevent excessive browning; remove foil last 15 minutes of baking. Bake 35 to 45 minutes or until crust is nicely browned. Serve slightly warm.

CONCORD GRAPE PIE

The Concord grape is an Eastern variety available in the fall. Since this pie is a bit time-consuming to make, plan it as a special treat when the grapes are in season.

4 cups Concord grapes
1 cup sugar
3 tablespoons flour
Pastry for 8-inch Two-crust Pie (page 8)
1 teaspoon lemon juice
Dash salt
1 tablespoon butter or margarine

Remove skins from grapes; set skins aside. In saucepan, heat pulp of grapes (without any water) just to boiling. While hot, rub through strainer to remove seeds. Mix strained pulp with the skins. Stir together sugar and flour; mix lightly with grape mixture.

Heat oven to 425°. Prepare pastry. Pour grape mixture into pastry-lined pie pan. Sprinkle with lemon juice and salt; dot with butter. Cover with top crust which has slits cut in it; seal and flute. Cover edge with 2- to 3-inch strip of aluminum foil to prevent excessive browning; remove foil last 15 minutes of baking. Bake 35 to 45 minutes or until crust is nicely browned and juice begins to bubble through slits in crust. Serve warm or cool.

CHERRY PIE

8-INCH PIE

Pastry for 8-inch Two-crust Pie (page 8)
1⅓ cups sugar
⅓ cup all-purpose flour
2 cans (1 pound each) pitted red tart cherries, drained
¼ teaspoon almond extract
2 tablespoons butter or margarine

9-INCH PIE

Pastry for 9-inch Two-crust Pie (page 8)
1⅓ cups sugar
⅓ cup all-purpose flour
2 cans (1 pound each) pitted red tart cherries, drained
¼ teaspoon almond extract
2 tablespoons butter or margarine

10-INCH PIE

Pastry for 10-inch Two-crust Pie (page 8)
1⅔ cups sugar
½ cup all-purpose flour
3 cans (1 pound each) pitted red tart cherries, drained
1 teaspoon almond extract
3 tablespoons butter or margarine

Heat oven to 425°. Prepare pastry. Stir together sugar and flour; mix lightly with cherries. Turn into pastry-lined pie pan. Sprinkle fruit with extract and dot with butter. Cover with top crust which has slits cut in it; seal and flute. Cover edge with 2- to 3-inch strip of aluminum foil to prevent excessive browning; remove foil last 15 minutes of baking. Bake 8- and 9-inch pies 35 to 45 minutes, 10-inch pie 40 to 50 minutes or until crust is nicely browned and juice begins to bubble through slits in crust. Serve warm.

Variations

Fresh Cherry Pie: Follow recipe for 9-inch Cherry Pie (above) except—substitute 4 cups fresh red tart cherries, washed, drained and pitted, for the canned cherries.

Frozen Cherry Pie: Follow recipe for 9-inch Cherry Pie (above) except—substitute 2 cans (1 pound 4 ounces each) frozen pitted red tart cherries, thawed and drained, for the canned cherries and decrease sugar to ½ cup.

ORANGE-GLAZED CHERRY PIE

Heat oven to 425°. Prepare Orange Variation of Pastry for 8-inch Two-crust Pie (page 17). Pour 1 can (1 pound 5 ounces) cherry pie filling into pastry-lined pie pan. Cover filling with Lattice Top (page 15). Cover edge with 2- to 3-inch strip of aluminum foil to prevent excessive browning; remove foil last 15 minutes of baking. Bake 35 to 40 minutes. Spoon Orange Glaze (page 25) over center of warm pie and garnish with a twisted orange slice.

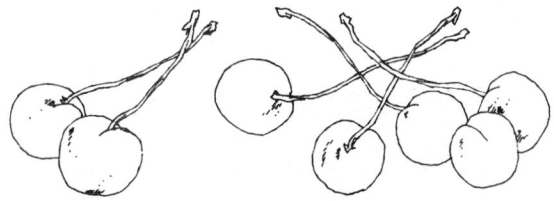

CHERRY BANANA PIE

9-inch Baked Pie Shell (page 11)
1 can (1 pound) pitted red tart cherries
1 cup sugar
3 tablespoons cornstarch
1 tablespoon butter or margarine
½ teaspoon cinnamon
1 teaspoon almond extract
2 medium bananas

Bake pie shell. In saucepan mix cherries (with liquid), sugar and cornstarch. Cook over medium heat, stirring constantly, until mixture thickens and boils. Boil and stir 1 minute. Stir in butter; cool. Stir in cinnamon and extract. Slice bananas into baked pie shell in layers. Pour filling over banana slices; chill until set. If desired, spoon wreath of whipped cream on filling; garnish with additional banana slices.

Cherry Banana Pie

Pear Mincemeat Pie

PEAR PIE

Summer or winter pears can be used for this pie . . . select firm and slightly underripe fruit for baking.

Pastry for 9-inch Two-crust Pie (page 8)
½ cup sugar
⅓ cup all-purpose flour
½ teaspoon mace, if desired
4 cups sliced pared pears (about 7 medium)
1 tablespoon lemon juice
2 tablespoons butter or margarine

Heat oven to 425°. Prepare pastry. Stir together sugar, flour and mace; mix lightly with pears. Turn into pastry-lined pie pan. Sprinkle pear slices with lemon juice and dot with butter. Cover with top crust which has slits cut in it; seal and flute. Cover edge with 2- to 3-inch strip of aluminum foil to prevent excessive browning; remove foil last 15 minutes of baking. Bake 40 to 50 minutes or until crust is nicely browned and juice begins to bubble through slits in crust. Serve slightly warm.

Variations

Canned Pear Pie: Follow recipe for Pear Pie (above) except—decrease sugar to ⅓ cup and substitute 2 cans (1 pound each) sliced pears, drained, for fresh pears.

Crumble-topped Pear Pie: Follow recipe for Pear Pie (above) except—prepare pastry for 9-inch One-crust Pie (page 8), omit butter and sprinkle top of pear filling with **Pecan Topping:** Mix ¾ cup all-purpose flour,° ⅓ cup firm butter or margarine, ⅓ cup brown sugar (packed) and ½ cup chopped pecans.

°*Do not use self-rising flour in this recipe.*

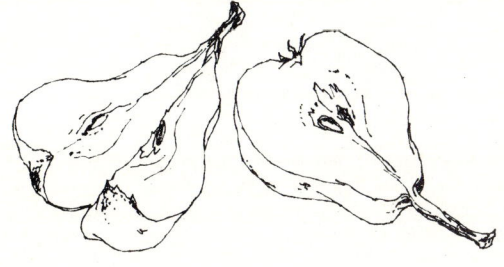

PEAR MINCEMEAT PIE

Pastry for 9-inch Two-crust Pie (page 8)
1 jar (28 ounces) prepared mincemeat (3 cups)
6 canned large pear halves
6 maraschino cherries

Heat oven to 425°. Prepare pastry. Spread mincemeat in pastry-lined pie pan. Press pear halves into mincemeat with cut sides up and narrow ends toward center. Place a cherry in hollow of each pear half. Cover with Lattice Top (page 15). Cover edge with 2- to 3-inch strip of aluminum foil to prevent excessive browning; remove foil last 15 minutes of baking. Bake 40 to 50 minutes or until crust is nicely browned. Serve slightly warm and, if desired, top servings with Whipped Cream Cheese (page 25) and Old-fashioned Lemon Sauce (page 23).

ALMOND-CRUNCH PINEAPPLE PIE

Pastry for 9-inch Two-crust Pie (page 8)
2 tablespoons cornstarch
2 tablespoons sugar
¼ teaspoon salt
1 can (1 pound 4½ ounces) crushed pineapple
½ cup sliced almonds
Corn Syrup Glaze (below)

Heat oven to 425°. Prepare pastry. In saucepan blend cornstarch, sugar and salt. Stir in pineapple (with syrup). Cook, stirring constantly, until mixture thickens and boils. Boil and stir 1 minute. Turn into pastry-lined pie pan. Cover with top crust which has slits cut in it; seal and flute. Cover edge with 2- to 3-inch strip of aluminum foil to prevent excessive browning. Bake 20 minutes. Remove pie from oven; remove foil and sprinkle almonds over top. Spoon hot glaze over nuts and bake 5 to 10 minutes longer or until crust is golden brown.

Corn Syrup Glaze

In small saucepan heat 2 tablespoons light corn syrup and 1 tablespoon butter over low heat.

FRESH PINEAPPLE PIE

2 medium pineapples
1 cup sugar
Pastry for 9-inch Two-crust Pie (page 8)
1 cup sugar
½ cup all-purpose flour
½ teaspoon grated lemon peel
1 tablespoon lemon juice
2 tablespoons butter or margarine

Cut a thick slice from top and one from bottom of each pineapple. Cut remaining pineapple into 1-inch-thick rings; remove rind and core. Cut slices into ¼-inch pieces. Place in shallow dish; sprinkle with 1 cup sugar. Cover; refrigerate at least 5 hours.

Heat oven to 425°. Drain pineapple and reserve ½ cup syrup. Prepare pastry. Spoon pineapple into pastry-lined pie pan. In small saucepan stir together 1 cup sugar and the flour. Stir in reserved syrup. Cook over medium heat, stirring constantly, until mixture thickens and boils. Boil and stir 1 minute. Remove from heat; stir in lemon peel and juice. Pour over pineapple in pie pan; dot with butter.

Cover with top crust which has slits cut in it; seal and flute. Cover edge with 2- to 3-inch strip of aluminum foil to prevent excessive browning; remove foil last 15 minutes of baking. Bake 35 to 45 minutes or until crust is nicely browned and juice begins to bubble through slits in crust. Serve slightly warm or cool.

FRUIT SALAD PIE

A colorful mixture of fresh, frozen and canned fruits, this delightful winter pie tastes like a summer fruit salad.

Pastry for 9-inch Two-crust Pie (page 8)
1 medium banana
1 package (10 ounces) frozen strawberries, thawed and drained (reserve syrup)
1 can (1 pound 4½ ounces) pineapple chunks, drained (reserve syrup)
1 tablespoon lemon juice
½ cup sugar
¼ cup quick-cooking tapioca
¼ teaspoon salt
2 tablespoons butter or margarine
Strawberry Sour Cream Topping (below)

Heat oven to 425°. Prepare pastry. Slice banana into bowl; add berries, pineapple chunks, lemon juice and ¼ cup of the reserved pineapple syrup. Stir together sugar, tapioca and salt; mix lightly with fruit mixture. Turn into pastry-lined pie pan; dot with butter. Cover with top crust which has slits cut in it; seal and flute. Cover edge with 2- to 3-inch strip of aluminum foil to prevent excessive browning; remove foil last 15 minutes of baking. Bake 40 to 50 minutes or until crust is nicely browned. Cool. Serve with Strawberry Sour Cream Topping.

Strawberry Sour Cream Topping

Blend 2 tablespoons reserved strawberry syrup and 1 cup dairy sour cream.

CHERRY-PINEAPPLE PIE

Heat oven to 425°. Prepare pastry for Two-crust Pie as directed on the pie crust mix package. Stir together 1 can (1 pound 5 ounces) cherry pie filling and 1 can (13½ ounces) pineapple tidbits, drained. Pour into pastry-lined pie pan. Dot with 1 tablespoon butter. Cover with top crust which has slits cut in it; seal and flute. Cover edge with 2- to 3-inch strip of aluminum foil to prevent excessive browning; remove foil last 15 minutes of baking. Bake 40 to 45 minutes.

Seasonal Fruit Chart

	JAN	FEB	MAR	APR	MAY	JUN	JUL	AUG	SEP	OCT	NOV	DEC
APPLES	✓	✓	✓	✓	✓	✓	✓	✓	✓	✓	✓	✓
APRICOTS						✓	✓	✓				
BANANAS	✓	✓	✓	✓	✓	✓	✓	✓	✓	✓	✓	✓
BERRIES						✓	✓	✓	✓	✓		
BLUEBERRIES						✓	✓	✓	✓			
CANTALOUPE					✓	✓	✓	✓	✓	✓		
CHERRIES						✓	✓	✓	✓			
CRANBERRIES									✓	✓	✓	✓
GRAPEFRUIT	✓	✓	✓	✓	✓	✓	✓	✓	✓	✓	✓	✓
GRAPES	✓	✓	✓	✓	✓	✓	✓	✓	✓	✓	✓	✓
HONEYDEW		✓	✓	✓	✓	✓	✓	✓	✓	✓		
LEMONS	✓	✓	✓	✓	✓	✓	✓	✓	✓	✓	✓	✓
LIMES	✓	✓	✓	✓	✓	✓	✓	✓	✓	✓	✓	✓
ORANGES	✓	✓	✓	✓	✓	✓	✓	✓	✓	✓	✓	✓
PEACHES						✓	✓	✓	✓			
PEARS	✓	✓	✓	✓	✓	✓	✓	✓	✓	✓	✓	✓
PINEAPPLES	✓	✓	✓	✓	✓	✓	✓	✓	✓	✓	✓	✓
PLUMS, PRUNES						✓	✓	✓	✓	✓		
STRAWBERRIES			✓	✓	✓	✓	✓	✓	✓	✓		
WATERMELON					✓	✓	✓	✓	✓	✓		

FRESH PEACH PIE

8-INCH PIE

Pastry for 8-inch Two-crust Pie (page 8)
4 cups sliced fresh peaches (about 6 medium)
1 teaspoon lemon juice
⅔ cup sugar
3 tablespoons flour
¼ teaspoon cinnamon
1 tablespoon butter or margarine

9-INCH PIE

Pastry for 9-inch Two-crust Pie (page 8)
5 cups sliced fresh peaches (about 8 medium)
1 teaspoon lemon juice
1 cup sugar
¼ cup all-purpose flour
¼ teaspoon cinnamon
2 tablespoons butter or margarine

10-INCH PIE

Pastry for 10-inch Two-crust Pie (page 8)
6 cups sliced fresh peaches (about 10 medium)
1 teaspoon lemon juice
1¼ cups sugar
⅓ cup all-purpose flour
¼ teaspoon cinnamon
3 tablespoons butter or margarine

Easy Peach Pie (page 78); Fresh Peach Pie; Summer Jewel Pie (page 66); Peach Melba Pie (page 66)

FRUIT PIES 65

Heat oven to 425°. Prepare pastry. Toss peaches and lemon juice. Stir together sugar, flour and cinnamon; mix lightly with sliced peaches. Turn into pastry-lined pie pan; dot with butter. Cover with top crust which has slits cut in it; seal and flute. Cover edge with 2- to 3-inch strip of aluminum foil to prevent excessive browning; remove foil last 15 minutes of baking. Bake 8- and 9-inch pies 35 to 45 minutes, 10-inch pie 40 to 50 minutes or until crust is nicely browned and juice begins to bubble through slits in crust. Serve warm.

Variations

Frozen Peach Pie: Follow recipe for 9-inch Fresh Peach Pie (left) except—substitute 3 packages (12 ounces each) frozen sliced peaches, partially thawed and drained, for the fresh peaches and decrease sugar to ½ cup.

Peach-Green Apple Pie: Follow recipe for 9-inch Fresh Peach Pie (left) except—reduce sliced peaches to 2 cups; add 2 cups thinly sliced pared green apples and ¼ cup sliced almonds and substitute ½ teaspoon salt for the cinnamon.

Canned Peach Pie: Follow recipe for 9-inch Fresh Peach Pie (left) except—substitute 2 cans (1 pound 13 ounces each) peach slices, drained, for fresh peaches and decrease sugar to ½ cup.

Brown Sugar Peach Pie: Follow recipe for 9-inch Fresh Peach Pie (left) except—substitute ¾ cup brown sugar (packed) for granulated sugar.

Apricot Pie: Follow recipe for 9-inch Fresh Peach Pie (left) except—substitute fresh apricot halves for peaches.

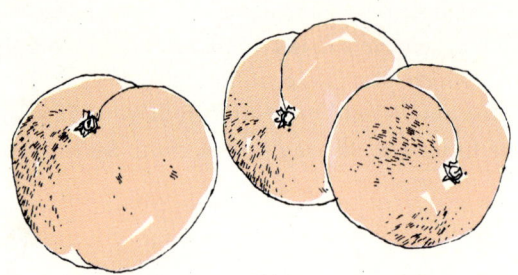

PEACH MELBA PIE

Pictured on page 65.

Pastry for 9-inch Two-crust Pie (page 8)
½ cup sugar
2 tablespoons cornstarch
3½ cups drained canned peach slices*
   (reserve ¼ cup syrup)
1 package (10 ounces) frozen red
   raspberries, thawed and drained
   (reserve syrup)
1 tablespoon butter or margarine
Vanilla ice cream
Melba Sauce (below)

Heat oven to 425°. Prepare pastry. Mix sugar, cornstarch and reserved peach syrup in saucepan. Heat to boiling over medium heat, stirring constantly. Boil and stir 1 minute; remove from heat. In bowl mix hot syrup with peach slices. Place raspberries evenly in pastry-lined pie pan; cover with peach mixture and dot with butter.

Cover with top crust which has slits cut in it; seal and flute. Cover edge with 2- to 3-inch strip of aluminum foil to prevent excessive browning; remove foil last 15 minutes of baking. Bake 40 to 45 minutes or until crust is nicely browned. Serve warm or cool with ice cream and Melba Sauce.

*1 can (1 pound 13 ounces) plus 1 can (1 pound 1 ounce) will measure 3½ cups drained peach slices.

Melba Sauce

In small saucepan mix 2 teaspoons cornstarch, ¼ cup currant jelly and ½ cup reserved raspberry syrup. Cook over medium heat, stirring constantly, until mixture thickens and boils. Boil and stir 1 minute. Cool.

SUMMER JEWEL PIE

A shortcake-type crust heaped with sparkling fresh fruit. Pictured on page 65.

Short Pie Crust (page 18)
Orange Glacé (below)
2 cups melon balls
1 cup raspberries or sliced strawberries
1 cup blueberries
1½ cups sliced peaches
½ cup sliced bananas
Whole strawberries

Bake pie crust. Prepare Orange Glacé. Place fruits (except whole strawberries) in bowl; pour glacé over them and toss lightly. Turn fruit mixture into pie crust. Garnish pie with whole strawberries. Chill before serving.

Orange Glacé

In saucepan blend ½ cup sugar, 2 tablespoons cornstarch and ⅛ teaspoon salt. Stir in ⅔ cup orange juice and ⅓ cup water. Cook over medium heat, stirring constantly, until mixture thickens and boils. Boil and stir 1 minute. Cool.

BLUEBERRY PEACH PIE

Pastry for 9-inch Two-crust Pie (page 8)
1½ cups sugar
⅓ cup all-purpose flour
½ teaspoon cinnamon
2 cups fresh blueberries
2½ cups sliced fresh peaches (about 3 medium)
1½ tablespoons butter or margarine

Heat oven to 425°. Prepare pastry. Stir together sugar, flour and cinnamon. Turn blueberries into pastry-lined pie pan. Sprinkle half of sugar mixture evenly over berries. Arrange peach slices over berries; sprinkle with remaining sugar mixture and dot with butter. Cover with top crust which has slits cut in it; seal and flute. Cover edge with 2- to 3-inch strip of aluminum foil to prevent excessive browning; remove foil last 15 minutes of baking. Bake 40 to 50 minutes or until crust is nicely browned. Cool.

PEACHES 'N CREAM PIE

Peach halves served sunny side up in a cream sauce.

Pastry for 9-inch One-crust Pie (page 8)
¾ cup sugar
3 tablespoons flour
5 medium peaches, peeled and halved
¾ cup whipping cream
¼ teaspoon cinnamon

Heat oven to 450°. Prepare pastry. Stir together sugar and flour; spread half of mixture over bottom of pastry-lined pie pan. Place peach halves cut side down, overlapping if necessary, on sugar. Sprinkle remaining sugar mixture over peaches. Pour cream over peaches; sprinkle with cinnamon. Cover edge with 2- to 3-inch strip of aluminum foil to prevent excessive browning; remove foil last 15 minutes of baking. Bake 10 minutes. *Reduce oven temperature to 350°;* bake 30 to 35 minutes longer. Cool.

PEACH BLOSSOM PIE

Pastry for 9-inch Two-crust Pie (page 8)
½ cup sugar
2 tablespoons cornstarch
3½ cups drained canned peach slices*
   (reserve ¼ cup syrup)
3 tablespoons red cinnamon candies
1 tablespoon butter or margarine

Heat oven to 425°. Prepare pastry. Mix sugar, cornstarch and reserved peach syrup in saucepan. Cook over medium heat, stirring constantly, until mixture thickens and boils. Boil and stir 1 minute. Pour hot syrup over peach slices. Add cinnamon candies and mix lightly. Pour into pastry-lined pie pan. Dot with butter.

Cover with top crust which has slits cut in it; seal and flute. Cover edge with 2- to 3-inch strip of aluminum foil to prevent excessive browning; remove foil last 15 minutes of baking. Bake 40 to 45 minutes.

*1 can (1 pound 13 ounces) plus 1 can (1 pound 1 ounce) will measure 3½ cups peach slices.

PLUM PIE

A rather tart but refreshing pie.

Pastry for 9-inch Two-crust Pie (page 8)
½ cup sugar
⅓ cup all-purpose flour
½ teaspoon cinnamon
4 cups fresh purple plum slices
1 tablespoon lemon juice
2 tablespoons butter or margarine

Heat oven to 425°. Prepare pastry. Stir together sugar, flour and cinnamon; mix lightly with plum slices. Turn into pastry-lined pie pan; sprinkle with lemon juice and dot with butter. Cover with top crust which has slits cut in it; seal and flute. Cover edge with 2- to 3-inch strip of aluminum foil to prevent excessive browning; remove foil last 15 minutes of baking. Bake 35 to 45 minutes or until crust is nicely browned and juice begins to bubble through slits in crust. Serve slightly warm.

APRICOT PRUNE PIE

8-inch Baked Pie Shell (page 11)
¼ pound (about ¾ cup) dried apricots
   (1 cup cooked)
½ pound (about 1½ cups) dried prunes
   (1 cup cooked)
½ cup sugar
2 tablespoons cornstarch
2 teaspoons lemon juice

Bake pie shell. In separate saucepans, cook apricots and prunes in water to cover until tender. Drain fruits, reserving liquid. Pit prunes and cut fruits into bite-size pieces. In small saucepan blend sugar and cornstarch. Measure reserved liquid and add enough water to measure 1 cup liquid. Stir into sugar-cornstarch mixture. Add lemon juice. Cook over medium heat, stirring constantly, until mixture thickens and boils. Boil and stir 1 minute. Stir in fruits. Cool. Turn into baked pie shell. If desired, top pie with whipped cream.

APPLE PIE

Pictured on page 70.

8-INCH PIE

Pastry for 8-inch Two-crust Pie (page 8)
½ cup sugar
3 tablespoons flour
¼ teaspoon nutmeg
¼ teaspoon cinnamon
Dash salt
5 cups thinly sliced pared tart apples (about 4 medium)
1 tablespoon butter or margarine

9-INCH PIE

Pastry for 9-inch Two-crust Pie (page 8)
¾ cup sugar
¼ cup all-purpose flour
½ teaspoon nutmeg
½ teaspoon cinnamon
Dash salt
6 cups thinly sliced pared tart apples (about 5 medium)
2 tablespoons butter or margarine

10-INCH PIE

Pastry for 10-inch Two-crust Pie (page 8)
1 cup sugar
⅓ cup all-purpose flour*
1 teaspoon nutmeg
1 teaspoon cinnamon
Dash salt
8 cups thinly sliced pared tart apples (about 7 medium)
3 tablespoons butter or margarine

If using self-rising flour, omit salt.

Heat oven to 425°. Prepare pastry. Stir together sugar, flour, nutmeg, cinnamon and salt; mix lightly with apples. Turn into pastry-lined pie pan; dot with butter. Cover with top crust which has slits cut in it; seal and flute. Cover edge with 2- to 3-inch strip of aluminum foil to prevent excessive browning; remove foil last 15 minutes of baking. Bake 40 to 50 minutes or until crust is nicely browned and juice begins to bubble through slits in crust. Serve warm and, if desired, with ice cream or wedges of cheese.

Variations

Canned Apple Pie: Follow recipe for 9-inch Apple Pie (above) except—substitute 2 cans (1 pound 4 ounces each) pie-sliced apples, drained, for the fresh apples.

Frozen Apple Pie: Follow recipe for 9-inch Apple Pie (above) except—substitute 1 package (1 pound 4 ounces) frozen sliced apples, partially thawed, for the fresh apples.

French Apple Pie: Follow recipe for 9-inch Apple Pie (above) except—prepare pastry for 9-inch One-crust Pie (page 8); omit butter and top filling with **Crumb Topping:** Mix 1 cup all-purpose flour,° ½ cup firm butter or margarine and ½ cup brown sugar (packed) with fork or pastry blender until crumbly. Increase baking time to 50 minutes. Cover Crumb Topping with foil last 10 minutes of baking if top browns too quickly.

°Do not use self-rising flour in this recipe.

Apple-Pecan Pie: Follow recipe for 10-inch Apple Pie (above) except—stir in ⅔ cup chopped pecans with the sugar; increase baking time to 50 to 60 minutes and spread hot pie with Crunchy Pecan Glaze (page 25).

Dutch Apple Pie: Follow recipe for 9-inch Apple Pie (above) except—make extra large slits in top crust; 5 minutes before pie is completely baked, pour ½ cup whipping cream through slits in top crust and bake 5 minutes.

Green Apple Pie: Follow recipe for 9-inch Apple Pie (above) except—increase sugar to 1¼ cups and use green apples.

Apple-Cheese Surprise Pie: Follow recipe for 9-inch Apple Pie (above) except—pour half of the apple mixture into pastry-lined pie pan; cover with 5 slices (1 ounce each) process American cheese and top with remaining apple mixture. Serve warm.

Apple Varieties

There are many different apple varieties; each has its own distinctive texture and flavor characteristics. The use determines the variety selected. Some apples are excellent for baking; others should be chosen for salads and for eating raw.
Apples for pies should be tart, firm and juicy. Almost any all-purpose apple can be used in a pie but certain varieties are especially good. Some of these are given here.

BALDWIN—Good all-purpose apple.

Bright red mottling over light yellow or greenish skin; juicy, mildly tart.

Season: October–January

GOLDEN DELICIOUS—Very good for pie, excellent for eating and salad.

Golden yellow, oval in shape, juicy and sweet.

Season: September–April

JONATHAN—Very good for pie, sauce, eating, salads, fair for baking.

Rich red skin overlaying a yellow background; juicy, slightly tart.

Season: September–January

McINTOSH—Very good for pie and sauce, fair for baking.

Bright deep red, striped with carmine; juicy, slightly tart and tender.

Season: September–April

NORTHERN SPY—Good all-purpose apple.

Bright red, striped over yellow; very juicy, tender.

Season: October–March

RHODE ISLAND GREENING—Excellent for pie and sauce.

Green or yellowish green, slightly tart, juicy, crisp.

Season: October–March

ROME BEAUTY—Very good for pie and sauce, excellent for baking.

Red apple with yellow or green markings; juicy, slightly tart, firm.

Season: October–April

STAYMAN—Good all-purpose apple.

Dull red striped with carmine; juicy, slightly tart, semifirm.

Season: October–March

WINESAP—Good all-purpose apple.

Bright deep red, juicy, firm, slightly tart.

Season: October–June

YORK IMPERIAL—Good for pie, sauce, baking.

Red over yellow background; tart, firm.

Season: October–May

Apple Pie (page 68); *Apple Meringue Pie*

BUTTERSCOTCH APPLE CRUMBLE PIE

It's mix easy! Pie crust mix makes the crust, thickens the filling, forms the special topping.

1 package (11 ounces) pie crust mix
⅓ cup brown sugar (packed)
1 package (6 ounces) butterscotch pieces
1 can (1 pound 4 ounces) pie-sliced apples, drained

Heat oven to 425°. Prepare pastry for 9-inch One-crust Pie as directed on package. With pastry blender mix remaining pie crust mix (or 1 stick) and the sugar until mixture is finely crumbled. Stir in butterscotch pieces; reserve 1½ cups crumbly mixture. Mix remaining crumbly mixture and pie-sliced apples. Turn into pastry-lined pie pan. Sprinkle reserved crumbly mixture over filling. Cover edge with 2- to 3-inch strip of aluminum foil to prevent excessive browning; remove foil last 15 minutes of baking. Bake 40 to 45 minutes.

APPLE MERINGUE PIE

No need to pare these apples—the peel will add a bit of color.

Pastry for 9-inch One-crust Pie (page 8)
1 cup sugar
2 tablespoons cornstarch
½ teaspoon cinnamon
½ teaspoon nutmeg
3 egg yolks
3 tablespoons butter or margarine, melted
½ cup light cream
2½ cups shredded tart apples (5 medium)
½ cup raisins
Meringue for 9-inch Pie (page 82)

Heat oven to 400°. Prepare pastry. Stir together sugar, cornstarch and spices. In small mixer bowl beat egg yolks until thick and lemon colored. Gradually beat in sugar-spice mixture, butter and cream. Fold in apples and raisins. Turn into pastry-lined pie pan. Cover edge with 2- to 3-inch strip of aluminum foil to prevent excessive browning; remove foil last 15 minutes of baking. Bake 35 to 40 minutes or until set. While hot, cover pie with meringue, carefully sealing the meringue onto edge of crust. Bake 8 to 10 minutes longer. Cool pie away from draft.

COCONUT APPLE PIE

1 egg
½ cup granulated sugar
¼ cup dairy sour cream
1¼ cups flaked coconut
Dash salt
Pastry for 9-inch One-crust Pie (page 8)
6 to 7 cups thinly sliced pared tart apples (about 6 medium)
½ cup brown sugar (packed)
½ teaspoon cinnamon
2 tablespoons butter or margarine

In small mixer bowl, beat egg thoroughly. Mix in granulated sugar, sour cream, coconut and salt. Set aside.

Heat oven to 425°. Prepare pastry. Layer apples in pastry-lined pie pan. Stir together brown sugar and cinnamon; sprinkle over apples and dot with butter. Cover edge with 2- to 3-inch strip aluminum foil to prevent excessive browning. Bake 25 minutes. Remove pie from oven; remove foil. Spoon coconut mixture over apples and spread evenly. Bake 25 minutes longer. Serve warm.

APPLE CIDER PIE

The Delicious variety of apple, normally not used for cooking, lives up to its name in this fluffy pie.

9-inch Baked Pie Shell (page 11)
1½ cups apple cider
2 tablespoons red cinnamon candies
1 package (3 ounces) lemon-flavored gelatin
2 medium-large Delicious apples
1 cup chilled whipping cream

Bake pie shell. In saucepan heat ¾ cup of the cider and the candies, stirring until candies are melted. Stir in gelatin until dissolved. Stir in remaining cider; chill until very thick. Beat with electric mixer until mixture is thick and fluffy or about double in volume. Pare and shred apples; immediately fold into gelatin mixture. In chilled bowl beat cream until stiff; fold into apple-gelatin mixture. Pour into baked pie shell; chill several hours until set.

APPLESCOTCH PIE

Buttery apples glazed with brown sugar fill this meltingly delicious pie.

5 cups thinly sliced pared tart apples
   (about 4 medium)
1 cup brown sugar (packed)
¼ cup water
1 tablespoon lemon juice
¼ cup all-purpose flour
2 tablespoons granulated sugar
¾ teaspoon salt
1 teaspoon vanilla
3 tablespoons butter or margarine
Pastry for 9-inch Two-crust Pie (page 8)

In saucepan combine apples, brown sugar, water and lemon juice. Cover; cook over medium heat 7 to 8 minutes or until apples are *just* tender. Stir together flour, granulated sugar and salt; stir into apple mixture in saucepan. Cook, stirring constantly, until mixture thickens and boils. Boil and stir 1 minute. Remove from heat; stir in vanilla and butter. Cool to room temperature.

Heat oven to 425°. Prepare pastry. Turn apple mixture into pastry-lined pie pan. Cover with crust which has slits cut in it; seal and flute. Cover edge with 2- to 3-inch strip of aluminum foil to prevent excessive browning; remove foil last 15 minutes of baking. Bake 40 to 45 minutes.

CRANBERRY APPLE PIE

Pastry for 9-inch Two-crust Pie (page 8)
1¾ to 2 cups sugar
⅓ cup all-purpose flour
3 cups sliced pared tart apples
   (about 3 medium)
2 cups fresh or frozen cranberries
2 tablespoons butter or margarine

Heat oven to 425°. Prepare pastry. Stir together sugar and flour. In pastry-lined pie pan, alternate layers of apples, cranberries and sugar mixture, beginning and ending with apples. Dot with butter. Cover with top crust which has slits cut in it; seal and flute. Cover edge with 2- to 3-inch strip of aluminum foil to prevent excessive browning; remove foil last 15 minutes of baking. Bake 40 to 50 minutes or until crust is nicely browned. Cool.

UPSIDE-DOWN APPLE-PECAN PIE

2 tablespoons soft butter or margarine
½ cup pecan halves
⅓ cup brown sugar (packed)
Pastry for 9-inch Two-crust Pie (page 8)
¾ cup granulated sugar
2 tablespoons flour
1 teaspoon cinnamon
½ teaspoon nutmeg
6 cups thinly sliced pared tart apples
   (about 5 medium)

Cut 13-inch circle from aluminum foil. Line 9-inch pie pan with circle, leaving a 1-inch overhanging edge. Spread butter over foil in pan. Press pecan halves rounded sides down on foil. Sprinkle brown sugar evenly over nuts and buttered foil.

Heat oven to 450°. Prepare pastry as directed except—ease lower crust over nuts and brown sugar in pie pan. Stir together granulated sugar, flour, cinnamon and nutmeg; mix lightly with apples. Turn into pastry-lined pie pan. Cover with top crust which has slits cut in it; seal and flute. Turn up overhanging foil edge. Bake 10 minutes. *Reduce oven temperature to 375°;* bake 35 to 40 minutes or until apples are tender. Allow pie to stand 5 minutes after removing from oven. Invert onto serving plate and serve warm.

FRESH RHUBARB PIE

For the best pies, choose pink, tender rhubarb. Use the lesser amount of sugar for early rhubarb as it is sweet and mild.

8-INCH PIE
Pastry for 8-inch Two-crust Pie (page 8)
1 to 1¼ cups sugar
¼ cup all-purpose flour
¼ teaspoon grated orange peel, if desired
3 cups cut-up rhubarb (½-inch pieces)
1 tablespoon butter or margarine
Sugar

9-INCH PIE
Pastry for 9-inch Two-crust Pie (page 8)
1⅓ to 1⅔ cups sugar
⅓ cup all-purpose flour
½ teaspoon grated orange peel, if desired
4 cups cut-up rhubarb (½-inch pieces)
2 tablespoons butter or margarine
Sugar

10-INCH PIE
Pastry for 10-inch Two-crust Pie (page 8)
1¾ to 2 cups sugar
½ cup all-purpose flour
½ teaspoon grated orange peel, if desired
5 cups cut-up rhubarb (½-inch pieces)
3 tablespoons butter or margarine
Sugar

Heat oven to 425°. Prepare pastry. Stir together sugar, flour and orange peel. Turn half of rhubarb into pastry-lined pie pan; sprinkle with half of sugar mixture. Repeat with remaining rhubarb and sugar mixture; dot with butter. Cover with top crust which has slits cut in it; seal and flute. Sprinkle sugar over top crust. Cover edge with 2- to 3-inch strip of aluminum foil to prevent excessive browning; remove foil last 15 minutes of baking. Bake 40 to 50 minutes or until crust is nicely browned and juice begins to bubble through slits in crust. Serve slightly warm. If desired, top with ice cream or whipped cream.

Variations

Frozen Rhubarb Pie: Follow recipe for 9-inch Fresh Rhubarb Pie (above) except—decrease sugar to ⅔ cup and substitute 2 packages (1 pound each) frozen rhubarb, partially thawed, for fresh rhubarb.

Rhubarb-Strawberry Pie: Follow recipe for Fresh Rhubarb Pie (above) except—substitute sliced fresh strawberries for half the rhubarb and use the lesser amount of sugar.

RHUBARB–PEAR PIE

Pastry for 9-inch Two-crust Pie (page 8)
1 cup sugar
⅓ cup all-purpose flour
3 cups cut-up rhubarb (½-inch pieces)
1 can (1 pound 13 ounces) pear halves, drained and cut into chunks
Vanilla ice cream

Heat oven to 425°. Prepare pastry. Stir together sugar and flour. Turn half of rhubarb into pastry-lined pie pan; top with half of the pear chunks. Sprinkle with half of the sugar mixture. Repeat with remaining rhubarb, pears and sugar mixture. Cover with top crust which has slits cut in it; seal and flute. Cover edge with 2- to 3-inch strip of aluminum foil to prevent excessive browning; remove foil last 15 minutes of baking. Bake 45 to 50 minutes or until crust is nicely browned and juice begins to bubble through slits. Serve pie topped with ice cream.

Custard, Cream and Meringue Pies

In contrast to the tart tangy taste of most fruit fillings, the custards, creams and meringues have a cool satiny texture and delicately sweet flavor. Unlike fruit pies, which are usually baked in a crust and often served warm, many of these delicious fillings are cooked separately and poured, semi-set, into a baked crust. All of our cream and meringue fillings are made by a new simplified method.

CUSTARD PIE

8-INCH PIE

Pastry for 8-inch
    One-crust Pie (page 8)
3 eggs
⅓ cup sugar
¼ teaspoon salt
¼ teaspoon nutmeg
1¾ cups milk
1 teaspoon vanilla

9-INCH PIE

Pastry for 9-inch
    One-crust Pie (page 8)
4 eggs
⅔ cup sugar
½ teaspoon salt
¼ teaspoon nutmeg
2⅔ cups milk
1 teaspoon vanilla

10-INCH PIE

Pastry for 10-inch One-crust
    Pie (page 8)
5 eggs
1 cup sugar
½ teaspoon salt
¼ teaspoon nutmeg
3 cups milk
1½ teaspoons vanilla

Heat oven to 450°. Prepare pastry. Beat eggs slightly with rotary beater. Beat in remaining ingredients; pour into pastry-lined pie pan. (To prevent spills, fill pie shell on oven rack or on open oven door.) Bake 20 minutes.

Reduce oven temperature to 350°. Bake 8-inch pie 10 minutes longer, 9-inch pie 15 to 20 minutes longer and 10-inch pie 30 minutes longer or until knife inserted halfway between center and edge of filling comes out clean. Serve slightly warm or cool.

SLIP–SLIDE CUSTARD PIE

9-inch Baked Pie Shell (page 11)
4 eggs
⅔ cup sugar
½ teaspoon salt
¼ teaspoon nutmeg
1 teaspoon vanilla
2⅔ cups milk

Bake pie shell. *Heat oven to 350°.* Beat eggs slightly with rotary beater. Beat in remaining ingredients; pour into ungreased 9-inch pie pan. Set pan in shallow pan of hot water. Bake about 65 minutes or until knife inserted halfway between center and edge of filling comes out clean. Cool to lukewarm. To slip baked filling into baked pie shell: 1) loosen custard around edge of pan with spatula; shake pan gently to loosen custard completely; 2) slip custard into shell and let settle a few minutes before serving.

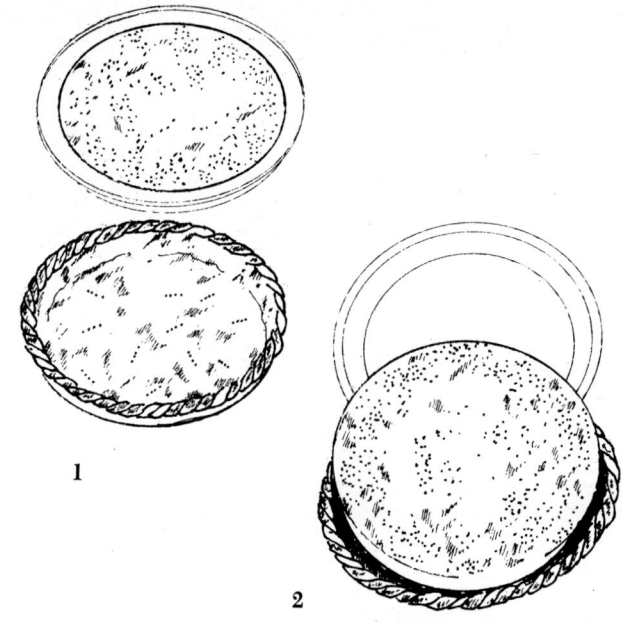

1

2

CUSTARD PIES 75

PERFECT PINEAPPLE PIE

A most unusual pie . . . golden pineapple custard baked under a lattice crust. Pictured above.

Pastry for 9-inch Two-crust Pie (page 8)
3 eggs
⅓ cup butter or margarine, melted
2 tablespoons lemon juice
½ cup water
1 cup sugar
¼ cup all-purpose flour
¼ teaspoon salt
1 can (1 pound 4½ ounces) crushed
 pineapple, drained

Heat oven to 400°. Prepare pastry. In small mixer bowl beat eggs slightly. Add butter, lemon juice and water; blend on low speed. Add sugar, flour and salt; beat until smooth. Stir in pineapple; pour into pastry-lined pie pan. Cover with Lattice Top (page 15). Cover edge with 2- to 3-inch strip of aluminum foil to prevent excessive browning; remove foil last 15 minutes of baking. Bake 35 to 40 minutes.

SPICY WALNUT RAISIN PIE

Those who enjoy pecan pie will like this rich version of dark custard pie.

Pastry for 9-inch One-crust Pie (page 8)
3 eggs
⅔ cup sugar
½ teaspoon salt
½ teaspoon cinnamon
½ teaspoon nutmeg
½ teaspoon cloves
1 cup light or dark corn syrup
⅓ cup butter or margarine, melted
½ cup coarsely chopped walnuts
½ cup raisins

Heat oven to 375°. Prepare pastry. With rotary beater, beat remaining ingredients except walnuts and raisins until blended. Stir in walnuts and raisins. Pour into pastry-lined pie pan. Bake 40 to 50 minutes or until filling is set and pastry is nicely browned. Serve slightly warm or cool.

Chocolate Cream Pie

VANILLA CREAM PIE

Here's our new streamlined method for making cream fillings.

8-INCH PIE
8-inch Baked Pie Shell (page 11)
½ cup sugar
3 tablespoons cornstarch
¼ teaspoon salt
2 cups milk
3 egg yolks, slightly beaten
1 tablespoon butter or margarine, softened
1 tablespoon vanilla
Sweetened whipped cream

9-INCH PIE
9-inch Baked Pie Shell (page 11) or Cookie Crumb Crust (page 19)
⅔ cup sugar
¼ cup cornstarch
½ teaspoon salt
3 cups milk
4 egg yolks, slightly beaten
2 tablespoons butter or margarine, softened
1 tablespoon plus 1 teaspoon vanilla
Sweetened whipped cream

10-INCH PIE
10-inch Baked Pie Shell (page 11)
¾ cup sugar
¼ cup plus 2 tablespoons cornstarch
1 teaspoon salt
4 cups milk
5 egg yolks, slightly beaten
3 tablespoons butter or margarine, softened
1 tablespoon plus 2 teaspoons vanilla
Sweetened whipped cream

Bake pie shell. In saucepan blend sugar, cornstarch and salt. Stir milk into egg yolks. Stir egg mixture slowly into dry ingredients. Cook, stirring constantly, over medium heat until mixture thickens and boils. Boil and stir 1 minute. Remove from heat; blend in butter and vanilla. Immediately pour into baked pie shell; press plastic wrap onto filling. Chill pie thoroughly (2 hours or longer). Just before serving, remove plastic wrap from filling; top pie with sweetened whipped cream.

Variations

Chocolate Cream Pie: Follow recipe for 9-inch Vanilla Cream Pie (above) except—increase sugar to 1½ cups and cornstarch to ⅓ cup. Add 2 squares (1 ounce each) unsweetened chocolate, cut up, or 2 envelopes (1 ounce each) premelted unsweetened chocolate after stirring in milk. Omit the butter.

Butterscotch Cream Pie: Follow recipe for 9-inch Vanilla Cream Pie (above) except—substitute 1 cup brown sugar (packed) for the granulated sugar and decrease vanilla to 1 teaspoon.

Banana Cream Pie: Follow recipe for 9-inch Vanilla Cream Pie (above) except—press plastic wrap onto filling in saucepan and cool to room temperature. Slice 2 large bananas into baked pie shell in layers; pour in cooled filling.

Coconut Cream Pie: Follow recipe for 9-inch Vanilla Cream Pie (above) except—decrease vanilla to 2 teaspoons and stir in ¾ cup flaked coconut. Sprinkle an additional ¼ cup flaked coconut over whipped cream on top of pie.

All of our cream and meringue pies feature a new method of cooking—it's faster and it means you use fewer utensils. In the past, these fillings were cooked without the egg yolks; then part of the hot mixture was stirred into the beaten yolks. Then the mixture was returned to the range and brought to boiling. In our recipes, the whole mixture is cooked and thickened in one step.

SILKEN SOUR CREAM PIE

Pastry for 9-inch One-crust Pie (page 8)
2 tablespoons lemon juice
1¾ cups light cream
⅔ cup sugar
3 tablespoons flour
¼ teaspoon salt
3 eggs, separated
2 teaspoons vanilla
Raspberry Sauce (below)

Heat oven to 425°. Prepare pastry. Combine lemon juice and cream; set aside. Stir together sugar, flour and salt. Beat egg yolks slightly. Stir cream, egg yolks and vanilla into sugar mixture. Beat egg whites until stiff; blend into egg yolk mixture. Pour into pastry-lined pie pan. Bake 10 minutes.

Reduce oven temperature to 325°. Bake 30 minutes longer or until a knife inserted 1 inch from edge comes out clean. Cool; serve with Raspberry Sauce. If not served immediately, refrigerate until serving time.

Raspberry Sauce

Thaw and drain 1 package (10 ounces) frozen raspberries, reserving syrup. Add water to reserved syrup to measure ⅔ cup liquid. Blend 2 tablespoons cornstarch into liquid in small saucepan. Cook over medium heat, stirring until mixture thickens and boils. Boil and stir 1 minute. Cool to lukewarm; stir in ½ cup grenadine syrup and the raspberries.

CHOCOLATE PUDDING PIE

Canned puddings are ready to serve and come in several flavors. Try this recipe for a quick pie filling.

9-inch Baked Pie Shell (page 11)
1 envelope (1 tablespoon) unflavored gelatin
⅔ cup cold water
1 can (18 ounces) chocolate or chocolate fudge pudding (room temperature)

Bake pie shell. Cool. In small saucepan, soften gelatin in water; place over low heat and stir until dissolved. In medium bowl, blend pudding and gelatin with rotary beater or spoon until smooth. Pour mixture into pie shell. Refrigerate at least 2 hours.

PEANUT-BUTTER PUDDING PIE

A pudding mix makes this a speedy palate pleaser.

9-inch Baked Pie Shell (page 11)
1 package (about 3½ ounces) vanilla pudding and pie filling
¼ cup peanut butter
2 medium bananas
Sweetened whipped cream

Bake pie shell. Prepare pie filling as directed on package except—use 1¾ cups milk and when pudding boils, immediately remove from heat; blend in peanut butter with rotary beater. Cool pie filling slightly. Arrange a layer of sliced bananas on side and bottom of pie shell. Pour filling over slices; let pie stand at room temperature about 30 minutes. Chill 2 to 3 hours. Garnish with whipped cream.

EASY PEACH PIE

Pictured on page 64.

Pastry for 9-inch One-crust Pie (page 8)
2 tablespoons finely chopped almonds
1 package (about 3½ ounces) vanilla instant pudding
1 cup milk
1 cup chilled whipping cream*
1 can (1 pound 4 ounces) sliced peaches, drained, or 4 fresh peaches, peeled and sliced

Prepare pastry as directed except—stir in almonds before adding water. Bake pie shell. In small mixing bowl blend pudding and milk at low speed. Add cream and beat at medium speed until soft peaks form, 3 to 5 minutes. Fold in peaches, reserving about ½ cup for garnish. (If using fresh peaches, dip peach slices for garnish in lemon juice to prevent darkening; drain on paper towels.) Pour into pie shell. Arrange reserved peach slices on top of pie. Refrigerate several hours or until filling is firm.

*One envelope (about 2 ounces) dessert topping mix can be substituted for the cream. Add dry topping mix and the amount of milk called for on the package to the pudding-milk mixture; beat until soft peaks form.

STRAWBERRY GLACÉ CREAM PIE

9-inch Graham Cracker Crust (page 19)
1 pint fresh strawberries, washed and hulled
Strawberry Glacé (below)
1 cup dairy sour cream
1 cup milk
1 package (about 3½ ounces) vanilla instant pudding

Prepare crust. Slice strawberries. Prepare Strawberry Glacé, reserving remaining strawberries. Beat sour cream and milk with rotary beater until smooth. Blend in pudding (dry mix) until mixture is smooth and slightly thickened. Pour into crust. Arrange remaining strawberries over filling. Cover with glacé and refrigerate until firm, about 2 hours.

Strawberry Glacé

Combine ½ cup of the sliced fresh strawberries and ¼ cup water in small saucepan; simmer about 3 minutes. Stir together ½ cup sugar and 1½ tablespoons cornstarch; blend in ¼ cup water. Stir into hot strawberry mixture. Cook, stirring constantly, until mixture thickens and boils. Boil and stir 1 minute. Cool.

Variations

Banana Sour Cream Pie: Follow recipe for Strawberry Glacé Cream Pie (above) except—omit strawberries and glacé. Slice 2 or 3 bananas into crust. Pour filling over bananas. At serving time, top with additional banana slices if desired.

Cherry-Chocolate Pudding Pie: Follow recipe for Strawberry Glacé Cream Pie (above) except—omit strawberries and glacé. Drain 1 can (1 pound 5 ounces) cherry pie filling, reserving ½ cup syrup. Spoon cherries into crust; spread reserved syrup over cherries. Substitute 1 package (about 4½ ounces) chocolate instant pudding for the vanilla instant pudding. Pour filling over cherries in crust.

VANILLA SOUR CREAM PIE

A real quickie . . . crumb crust with a pudding mix filling.

8-inch Graham Cracker Crust (page 19)
1 cup dairy sour cream
1 cup milk
1 package (about 3½ ounces) vanilla instant pudding

Prepare crust. Beat sour cream and milk with rotary beater until smooth. Blend in pudding (dry mix) until mixture is smooth and slightly thickened. Pour into crust. Chill at least 1 hour or until set. If desired, serve with sweetened whipped cream.

Variations

Chocolate Sour Cream Pie: Follow recipe for Vanilla Sour Cream Pie (above) except—substitute 1 package (about 4½ ounces) chocolate instant pudding for the vanilla instant pudding.

Fruit Cream Pie: Follow recipe for Vanilla Sour Cream Pie (above) except—after pie has been chilled, top with sliced strawberries, peaches or drained crushed pineapple, or spread with a thin layer of cherry, strawberry or blueberry preserves.

LEMON MERINGUE PIE

Tender meringue atop a tangy citrus filling adds up to a favorite dessert with just about everyone.

8-INCH PIE

8-inch Baked Pie Shell (page 11)
1 cup sugar
¼ cup cornstarch
1 cup water
2 egg yolks, slightly beaten
2 tablespoons butter or margarine
1 teaspoon grated lemon peel
⅓ cup lemon juice
1 or 2 drops yellow food coloring, if desired
Meringue for 8-inch Pie (page 82)

9-INCH PIE

9-inch Baked Pie Shell (page 11)
1½ cups sugar
⅓ cup plus 1 tablespoon cornstarch
1½ cups water
3 egg yolks, slightly beaten
3 tablespoons butter or margarine
2 teaspoons grated lemon peel
½ cup lemon juice
1 or 2 drops yellow food coloring, if desired
Meringue for 9-inch Pie (page 82)

10-INCH PIE

10-inch Baked Pie Shell (page 11)
2 cups sugar
½ cup cornstarch
2 cups water
4 egg yolks, slightly beaten
¼ cup butter or margarine
2 teaspoons grated lemon peel
⅔ cup lemon juice
1 or 2 drops yellow food coloring, if desired
Meringue for 10-inch Pie (page 82)

Lemon Meringue Pie

Orange Meringue Pie (page 82)

Bake pie shell. *Heat oven to 400°.* In saucepan blend sugar and cornstarch. Gradually stir in water. Cook, stirring constantly, over medium heat until mixture thickens and boils. Boil and stir 1 minute. Gradually stir at least half the hot mixture into egg yolks. Blend into hot mixture in pan. Boil and stir 1 minute (2 minutes for 10-inch). Remove from heat; stir in butter, lemon peel and juice and food coloring. Immediately pour into baked pie shell. Heap meringue on hot pie filling; spread over filling, carefully sealing the meringue onto edge of crust to prevent shrinking or weeping. Bake about 10 minutes or until delicately browned. Cool pie away from draft.

Variation

Lime Meringue Pie: Follow recipe for 9-inch Lemon Meringue Pie (left) except—decrease cornstarch to ⅓ cup and omit butter. Substitute 2 teaspoons grated lime peel and ¼ cup lime juice for the lemon peel and juice and green food coloring for the yellow.

Lime Meringue Pie

PIE MERINGUE

Separate eggs carefully; even the smallest amount of egg yolk can prevent the whites from whipping.

FOR 8-INCH PIE
2 egg whites
¼ teaspoon cream of tartar
¼ cup sugar
¼ teaspoon vanilla

FOR 9-INCH PIE
3 egg whites
¼ teaspoon cream of tartar
6 tablespoons sugar
½ teaspoon vanilla

FOR 10-INCH PIE
4 egg whites
¼ teaspoon cream of tartar
½ cup sugar
¾ teaspoon vanilla

Beat egg whites and cream of tartar until frothy. Beat in sugar, 1 tablespoon at a time; continue beating until stiff and glossy. *Do not underbeat.* Beat in vanilla.

Variation
Brown Sugar Meringue: Prepare meringue as directed at left except—substitute brown sugar (packed) for granulated sugar.

ORANGE MERINGUE PIE

Pictured on page 81.

**9-inch Baked Pie Shell (page 11) or
 Toasted Coconut Crust (page 18)**
1 cup sugar
3 tablespoons cornstarch
3 egg yolks, slightly beaten
1 cup orange juice
½ cup water
3 tablespoons butter or margarine
1 tablespoon lemon juice
1 tablespoon grated orange peel
Meringue for 9-inch Pie (above)

Bake pie shell. *Heat oven to 400°.* In saucepan blend sugar and cornstarch. Combine egg yolks, orange juice and water; stir gradually into sugar mixture. Cook, stirring constantly, over medium heat until mixture thickens and boils. Boil and stir 1 minute. Remove from heat; stir in butter, lemon juice and orange peel. (If a more intense orange color is desired, stir in red and yellow food coloring.) Immediately pour into baked pie shell. Heap meringue on hot pie filling; spread over filling, carefully sealing the meringue onto edge of crust. Bake about 10 minutes or until delicately browned. Cool pie away from draft.

SOUR CREAM RAISIN MERINGUE PIE

9-inch Baked Pie Shell (page 11)
1½ tablespoons cornstarch
1 cup plus 2 tablespoons sugar
¼ teaspoon salt
¾ teaspoon nutmeg
1½ cups dairy sour cream
3 egg yolks, slightly beaten
1½ cups raisins
1 tablespoon lemon juice
**Brown Sugar Meringue for 9-inch Pie
 (above)**

Bake pie shell. *Heat oven to 400°.* In saucepan blend cornstarch, sugar, salt and nutmeg. Blend in sour cream. Stir in egg yolks, raisins and lemon juice. Cook over medium heat, stirring constantly, until mixture thickens and boils. Boil and stir 1 minute. Immediately pour into baked pie shell. Heap brown sugar meringue on hot pie filling; spread over filling, carefully sealing the meringue onto edge of crust. Bake about 10 minutes or until lightly browned. Cool pie away from draft.

Chiffon Pies

A perfect ending for a luncheon or a hearty dinner is an airy, foamy chiffon pie, light as a feather and a special favorite of women. Served without topping to display its delicate filling or surmounted with snowy peaks of whipped cream, a chiffon pie is a thing of beauty. Flavors run the full gamut from the traditional lemon (or lime or orange) through strawberry, chocolate and caramel all the way to mincemeat and Nesselrode.

Just remember that you'll give extra loft to your pie if you chill the filling for a few minutes before putting it into the pie shell. And if you want to reach fantastic heights, do try our Mile High Lemon Pie, the tallest treat of all.

LEMON CHIFFON PIE

The glamour queen of all pies, a billowy chiffon with sunshine flavor—choose lemon, lime or orange.

8-INCH PIE
- 8-inch Baked Pie Shell (page 11)
- 3 egg yolks, slightly beaten
- ⅓ cup sugar
- 2 teaspoons unflavored gelatin
- ½ cup water
- ¼ cup lemon juice
- 2 teaspoons grated lemon peel
- 3 egg whites
- ¼ teaspoon cream of tartar
- ⅓ cup sugar

9-INCH PIE
- 9-inch Baked Pie Shell (page 11)
- 4 egg yolks, slightly beaten
- ½ cup sugar
- 1 envelope (1 tablespoon) unflavored gelatin
- ⅔ cup water
- ⅓ cup lemon juice
- 1 tablespoon grated lemon peel
- 4 egg whites
- ½ teaspoon cream of tartar
- ½ cup sugar

10-INCH PIE
- 10-inch Baked Pie Shell (page 11)
- 5 egg yolks, slightly beaten
- ⅔ cup sugar
- 4 teaspoons unflavored gelatin
- ¾ cup water
- ½ cup lemon juice
- 4 teaspoons grated lemon peel
- 5 egg whites
- ½ teaspoon cream of tartar
- ½ cup sugar

Bake pie shell. In saucepan blend yolks, ½ cup sugar, the gelatin, water and lemon juice. Cook over medium heat, stirring constantly, *just* until mixture boils. Stir in lemon peel. Place pan in bowl of ice and water or chill in refrigerator, stirring occasionally, until mixture mounds when dropped from a spoon (page 84).

Beat egg whites and cream of tartar until frothy. Beat in ½ cup sugar, 1 tablespoon at a time; continue beating until stiff and glossy. *Do not underbeat.* Fold in lemon mixture; pile into pie shell. Chill several hours until set. If desired, serve with sweetened whipped cream or garnish with Lemon Roses (page 27).

Variations

Lime Chiffon Pie: Follow recipe for Lemon Chiffon Pie (above) except—substitute lime juice and grated lime peel for the lemon juice and peel.

Orange Chiffon Pie: Follow recipe for Lemon Chiffon Pie (above) except—substitute orange juice for the water and lemon juice, orange peel for the lemon peel.

COFFEE CHIFFON PIE

9-inch Baked Pie Shell (page 11)
3 egg yolks, slightly beaten
½ cup sugar
3 tablespoons instant coffee
1 envelope (1 tablespoon) unflavored gelatin
½ teaspoon salt
1½ cups milk
1 teaspoon vanilla
3 egg whites
¼ teaspoon cream of tartar
½ cup sugar
½ cup chilled whipping cream

Bake pie shell. In saucepan blend egg yolks, ½ cup sugar, the instant coffee, gelatin, salt and milk. Cook over medium heat, stirring constantly, *just* until mixture boils. Stir in vanilla. Place pan in bowl of ice and water or chill in refrigerator, stirring occasionally, until mixture mounds when dropped from a spoon.

Beat egg whites and cream of tartar until frothy. Beat in ½ cup sugar, 1 tablespoon at a time; continue beating until stiff and glossy. *Do not underbeat.* In chilled bowl, beat cream until stiff; fold into coffee mixture. Fold mixture into meringue; pile into pie shell. Chill several hours until set.

TUTTI-FRUTTI PIE

Whipped evaporated milk adds airy goodness to this fruit-rich pie.

9-inch Baked Pie Shell (page 11)
1 cup chilled evaporated milk
1 can (8¾ ounces) crushed pineapple
¼ cup maraschino cherry juice
1 package (3 ounces) lemon-flavored gelatin
½ cup sugar
1 tablespoon lemon juice
¼ cup maraschino cherries, quartered

Bake pie shell. To insure whipping quality of evaporated milk, have it *well chilled.* (For quick chilling, pour into 8-inch square pan or 9-inch pie pan and freeze until crystals form around the outside edge.)

In saucepan combine pineapple (with syrup), cherry juice, gelatin and sugar. Cook over medium heat, stirring constantly, *just* until mixture boils. Place pan in bowl of ice and water or chill in refrigerator, stirring occasionally, until mixture mounds when dropped from a spoon. Whip milk and lemon juice until stiff. Fold in fruit mixture and cherries; pile into pie shell. Chill several hours until firm.

Chiffon Mixtures

Place pan in bowl of ice and water or chill in refrigerator, stirring occasionally, until mixture mounds slightly when dropped from a spoon (mixture should be slightly thicker than unbeaten egg whites). Do not let mixture get too firm.

Beat egg whites and cream of tartar until frothy. Beat in sugar, 1 tablespoon at a time; continue beating until stiff and glossy.

Stir gelatin mixture until blended. Carefully fold gelatin mixture into meringue, bringing rubber scraper across bottom of bowl, up the side and over, cutting through center occasionally. Turn bowl and continue folding until mixture is blended.

MILE HIGH LEMON PIE

Tall and elegant—it's the angel food of the pie world.

9-inch Baked Pie Shell (page 11)
8 egg yolks, slightly beaten
1 cup sugar
1 envelope (1 tablespoon) unflavored gelatin
½ cup water
1 tablespoon grated lemon peel
½ cup lemon juice
¼ teaspoon salt
8 egg whites
¼ teaspoon cream of tartar
1 cup sugar

Bake pie shell. In saucepan blend egg yolks, 1 cup sugar, the gelatin, water, lemon peel, juice and salt. Cook over medium heat, stirring constantly, *just* until mixture boils. Place pan in bowl of ice and water or chill in refrigerator, stirring occasionally, until mixture mounds when dropped from a spoon (page 84).

Beat egg whites and cream of tartar until frothy. Beat in 1 cup sugar, 1 tablespoon at a time; continue beating until stiff and glossy. *Do not underbeat.* Fold in lemon mixture; pile into pie shell. Chill several hours until set.

Chocolate Chiffon Pie; Raspberry Chiffon Pie

CHIFFON PIES

CHOCOLATE CHIFFON PIE

9-inch Graham Cracker Crust (page 19)
1 envelope (1 tablespoon) unflavored
    gelatin
½ cup sugar
½ teaspoon salt
1⅓ cups water
2 squares (1 ounce each) unsweetened
    chocolate, cut up, or 2 envelopes
    (1 ounce each) premelted unsweetened
    chocolate
3 eggs, separated
1 teaspoon vanilla
¼ teaspoon cream of tartar
½ cup sugar
½ cup chilled whipping cream

    Prepare crust. In saucepan mix gelatin, ½ cup sugar, the salt, water and chocolate. Cook over medium heat, stirring constantly, until chocolate melts. Remove from heat. Beat egg yolks slightly; stir chocolate mixture slowly into yolks. Return mixture to saucepan. Cook over medium heat, stirring constantly, *just* until mixture boils. Remove from heat. Place pan in bowl of ice and water or chill in refrigerator, stirring occasionally, until mixture mounds when dropped from a spoon (page 84). Stir in vanilla.
    Beat egg whites and cream of tartar until frothy. Beat in ½ cup sugar, 1 tablespoon at a time; continue beating until stiff and glossy. *Do not underbeat.* In chilled bowl, beat cream until stiff; fold into chocolate mixture. Fold mixture into meringue; pile into pie shell. Chill several hours until set. If desired, garnish with whipped cream and chocolate curls.

STRAWBERRY CHIFFON PIE

9-inch Baked Pie Shell (page 11)
⅔ cup sugar
1 envelope (1 tablespoon) unflavored
    gelatin
1 pint fresh strawberries, crushed
3 egg whites
¼ teaspoon cream of tartar
⅓ cup sugar
½ cup chilled whipping cream

    Bake pie shell. In saucepan blend ⅔ cup sugar, the gelatin and strawberries. Cook over medium heat, stirring constantly, *just* until mixture boils. Place pan in bowl of ice and water or chill in refrigerator, stirring occasionally, until mixture mounds when dropped from a spoon (page 84).
    Beat egg whites and cream of tartar until frothy. Beat in ⅓ cup sugar, 1 tablespoon at a time; continue beating until stiff and glossy. *Do not underbeat.* In chilled bowl beat cream until stiff; fold into strawberry mixture. Fold mixture into meringue; pile into pie shell. Chill several hours until set.

Variations

Frozen Strawberry Chiffon Pie: Follow recipe for Strawberry Chiffon Pie (above) except—substitute 1 package (10 ounces) frozen strawberry halves, thawed, for fresh strawberries and decrease sugar to ¼ cup.

Raspberry Chiffon Pie: Follow recipe for Strawberry Chiffon Pie (above) except—substitute 1 pint fresh raspberries, crushed, or 1 package (10 ounces) frozen raspberries, thawed, for the strawberries. If using frozen raspberries, decrease sugar to ¼ cup.

LEMON-LIME CHIFFON PIE

No rolling, no grating, no squeezing; a simply delicious pie that's a delight for the cook.

10-inch Graham Cracker Crust (page 19)
2 egg yolks, slightly beaten
1 package (3½ ounces) lemon pie filling
1 package (3 ounces) lime-flavored gelatin
2¼ cups water
2 egg whites
¼ teaspoon cream of tartar
¼ cup sugar

Prepare crust. In saucepan blend egg yolks, pie filling, gelatin and water. Cook over medium heat, stirring constantly, *just* until mixture boils. Place pan in bowl of ice and water or chill in refrigerator, stirring occasionally, until mixture mounds when dropped from a spoon (page 84).

Beat egg whites and cream of tartar until frothy. Beat in sugar, 1 tablespoon at a time; continue beating until stiff and glossy. *Do not underbeat.* Fold in gelatin mixture; pile into pie shell. Chill several hours until set.

LEMONADE PIE

8-inch Baked Pie Shell (page 11)
3 egg yolks, slightly beaten
1 can (6 ounces) frozen lemonade concentrate, thawed
2 teaspoons unflavored gelatin
3 egg whites
¼ teaspoon cream of tartar
½ cup sugar
1 cup chilled whipping cream

Bake pie shell. In saucepan blend egg yolks, lemonade concentrate and gelatin. Cook over medium heat, stirring constantly, *just* until mixture boils. Place pan in bowl of ice and water or chill in refrigerator, stirring occasionally, until mixture mounds when dropped from a spoon (page 84).

Beat egg whites and cream of tartar until frothy. Beat in sugar, 1 tablespoon at a time; continue beating until stiff and glossy. *Do not underbeat.* In chilled bowl, beat cream until stiff; fold into lemonade mixture. Fold mixture into meringue; pile into pie shell. Chill several hours until set.

NESSELRODE PIE

9-inch Baked Pie Shell (page 11)
2 egg yolks, slightly beaten
½ cup sugar
1 envelope (1 tablespoon) unflavored gelatin
½ teaspoon salt
1 cup milk
¼ teaspoon almond extract
2 egg whites
¼ teaspoon cream of tartar
⅓ cup sugar
½ cup chilled whipping cream
1 jar (10 ounces) Nesselrode

Bake pie shell. In saucepan blend egg yolks, ½ cup sugar, the gelatin, salt and milk. Cook over medium heat, stirring constantly, *just* until mixture boils. Place pan in bowl of ice and water or chill in refrigerator, stirring occasionally, until mixture mounds when dropped from a spoon (page 84). Stir in almond extract.

Beat egg whites and cream of tartar until frothy. Beat in ⅓ cup sugar, 1 tablespoon at a time; continue beating until stiff and glossy. *Do not underbeat.* In chilled bowl, beat cream until stiff; fold into gelatin mixture. Fold Nesselrode into gelatin mixture. Carefully fold Nesselrode mixture into meringue; pile into pie shell. Chill several hours until set.

CHOCOLATE MARVEL PIE

9-inch Baked Pie Shell (page 11)
1 package (6 ounces) semisweet chocolate pieces
2 tablespoons sugar
3 tablespoons milk
4 eggs, separated
1 teaspoon vanilla
¼ teaspoon cream of tartar

Bake pie shell. In saucepan heat chocolate pieces, sugar and milk over low heat, stirring until chocolate is melted. Cool. Beat in egg yolks, one at a time. Stir in vanilla. Beat egg whites and cream of tartar until stiff. Fold in chocolate mixture. Pour into baked pie shell. Refrigerate several hours or overnight. If desired, garnish with whipped cream and sprinkle with roasted diced almonds.

MINCEMEAT CHIFFON PIE

9-inch Cookie Crust (page 18)
1 envelope (1 tablespoon) unflavored
   gelatin
½ cup water
1 jar (28 ounces) prepared mincemeat
3 egg whites
¼ teaspoon cream of tartar
½ cup sugar

Prepare crust. Soften gelatin in water in saucepan. Cook over low heat, stirring constantly, until gelatin is dissolved. Remove from heat; stir in mincemeat. Place pan in bowl of ice and water or chill in refrigerator, stirring occasionally, until mixture mounds when dropped from a spoon (page 84).

Beat egg whites and cream of tartar until frothy. Beat in sugar, 1 tablespoon at a time; continue beating until stiff and glossy. *Do not underbeat.* Fold in mincemeat mixture; pile into pie shell. Chill several hours until set.

CHERRY JUBILEE CHIFFON PIE

9-inch Baked Pie Shell (page 11)
1 can (1 pound) pitted dark sweet cherries,
   drained (reserve syrup)
1 package (3 ounces) cherry-flavored
   gelatin
1 cup chilled whipping cream or 1 envelope
   (about 2 ounces) dessert topping mix

Bake pie shell. In saucepan combine reserved syrup and enough water to measure 1½ cups and the gelatin. Cook over medium heat, stirring constantly, *just* until mixture boils. Place pan in bowl of ice and water or chill in refrigerator, stirring occasionally, until mixture mounds when dropped from a spoon (page 84). Cut cherries in half.

In chilled bowl beat cream until stiff. (If using dessert topping mix, prepare as directed on package.) Fold in gelatin mixture and cherries; pile into pie shell. Chill several hours until set.

CARAMEL NUT CHIFFON PIE

A blending of pecans, caramelized sugar and a brown sugar meringue results in this unusual chiffon pie.

9-inch Baked Pie Shell (page 11)
½ cup granulated sugar
3 egg yolks, slightly beaten
1½ cups milk
1 envelope (1 tablespoon) unflavored
   gelatin
½ teaspoon salt
1 teaspoon vanilla
½ cup toasted chopped pecans
3 egg whites
¼ teaspoon cream of tartar
¼ cup granulated sugar
¼ cup brown sugar (packed)

Bake pie shell. In saucepan cook and stir ½ cup granulated sugar over low heat until melted and golden brown. Blend egg yolks, milk, gelatin and salt; stir into melted sugar. (Sugar will crystallize, then dissolve with continued cooking.) Cook over medium heat, stirring constantly, until mixture boils. Continue to cook and stir until brittle sugar dissolves. Stir in vanilla and pecans. Place pan in bowl of ice and water or chill in refrigerator, stirring occasionally, until mixture mounds when dropped from a spoon (page 84).

Beat egg whites and cream of tartar until frothy. Beat in ¼ cup granulated sugar and the brown sugar, 1 tablespoon at a time; continue beating until stiff and glossy. *Do not underbeat.* Fold in caramel mixture; pile into pie shell. Chill several hours until set. If desired, sprinkle with chopped pecans just before serving.

Refrigerated and Frozen Pies

Pies that come to the table from the refrigerator or freezer have a set of special virtues all their own. All can be made well ahead and simply whisked out at dessert time (but do allow fifteen minutes or so out of the freezer for frozen pies to soften). The crust can be a regular pastry shell, meringue, cookie or graham cracker, and the fillings range all the way from super-rich Frozen Chocolate Pie and Chocolate Pie Deluxe to the Low-calorie Pie. This pie's whipped filling is so astonishingly low in calories that the most dedicated dieter can enjoy it.

When you want a special treat for the children, Candy Mallow Pie, combining marshmallows, chocolate bar and almonds, is a sure-fire hit with the small fry. If you're casting about for something exotic, either Grasshopper Pie flavored with crème de menthe or Alexander Pie laced with crème de cacao and brandy strikes a gourmet note.

STRAWBERRY MERINGUE TORTE

Made with a special cracker-pecan meringue shell.

3 egg whites
½ teaspoon baking powder
1 cup granulated sugar
10 soda crackers (each 2 inches square), crushed and rolled into fine crumbs
½ cup chopped pecans
3 cups sliced fresh strawberries
1 cup chilled whipping cream
2 tablespoons confectioners' sugar

Heat oven to 300°. Butter 9-inch pie pan. In small mixer bowl, beat egg whites and baking powder until frothy. Beat in granulated sugar, 1 tablespoon at a time; continue beating until stiff and glossy. *Do not underbeat.* Fold in cracker crumbs and pecans. Pile into prepared pan, pressing meringue up against side of pan. Bake 30 minutes. Turn off oven; leave meringue in oven with door closed 1 hour. Remove from oven; finish cooling meringue away from draft.

Just before serving, fill meringue shell with strawberries. In chilled bowl whip cream and confectioners' sugar until stiff. Spread over strawberries. If desired, garnish pie with fresh whole strawberries.

STRAWBERRY GLACÉ PIE

9-inch Baked Pie Shell (page 11)
6 cups strawberries, washed and hulled (about 1½ quarts)
1 cup sugar
3 tablespoons cornstarch
½ cup water
1 package (3 ounces) cream cheese, softened

Bake pie shell. Mash enough berries to measure 1 cup. Blend sugar and cornstarch; stir in water and crushed berries. Cook, stirring constantly, until mixture thickens and boils. Boil and stir 1 minute. Cool. Beat cream cheese until smooth; spread on bottom of baked pie shell. Fill shell with remaining berries; pour cooked berry mixture over top. Refrigerate several hours or until set.

Variations

Raspberry Glacé Pie: Follow recipe for Strawberry Glacé Pie (above) except—substitute 6 cups raspberries for the strawberries.

Peach Glacé Pie: Follow recipe for Strawberry Glacé Pie (above) except—substitute 5 cups sliced fresh peaches (7 medium) for the strawberries. To prevent peaches from darkening, use a commercial preparation and follow the instructions on the package.

Strawberry Glacé Pie

FROZEN CHOCOLATE PIE

Chocolate lovers rejoice! Here's our recipe for the richest of all chocolate pies.

- 9-inch Baked Pie Shell (page 11)
- 1 cup confectioners' sugar
- ½ cup soft butter
- 6 squares (1 ounce each) semisweet chocolate, melted
- 1 teaspoon vanilla
- 4 eggs
- 1 cup chilled whipping cream
- 2 tablespoons confectioners' sugar

Bake pie shell. In small mixer bowl, blend 1 cup confectioners' sugar and the butter on low speed until fluffy. Blend in chocolate and vanilla. On high speed beat in eggs, one at a time, beating thoroughly after each addition. Pour into pie shell. Cover pie with plastic wrap; freeze several hours or overnight. Remove pie 15 minutes before serving. Remove plastic wrap.

In chilled bowl, whip cream and 2 tablespoons confectioners' sugar until stiff. Pile onto pie and, if desired, garnish with chocolate curls.   *8 servings.*

STRAWBERRY MINUTE PIE

8-inch Baked Pie Shell (page 11)
1 package (3 ounces) strawberry-flavored gelatin
1 cup boiling water
1 package (16 ounces) frozen sliced strawberries

Bake pie shell. Dissolve gelatin in water. Add frozen strawberries; stir with fork to break berries apart. When mixture is partially set, pour into baked pie shell. Chill until set. If desired, serve with sweetened whipped cream.

Variation

Raspberry Minute Pie: Follow recipe above except— substitute 1 package (3 ounces) raspberry-flavored gelatin for strawberry-flavored gelatin and 2 packages (10 ounces each) frozen raspberries for the strawberries.

CRANBERRY FLUFF PIE

9-inch Baked Pie Shell (page 11)
⅔ cup evaporated milk
2 cups cranberries
½ cup water
1 cup sugar
1 teaspoon grated orange peel
1 orange, pared and sectioned
½ cup chopped pecans
¼ cup sugar
1 egg white
1 tablespoon lemon juice

Bake pie shell. Pour milk into refrigerator tray or baking pan; chill in freezer until soft crystals form around edge, 25 to 30 minutes. Cook cranberries in water until skins are broken. Add 1 cup sugar; heat to boiling, stirring constantly. Boil 10 to 15 minutes, stirring frequently, until a small portion dropped from spoon onto a cold plate jells. Remove from heat; cool. Add orange peel. Cut orange sections into fourths; stir cut-up sections and pecans into cranberry mixture. Beat chilled milk, ¼ cup sugar and the egg white until fluffy; add lemon juice and continue beating until stiff. Fold into cranberry mixture; pile into pie shell. Chill several hours until set.

CHOCOLATE ANGEL PIE

Meringue Pie Shell (page 19)
⅔ cup granulated sugar
2 tablespoons cornstarch
⅛ teaspoon salt
3 egg yolks, slightly beaten
1½ cups milk
2 squares (1 ounce each) unsweetened chocolate, melted, or 2 envelopes (1 ounce each) premelted unsweetened chocolate
1 teaspoon vanilla
1 cup chilled whipping cream
¼ cup confectioners' sugar

Bake meringue shell. In saucepan blend granulated sugar, cornstarch and salt. Combine egg yolks and milk; stir gradually into sugar mixture. Stir in chocolate. Cook, stirring constantly, over medium heat until mixture thickens and boils. Boil and stir 1 minute. Remove from heat; stir in vanilla. Press plastic wrap onto filling; cool thoroughly. Refrigerate 1 hour. Spoon into meringue shell. Press plastic wrap onto filling. Refrigerate 12 hours. Remove plastic wrap. In chilled bowl whip cream and confectioners' sugar until stiff; spread over filling. *8 to 10 servings.*

CHOCOLATE PIE DELUXE

Cut this pie in small pieces; it's very rich.

9-inch Graham Cracker Crust (page 19)
16 large marshmallows or 1½ cups miniature marshmallows
½ cup milk
7 bars (1⅜ ounces each) milk chocolate
1 cup chilled whipping cream or 1 envelope (about 2 ounces) dessert topping mix

Prepare crust. In saucepan heat marshmallows, milk and chocolate over medium heat, stirring constantly, *just* until marshmallows and chocolate are melted and blended. Chill until thickened. In chilled bowl beat cream until stiff. (If using dessert topping mix, prepare as directed on package.) Stir marshmallow mixture until blended; fold in whipped cream. Pour into crust. Chill several hours until set. If desired, garnish with toasted slivered almonds.

LEMON ANGEL PIE

Meringue Pie Shell (page 19)
¾ cup granulated sugar
3 tablespoons cornstarch
¼ teaspoon salt
¾ cup water
3 egg yolks, slightly beaten
1 tablespoon butter or margarine
1 teaspoon grated lemon peel
⅓ cup lemon juice
1 cup chilled whipping cream
¼ cup confectioners' sugar

Bake meringue shell. In saucepan blend granulated sugar, cornstarch and salt. Gradually stir in water. Cook, stirring constantly, over medium heat until mixture thickens and boils. Boil and stir 1 minute. Gradually stir at least half the hot mixture into egg yolks. Blend into hot mixture in pan. Boil and stir 1 minute. Remove from heat; stir in butter, peel and juice. Press plastic wrap onto filling; cool thoroughly. Spoon into meringue shell. Press plastic wrap onto filling. Refrigerate 12 hours. Remove plastic wrap. In chilled bowl whip cream and confectioners' sugar until stiff; spread over filling. *8 to 10 servings.*

PINEAPPLE MALLOW PIE

9-inch Graham Cracker Crust (page 19)
32 large marshmallows or 3 cups miniature marshmallows
1 can (1 pound 4½ ounces) crushed pineapple, drained (reserve ½ cup syrup)
1 teaspoon vanilla
¼ teaspoon salt
1 cup chilled whipping cream or 1 envelope (about 2 ounces) dessert topping mix

Prepare crust. In saucepan heat marshmallows and reserved pineapple syrup over medium heat, stirring constantly, *just* until marshmallows are melted. Remove from heat; stir in vanilla and salt. Chill until thickened. In chilled bowl beat cream until stiff. (If using dessert topping mix, prepare as directed on package.) Stir marshmallow mixture until blended. Reserving ½ cup crushed pineapple for garnish, fold remaining crushed pineapple and the whipped cream into marshmallow mixture. Pour into crust; garnish with reserved pineapple. Chill several hours until set.

LOW-CALORIE PIE

Too good to be true! A beautiful, flavorful pie with only 148 calories per serving.

Meringue Pie Shell (page 19)
1 teaspoon unflavored gelatin
⅓ cup sugar
⅔ cup unsweetened pineapple juice
3 egg yolks (reserve 1 egg white for the filling)
¼ teaspoon vanilla
Low-calorie Whipped Filling (below)
1 cup halved strawberries

Bake meringue shell. In small saucepan dissolve gelatin and sugar in pineapple juice. In small mixer bowl beat egg yolks until thick and lemon colored. Stir into gelatin mixture. Cook, stirring constantly, until mixture boils. Boil and stir 1 minute. Stir in vanilla. Place pan in bowl of ice and water or chill in refrigerator, stirring occasionally, until mixture mounds when dropped from a spoon (see page 84 for step pictures). Prepare filling; fold into gelatin mixture. Pile into meringue shell. Chill several hours until set. Just before serving, place halved strawberries over top of pie. *8 servings.*

Low-calorie Whipped Filling

¼ cup nonfat dry milk
¼ cup iced water
1 egg white
1 teaspoon lemon juice
2 tablespoons sugar
¼ teaspoon vanilla

In small mixer bowl whip nonfat dry milk, water and egg white 3 minutes on high speed. Add lemon juice; whip 1 minute longer on high speed. Add sugar and vanilla gradually; blend on low speed 1 minute.

Low-calorie Pie

GRASSHOPPER PIE

Pictured above.

Chocolate Cookie Crust (page 19)
32 large marshmallows
½ cup milk
¼ cup crème de menthe
3 tablespoons white crème de cacao
1½ cups chilled whipping cream
Few drops green food coloring, if desired

Prepare crust. In saucepan heat marshmallows and milk over medium heat, stirring constantly, *just* until marshmallows melt. Chill until thickened; blend in liqueurs. In chilled bowl beat cream until stiff. Fold whipped cream into marshmallow mixture; fold in food coloring. Pour into crust. If desired, sprinkle grated chocolate over top. Chill several hours until set.

Variation

Alexander Pie: Follow recipe above except—substitute ¼ cup dark crème de cacao for crème de menthe and 3 tablespoons brandy for crème de cacao.

CREAMY CHEESECAKE PIE

9-inch Graham Cracker Crust (page 19)
2 packages (8 ounces each) cream cheese, softened
2 eggs
¾ cup sugar
2 teaspoons vanilla
½ teaspoon grated lemon peel
Cheesecake Topping (below)

Heat oven to 350°. Prepare crust. Beat cream cheese slightly. Add eggs, sugar, vanilla and lemon peel; beat until light and fluffy. Pour into crust. Bake 25 minutes or until firm. Spread Cheesecake Topping carefully over cheesecake pie. Cool. Refrigerate several hours or overnight. Serve plain or, if desired, with sweetened strawberries. *8 servings.*

Cheesecake Topping

Blend 1 cup dairy sour cream, 2 tablespoons sugar and 2 teaspoons vanilla.

CREAMY LEMON PIE

So smooth, so refreshing, so easy.

9-inch Baked Pie Shell (page 11)
24 large marshmallows or 2¼ cups
    miniature marshmallows
2 teaspoons grated lemon peel
⅓ cup lemon juice
⅓ cup water
5 or 6 drops yellow food coloring, if desired
1½ cups chilled whipping cream

Bake pie shell. In saucepan heat marshmallows, lemon peel and juice and water over medium heat, stirring constantly, *just* until marshmallows are melted. Remove from heat; stir in food coloring. Chill until thickened. In chilled bowl beat cream until stiff. Stir marshmallow mixture until blended; fold in whipped cream. Pour into pie shell. Chill several hours until set. If desired, garnish with whipped cream and sprinkle top with shredded lemon peel.

CANDY-MALLOW PIE

Creamy milk chocolate and fluffy white marshmallows create a tasty pie.

9-inch Graham Cracker Crust (page 19)
32 large marshmallows or 3 cups miniature
    marshmallows
½ cup milk
¼ teaspoon almond extract
½ teaspoon vanilla
1 cup chilled whipping cream or 1 envelope
    (about 2 ounces) dessert topping mix
1 bar (4½ ounces) milk chocolate, grated
½ cup toasted slivered almonds

Prepare crust. In saucepan heat marshmallows and milk over medium heat, stirring constantly, *just* until marshmallows are melted. Remove from heat; stir in almond extract and vanilla. Chill until thickened. In chilled bowl beat cream until stiff. (If using dessert topping mix, prepare as directed on package.) Stir marshmallow mixture until blended; fold in whipped cream and chocolate. Pour into crust. Chill several hours until set. Garnish with almonds.

IMPERIAL CHERRY CREAM PIE

8- or 9-inch Baked Pie Shell (page 11)
1 package (about 3½ ounces) vanilla
    instant pudding
1 envelope (about 2 ounces) dessert
    topping mix
1½ cups milk
1 can (1 pound 5 ounces) cherry pie
    filling, drained (reserve thickened syrup)

Bake pie shell. In large mixer bowl blend pudding, dessert topping mix and milk at low speed. Beat at high speed until soft peaks form, about 3 minutes. Fold in cherries. Pour into pie shell; refrigerate 2 hours or until firm. Serve topped with reserved thickened syrup.

FROZEN LEMON PIE

9-inch Graham Cracker Crust (page 19)
3 eggs, separated
½ cup sugar
1 cup chilled whipping cream or 1 envelope
    (about 2 ounces) dessert topping mix
2 teaspoons grated lemon peel
¼ cup lemon juice

Prepare crust as directed except—reserve 2 tablespoons crumbs for garnish. Beat egg whites until frothy. Beat in sugar, 1 tablespoon at a time; continue beating until stiff and glossy. Beat egg yolks until thick. Fold into egg white mixture.

In chilled bowl beat whipping cream until stiff. (If using dessert topping mix, prepare as directed on package.) Fold whipped cream, lemon peel and juice into egg mixture. Pour into crust; sprinkle reserved crumbs over top. Freeze. Remove from freezer about 15 minutes before serving.

Any pie that's frozen will taste better if it's removed from the freezer to soften 15 minutes before serving. Otherwise taste buds are chilled and the pie's special flavor isn't appreciated.

Pies from Coast to Coast

Although pie *per se* may date back as far as ancient Greece, the shallow round dessert pie seems to have been an American invention. The very first of these all-American pies, however, bore little resemblance to today's crusty confections. Accounts of the lean early years in New England describe pumpkin "pyes" which were simply whole pumpkins with the fiber and seeds scooped out, filled with milk and baked on the open hearth. But as the colonies prospered the pies became richer and more varied. And when the population spread first southward and then westward, enterprising cooks began putting the fruits and nuts indigenous to these new areas in crusts, thus creating a whole new vocabulary of regional pies.

In this chapter we've included samplings from each region. From New England there are Colonial Innkeeper's Pie (really a cake batter baked in a pie shell), Boston Cream Pie (a custard-filled cake) and Marlborough Pie (a Thanksgiving dessert traditional in early Boston). The Pennsylvania Dutch contributed the legendary Shoo-Fly Pie with its spiced-molasses filling, Raisin Pie with its somber sobriquet "Funeral Pie" and Lemon Cake Pie. The Deep South is responsible for mouth-watering Pecan Pie, a Sweet Potato Pie closely akin to Pumpkin Pie and Florida's unique Key Lime Pie. From the Midwest come Apple Crumble Pizza and Double-crust Lemon Pie and from the Far West Ice-Cream Date Pie, Black Bottom Pie and the marvelous medley of fresh fruits in Fruit Platter Pie.

The expression "as American as apple pie" finds documentation in every part of the country—in New England's Apple Pandowdy, the Pennsylvania Dutch Schnitz Pie and the midwestern favorite, Deep Dish Apple Pie.

Although they are regional in origin, we've adapted the recipes in this section so they are no longer confined to one part of the country or one time of the year. In the few instances where a strictly seasonal or strictly local fruit is one of the ingredients, we've suggested a variation substituting a canned or frozen product which is available year 'round in all areas.

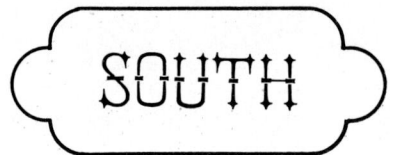

SOUTH

PECAN PIE

The South's rich contribution to good eating.

Pastry for 9-inch One-crust Pie (page 8)
3 eggs
⅔ cup sugar
½ teaspoon salt
⅓ cup butter or margarine, melted
1 cup dark or light corn syrup
1 cup pecan halves or broken pecans

Heat oven to 375°. Prepare pastry. Combine eggs, sugar, salt, butter and syrup; beat thoroughly. Stir in nuts. Pour into pastry-lined pie pan. Bake 40 to 50 minutes or until filling is set and pastry is nicely browned. Cool.

CHOCOLATE PECAN PIE

Pastry for 9-inch One-crust Pie (page 8)
1¼ cups light corn syrup
½ cup sugar
1 bar (4 ounces) sweet cooking chocolate, cut up
½ cup evaporated milk
3 eggs, slightly beaten
1 cup pecan halves

Heat oven to 350°. Prepare pastry. In saucepan combine corn syrup, sugar, chocolate and milk. Heat, stirring constantly, *just* until chocolate melts. Gradually stir hot mixture into eggs. Stir in pecan halves. Pour into pastry-lined pie pan. Bake 50 to 60 minutes. (Center will appear soft.) Cool several hours.

10 servings.

Pecan Pie is delightful proof that necessity is the mother of invention! Because the nuts are so plentiful in the South, ingenious cooks dreamed up the recipe—a joy for the sweet-tooth brigade.

DELUXE PECAN PIE

Extra-special! Crunchy-good pecan pie with the bonus of brandy and whipping cream added to the filling.

Pastry for 9-inch One-crust Pie (page 8)
3 eggs
1 cup sugar
½ teaspoon salt
2 tablespoons butter, melted
½ cup dark corn syrup
½ cup whipping cream
1 teaspoon vanilla
¼ cup brandy
1 cup pecan halves

Heat oven to 375°. Prepare pastry. In small mixer bowl beat eggs, sugar, salt, butter, syrup and cream. Stir in vanilla, brandy and pecans. Pour into pastry-lined pie pan. Bake 40 to 50 minutes or until filling is set and pastry is nicely browned. Cool.

10 to 12 servings.

SWEET POTATO PIE

This Southern favorite is the first cousin to pumpkin pie.

Pastry for 9-inch One-crust Pie (page 8)
2 eggs
2 cups mashed cooked sweet potato
¾ cup sugar
1 teaspoon cinnamon
½ teaspoon salt
½ teaspoon ginger
¼ teaspoon cloves
1⅔ cups evaporated milk or light cream

Heat oven to 425°. Prepare pastry. In mixing bowl beat eggs slightly; mix in remaining ingredients and pour into pastry-lined pie pan. Bake 15 minutes.

Reduce oven temperature to 350°. Bake 45 minutes longer or until knife inserted in center comes out clean.

Pecan Pie

Key Lime Pie

CHESS PIE

Pastry for 9-inch One-crust Pie (page 8)
3 egg yolks
⅔ cup sugar
1 tablespoon flour
½ teaspoon salt
1⅓ cups whipping cream
1 teaspoon vanilla
1 cup cut-up dates
1 cup chopped walnuts

Heat oven to 350°. Prepare pastry. In small mixer bowl beat egg yolks, sugar, flour and salt on medium speed until thick and lemon colored. On low speed blend in whipping cream and vanilla. Stir in dates and walnuts. Pour into pastry-lined pie pan. Bake 50 to 60 minutes or until top is golden and pastry is nicely browned.

Early versions of this English recipe contained cheese; over the years, the name became Chess. Now, the name remains but the cheese is gone.

KEY LIME PIE

Here is a version of Florida's famous pie.

9-inch Baked Pie Shell (page 11)
1 can (14 ounces) sweetened condensed milk
1 tablespoon grated lemon peel
½ teaspoon grated lime peel
¼ cup fresh lime juice
¼ cup fresh lemon juice
3 or 4 drops green food coloring
3 eggs, separated
¼ teaspoon cream of tartar
¼ cup shredded coconut, toasted

Bake pie shell. Blend milk, fruit peel, juices and food coloring. Beat egg yolks slightly; stir into juice mixture. Set aside. Beat egg whites and cream of tartar until stiff and glossy. Fold gently into lemon-lime mixture; pile into pie shell. Chill several hours until set. Sprinkle coconut over top just before serving.

COLONIAL INNKEEPER'S PIE

This rich pudding-cake baked in a pie shell originated with the early American custom of baking cake batter in pastry.

Pastry for 9-inch One-crust Pie (page 11)
1½ squares (1½ ounces) unsweetened chocolate
½ cup water
⅔ cup sugar
¼ cup butter or margarine
1½ teaspoons vanilla
1 cup all-purpose flour*
¾ cup sugar
1 teaspoon baking powder
½ teaspoon salt
¼ cup shortening
½ cup milk
½ teaspoon vanilla
1 egg
½ cup finely chopped nuts

Heat oven to 350°. Prepare pastry. In small saucepan melt chocolate with water. Add ⅔ cup sugar; heat to boiling, stirring constantly. Remove from heat; stir in butter and 1½ teaspoons vanilla. Set mixture aside.

In small mixer bowl blend remaining ingredients except egg and nuts on low speed. Beat 2 minutes on medium speed, scraping side and bottom of bowl constantly. Add egg; beat 2 minutes longer, scraping bowl frequently. Pour batter into pastry-lined pie pan. Stir chocolate mixture and pour over batter in pie pan. Sprinkle with nuts. Bake 55 to 60 minutes or until wooden pick inserted in center comes out clean. Serve warm. If desired, garnish pie with whipped cream.

Do not use self-rising flour in this recipe.

BOSTON CREAM PIE

A New England specialty, this "pie" is actually a custard-filled cake topped with icing.

1½ cups cake flour or 1¼ cups
    all-purpose flour*
1 cup sugar
1½ teaspoons baking powder
½ teaspoon salt
¾ cup milk
⅓ cup shortening
1 egg
1 teaspoon vanilla
Cream Filling (right)
Chocolate Glaze (right)

Heat oven to 350°. Grease and flour round layer pan, 9x1½ inches. Measure all ingredients except Cream Filling and Chocolate Glaze into large mixer bowl. Blend 30 seconds on low speed, scraping bowl constantly. Beat 3 minutes on medium speed, scraping bowl occasionally. Pour into prepared pan. Bake 35 minutes or until wooden pick inserted in center comes out clean. Cool. Split cake to make 2 thin layers. Fill layers with Cream Filling; spread Chocolate Glaze over top. Serve in wedges. Refrigerate remaining cake.   8 to 10 servings.

*If using self-rising flour, omit baking powder and salt.

Cream Filling

⅓ cup sugar
2 tablespoons cornstarch
⅛ teaspoon salt
1½ cups milk
2 egg yolks, slightly beaten
2 teaspoons vanilla

In saucepan stir together sugar, cornstarch and salt thoroughly. Add milk gradually to egg yolks; stir egg mixture slowly into dry ingredients. Cook, stirring constantly, over medium heat until mixture thickens and boils. Boil and stir 1 minute. Remove from heat; stir in vanilla. Press plastic wrap onto surface of filling; cool thoroughly.

Chocolate Glaze

Melt 3 tablespoons butter or margarine and 2 squares (1 ounce each) unsweetened chocolate or 2 envelopes (1 ounce each) premelted unsweetened chocolate. Blend in 1 cup confectioners' sugar and ¾ teaspoon vanilla. Stir in about 2 tablespoons hot water, 1 teaspoon at a time, until glaze has spreading consistency and is smooth.

Variation

Washington Pie: Follow recipe for Boston Cream Pie (left) except—substitute 1 cup jelly for the Cream Filling. Omit Chocolate Glaze and sprinkle top with confectioners' sugar.

The Cream Filling for Boston Cream Pie can be varied in a number of ways; two of our favorites are Almond Cream and Chocolate Cream. For the Almond, decrease vanilla to ½ teaspoon; stir in 1 teaspoon almond extract and ½ cup toasted slivered almonds. To make Chocolate Cream Filling, increase sugar to ⅔ cup and add 1 square (1 ounce) unsweetened chocolate after stirring in egg mixture. Or use 1 envelope (1 ounce) premelted unsweetened chocolate; stir in with the vanilla.

LEMON CAKE PIE

A refreshing pudding cake in pastry—called Lemon Sponge Pie by the Pennsylvania Dutch.

Pastry for 9-inch One-crust Pie (page 8)
2 eggs, separated
1 to 2 tablespoons grated lemon peel
½ cup lemon juice
1 cup milk
1 cup sugar
¼ cup all-purpose flour
¼ teaspoon salt

Heat oven to 350°. Prepare pastry. Beat egg whites until stiff peaks form. Beat egg yolks. Add lemon peel and juice and milk; beat. Add sugar, flour and salt; beat until smooth. Fold into egg whites. Pour into pastry-lined pie pan. Bake 45 to 50 minutes. Serve warm or cool; if desired, top with whipped cream.

SCHNITZ PIE

A dried apple pie originated by the Pennsylvania Dutch.

½ pound dried apples
2 cups cold water
1 tablespoon grated orange peel
¼ cup orange juice
½ teaspoon cinnamon
½ teaspoon nutmeg
¼ teaspoon salt
1 cup sugar
Pastry for 9-inch Two-crust Pie (page 8)

Combine apples and water in large saucepan. Cover and cook over low heat about 15 minutes or until tender. Stir in orange peel, juice, cinnamon, nutmeg, salt and sugar. Cool.

Heat oven to 425°. Prepare pastry. Pour apple mixture into pastry-lined pie pan. Cover with top crust which has slits cut in it; seal and flute. Cover edge with 2- to 3-inch strip of aluminum foil to prevent excessive browning; remove foil last 15 minutes of baking. Bake 40 to 45 minutes.

RAISIN PIE

Called Funeral Pie by the Pennsylvania Dutch because it was served to mourners.

Pastry for 9-inch Two-crust Pie (page 8)
2 cups raisins
2 cups water
½ cup sugar
2 tablespoons flour
½ cup finely chopped nuts
2 teaspoons grated lemon peel
3 tablespoons lemon juice

Heat oven to 425°. Prepare pastry. In saucepan heat raisins and water to boiling; cook 5 minutes. Blend sugar and flour; stir into raisin mixture. Heat to boiling over medium heat, stirring constantly. Boil and stir 1 minute. Remove from heat. Stir in nuts, lemon peel and juice. Pour hot filling into pastry-lined pie pan. Cover with top crust which has slits cut in it; seal and flute. Cover edge with 2- to 3-inch strip of aluminum foil to prevent excessive browning; remove foil last 15 minutes of baking. Bake 30 to 40 minutes or until crust is nicely browned and juice begins to bubble through slits in crust. Serve slightly warm.

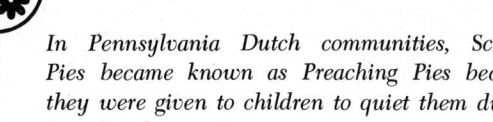

In Pennsylvania Dutch communities, Schnitz Pies became known as Preaching Pies because they were given to children to quiet them during long Sunday services.

SHOO-FLY PIE

This cake-like pie was named by Pennsylvania Dutch cooks angry with flies attracted to the molasses filling.

Pastry for 9-inch One-crust Pie (page 8)
¾ cup all-purpose flour*
½ teaspoon salt
½ teaspoon cinnamon
½ teaspoon ginger
¼ teaspoon nutmeg
¼ teaspoon cloves
½ cup brown sugar (packed)
3 tablespoons butter or margarine
½ teaspoon soda
¾ cup boiling water
½ cup dark molasses
1 egg yolk, well beaten

Heat oven to 400°. Prepare pastry. Measure flour, salt, spices and sugar into mixing bowl. Add butter; with hands work into dry ingredients until mixture is crumbly. In another bowl dissolve soda in water; stir in molasses and egg yolk. Pour into pastry-lined pie pan. Sprinkle crumbly mixture over top. Bake 10 minutes. *Reduce oven temperature to 325°*; bake 25 minutes longer. Serve warm or cool. If desired, serve with whipped cream.

If using self-rising flour, omit salt.

APPLE PANDOWDY

This pie was so popular among New Englanders during the early days of our country that it was sometimes served for breakfast.

Pastry for 8-inch Two-crust Pie (page 8)
1 can (1 pound 4 ounces) pie-sliced apples, drained
½ cup brown sugar (packed)
3 tablespoons butter or margarine, melted
6 tablespoons maple syrup

Heat oven to 425°. Prepare pastry. Stir together apple slices and brown sugar; turn into pastry-lined pie pan. Top with butter and 3 tablespoons of the syrup. Cover with top crust which has slits cut in it; seal and flute. Bake 15 minutes. Remove from oven; make crisscross cuts about 1 inch apart through top crust and apple slices. Pour remaining syrup over top. Cover edge with 2- to 3-inch strip of aluminum foil to prevent excessive browning. Bake 25 minutes longer. Serve warm; if desired, top with maple syrup.

Variation

Molasses Apple Pandowdy: Follow recipe above except—substitute 3 tablespoons corn syrup for first 3 tablespoons maple syrup and 3 tablespoons molasses for the second addition.

MARLBOROUGH PIE

An applesauce custard pie which Bostonians of earlier times enjoyed as a Thanksgiving specialty.

Pastry for 9-inch One-crust Pie (page 8)
1 cup applesauce
2 tablespoons lemon juice
1 cup sugar
4 eggs, slightly beaten
2 tablespoons butter or margarine, melted
½ teaspoon nutmeg
½ teaspoon salt

Heat oven to 450°. Prepare pastry. Blend remaining ingredients in bowl; pour into pastry-lined pie pan. Bake 15 minutes. *Reduce oven temperature to 325°* and bake 30 minutes longer or until a knife inserted 1 inch from edge of filling comes out clean. Cool.

Apple Pandowdy

Midwest

DEEP DISH APPLE PIE

Apples are a country-wide favorite for pie-making, particularly in the Midwest. Kansas is noted for deep dish apple pie.

1½ cups sugar
½ cup all-purpose flour*
1 teaspoon nutmeg
1 teaspoon cinnamon
¼ teaspoon salt
12 cups thinly sliced pared apples
   (about 10 medium)
2 tablespoons butter
Pastry for 9-inch One-crust Pie (page 8)

Stir together sugar, flour, nutmeg, cinnamon and salt. Mix lightly with apples. Pour into square pan, 9x9x2 inches. Dot fruit with butter.

Heat oven to 425°. Prepare pastry as directed except—roll to 10-inch square. Fold pastry in half; cut slits near center. Unfold over fruit in pan; fold edges under just inside edge of pan. Bake 1 hour or until juice begins to bubble through slits in crust. Serve warm.

*If using self-rising flour, omit salt.

Variations

Frozen Deep Dish Apple Pie: Follow recipe for Deep Dish Apple Pie (above) except—substitute 2 packages (1 pound 4 ounces each) frozen sliced apples, partially thawed, for fresh apples; bake 50 to 60 minutes.

Canned Deep Dish Apple Pie: Follow recipe for Deep Dish Apple Pie (above) except—substitute 3 cans (1 pound 4 ounces each) pie-sliced apples, drained, for fresh apples; use half the amounts of sugar, flour, nutmeg, cinnamon and salt. Bake 45 minutes.

APPLE CRUMBLE PIZZA PIE

No pizza pan? Roll dough into a 13- to 14-inch circle; place on baking sheet and flute.

**Pastry for 8- or 9-inch Two-crust Pie
   (page 8)**
6 or 7 medium tart apples
½ cup sugar
1 teaspoon cinnamon
¼ teaspoon nutmeg
Crumble Topping (below)

Heat oven to 450°. Prepare pastry as directed except—roll one inch larger than 12- or 13-inch pizza pan. Ease into pizza pan; flute edge. Core apples, but do not pare; cut into slices about ½ inch thick. Cover crust with apple slices, beginning at outer edge and overlapping slices. Mix sugar and spices; sprinkle over apple slices. Top with Crumble Topping. Bake 30 to 40 minutes or until edge is golden brown and apples are tender. Serve warm and, if desired, top with cinnamon ice cream. *8 to 10 servings.*

Crumble Topping

With fork, mix ¾ cup all-purpose flour,* ½ cup sugar and ½ cup firm butter until crumbly.

*Do not use self-rising flour in this recipe.

DOUBLE-CRUST LEMON PIE

This unusual dessert is made with lemon slices. Originated by Shakers who settled in Ohio, it ranks among the most deliciously tart of all lemon pies.

2 teaspoons grated lemon peel
2 large lemons
2 cups sugar
1 teaspoon salt
Pastry for 9-inch Two-crust Pie (page 8)
4 eggs

Grate peel from lemons; reserve. Peel lemons, removing all white membrane; cut lemons into very thin slices. Place slices and the grated peel in bowl; stir in sugar and salt. Set mixture aside.

Heat oven to 425°. Prepare pastry. Beat eggs thoroughly. Pour over lemon slices and sugar; mix well. Pour into pastry-lined pie pan. Cover with top crust which has slits cut in it; seal and flute. Cover edge with 2- to 3-inch strip of aluminum foil to prevent excessive browning; remove foil last 15 minutes of baking. Bake 45 to 50 minutes or until knife inserted near edge of pie comes out clean. Cool.

RHUBARB CUSTARD PIE

Pastry for 9-inch Two-crust Pie (page 8)
3 eggs
2 cups sugar
3 tablespoons milk
¼ cup all-purpose flour
½ teaspoon nutmeg
4 cups diced rhubarb
1 tablespoon butter or margarine

Heat oven to 400°. Prepare pastry. Beat eggs slightly; add remaining ingredients except butter and mix thoroughly. Pour into pastry-lined pie pan. Dot with butter. Cover with Lattice Top (page 15).

Cover edge with 2- to 3-inch strip of aluminum foil to prevent excessive browning; remove foil last 15 minutes of baking. Bake 50 to 60 minutes or until nicely browned. Serve slightly warm.

BLACK BOTTOM PIE

The creation of a famous restaurant on the West Coast, this double dessert is rich and chocolaty on the bottom, light and rum-flavored on the top . . . sure to bring praise from your guests.

9-inch Baked Pie Shell (page 11)
½ cup sugar
2 tablespoons cornstarch
½ teaspoon salt
2 cups milk
2 egg yolks, slightly beaten
2 teaspoons unflavored gelatin
3 tablespoons cold water
2 tablespoons rum or 2 teaspoons rum flavoring
1 square (1 ounce) unsweetened chocolate, melted, or 1 envelope (1 ounce) premelted unsweetened chocolate
2 egg whites
¼ teaspoon cream of tartar
⅓ cup sugar

Bake pie shell. In saucepan blend ½ cup sugar, the cornstarch, salt, milk and egg yolks. Cook over medium heat, stirring constantly, *just* until mixture boils. Remove 1 cup mixture and set aside. Soften gelatin in cold water; stir into remaining hot mixture. Stir in rum. Place pan in bowl of ice and water or chill in refrigerator, stirring occasionally, until mixture mounds when dropped from a spoon (page 84). Combine chocolate and the 1 cup custard mixture; pour into cooled pie shell.

Beat egg whites and cream of tartar until frothy. Beat in ⅓ cup sugar, 1 tablespoon at a time; continue beating until stiff and glossy. *Do not underbeat.* Fold in gelatin mixture. Pile into pie shell on top of chocolate mixture. Chill several hours until set. If desired, spread whipped cream over top of pie; sprinkle with shaved chocolate.

FRUIT PLATTER PIE

The Western states are well represented with this rainbow of fresh fruit, featuring California's always-available strawberries. Try this for a spectacular luncheon centerpiece.

Pastry for 8- or 9-inch Two-crust Pie (page 8)
⅔ cup shredded sharp natural Cheddar cheese
Clear Orange Sauce (below)
1 pint fresh strawberries (reserve 7 whole berries), washed and halved
3 medium peaches, peeled and sliced
1½ cups seedless green grapes, washed and drained on paper towels
1 medium banana, peeled and cut into ⅛-inch slices
2 tablespoons sugar
Sweetened whipped cream

Heat oven to 475°. Prepare pastry as directed except—stir the shredded cheese into the flour before adding water; roll 1 inch larger than 14-inch pizza pan. (Pastry can be baked on baking sheet. Roll dough into 15-inch circle; place on baking sheet and flute.) Ease into pizza pan; flute edge. Prick bottom and side of pastry. Bake 8 to 10 minutes. Cool.

Prepare Clear Orange Sauce. Arrange strawberry halves around outside edge of pastry shell. Place peach slices in a circle next to strawberries. Mound grapes in a circle next to peach slices; then arrange a circle of overlapping banana slices. Place reserved berries in center. Sprinkle fruits with sugar. Spoon part of orange sauce over fruit. Cut into wedges; serve with whipped cream and remainder of sauce. *12 to 14 servings.*

Clear Orange Sauce

In small saucepan mix 1 cup sugar, ¼ teaspoon salt and 2 tablespoons cornstarch. Stir in 1 cup orange juice, ¼ cup lemon juice and ¾ cup water. Cook, stirring constantly, until mixture thickens and boils. Boil and stir 1 minute. Remove from heat. Stir in ½ teaspoon *each* grated orange and lemon peel. Cool.

ICE-CREAM DATE PIE

A representative of sunny California, teaming that state's plentiful dates with ice cream in a crunchy crumb crust.

Heat oven to 400°. Mix ¼ cup soft butter or margarine and crumbly mix from 1 package (14 ounces) date bar mix with fork. Spread in oblong pan, 13x9x2 inches. Bake 10 minutes. *Do not overbake.* Remove from oven; crumble with fork. Press hot crumbled mixture on bottom and against side of 9-inch pie pan, reserving ½ cup for topping. Cool. Stir ½ cup hot water into date filling; cool. Spoon 1 quart slightly softened vanilla or lemon custard ice cream into pie shell; spread date filling over ice cream. Sprinkle remaining crumbled mixture over top. Freeze until firm.

FRESH ITALIAN PRUNE PIE

The Italian prune is a variety of plum, sometimes referred to as purple plum or prune plum . . . available in the fall. Most supplies of the Italian variety come from Idaho, Washington and Oregon.

Pastry for 9-inch Two-crust Pie (page 8)
¾ cup sugar
2 tablespoons cornstarch
3 cups sliced pitted Italian prune plums (about 1 pound)
1 tablespoon lemon juice
Vanilla ice cream

Heat oven to 400°. Prepare pastry. Stir together sugar and cornstarch; mix lightly with plums. Turn into pastry-lined pie pan and sprinkle fruit with lemon juice. Cover with top crust which has slits cut in it. Cover edge with 2- to 3-inch strip of aluminum foil to prevent excessive browning; remove foil last 15 minutes of baking. Bake 50 to 60 minutes or until crust is nicely browned. Serve warm with ice cream.

Ice-Cream Date Pie

Pie in the Sky

Certain great-occasion feasts call for something spectacular in the way of a finale, a dessert that's as extravagantly good looking as it is good tasting. It should definitely be a dessert to serve at the table with a flourish. And the pies in this section have been chosen to play this role to perfection. Those in the first group are specifically holiday pies, reflecting the traditions of all American fete days from New Year's around the calendar to Christmas. You can strike a sentimental note for Valentine's Day with a pie that frames ruby red cherries in fluffy white meringue and pay a sweet tribute to mother on her day with dainty little tarts filled with fresh strawberries and whipped cream.

For Thanksgiving we've assembled seven pumpkin recipes and seven mince, and suggest that you make it a two-pie holiday with one of each. Crown Christmas dinner with a cranberry studded Partridge-in-a-Pear-Tree Pie or a Della Robbia Pie rich with fruits and nuts; then see the old year out or the new year in with our Eggnog Pie.

But, as everyone knows, some of the greatest causes for celebration are the private ones—the very special birthday or long awaited reunion; the "meet the new in-laws" dinner or the "welcome home to a serviceman" party. And obviously at such times a super Pie in the Sky is indicated. Some of the ones we've selected for these happiest of all get-togethers are pies proper, some pastry production numbers of other sorts. But whether the holiday is a public or personal one and whether you choose a pie or a non-pie, all the recipes that follow are worthy of any extra touches of festivity you care to add.

Ring a cloud-light meringue pie with shiny green lemon leaves or a garland of ivy. Or you might submerge a little lapel vase in the center (after browning) and use it to hold three white daisies or one red rose. Light up your table with tiny birthday candles in a Baked Alaska Spumoni Pie, for example, or sugar cubes soaked in brandy or lemon extract and ignited on a mincemeat pie. Or have Flaming Orange Sauce (page 23) poured over an ice-cream pie. Turn Pink Peppermint Pie into the center attraction for a children's party or use the White Christmas Pie, a glamorous coconut chiffon pie, as the cool finale on a warm summer evening.

Finally, review these pies when you're planning a dessert and coffee party since every one of them is dramatic enough to serve as solo refreshment for guests.

New Year's Day Meringue Parfait Pie

Holiday Pies

In the section that follows you'll find a selection of pies particularly appropriate to a particular holiday. But of course there's no law that says you can't ring a slight variation on any one of them to tailor it to another festive day. To demonstrate the possibilities, we've taken a single pie—Meringue Parfait Pie—and with simple changes of ice-cream flavor and sauce, suited it perfectly to eleven different holidays. And you can do the same with virtually any of the pies in this book, by varying the shape, color or decoration to fit the occasion. Use cookie cutters to shape appropriate symbols of the season—hearts, stars, Christmas trees or shamrocks—and top a pie with pastry cutouts. Take advantage of the penny candies that proliferate at many holiday seasons—the cinnamon hearts, the jelly bean "eggs," the corn candies and the tiniest candy canes—to key your pie to the day. Or easiest of all, use a few drops of food coloring in a meringue or whipped cream topping—pink for Valentine's Day, green for St. Patrick's Day, yellow for Easter or orange for Halloween—to match the seasonal mood.

MERINGUE PARFAIT PIE

This magnificent meringue parfait pie is easily converted to any occasion by changing ice-cream flavors and sauces. Choose from one of the holidays below or create your own combination of flavors to please a special guest.

For each pie, prepare Meringue Pie Shell (page 19) and fill with 1 quart ice cream just before serving.

Variations

New Year's Day Pie: Fill Meringue Pie Shell with vanilla or eggnog ice cream; sprinkle with multicolored candies. Cut into wedges; top with Flaming Orange Sauce (page 23).

Valentine's Day Pie: Fill Meringue Pie Shell with pink peppermint ice cream and top with hot Fudge Sauce (page 24). Sprinkle with candy hearts or red cinnamon candies.

Washington's Birthday Pie: Fill Meringue Pie Shell with vanilla ice cream and top with Dark Sweet Cherry Sauce (page 23).

St. Patrick's Day Pie: Fill Meringue Pie Shell with green peppermint or pistachio ice cream. Top with **Marshmallow Crème Sauce:** Thin ½ cup marshmallow crème with ½ teaspoon water. Decorate top of pie with green shamrock candies.

Easter Pie: Fill Meringue Pie Shell with strawberry ice cream and top with Marshmallow Crème Sauce (left). Top with nest of colored coconut: Shake 1 cup shredded coconut with 3 drops green food coloring in plastic bag until evenly colored. Decorate nest with jelly beans.

Mother's Day Pie: Fill Meringue Pie Shell with vanilla or strawberry ice cream and top with Strawberry Sauce (page 23). Garnish with whipped cream and about 5 whole strawberries.

Father's Day Pie: Fill Meringue Pie Shell with vanilla or chocolate chip ice cream and top with Browned Butter-Rum Sauce (page 24).

Fourth of July Pie: Fill Meringue Pie Shell with vanilla ice cream and top with Cinnamon Blueberry Sauce (page 23). If desired, decorate with red candles.

Halloween Pie: Fill Meringue Pie Shell with pumpkin-flavored ice cream: Soften 1 quart vanilla ice cream. Stir in 1 cup canned pumpkin and ¼ teaspoon pumpkin pie spice; freeze. Top with ½ cup chocolate syrup and decorate with candy pumpkins.

Thanksgiving Day Pie: Fill Meringue Pie Shell with vanilla or butter pecan ice cream. Cut into wedges; top with Tangy Mincemeat Sauce (page 24).

Christmas Day Pie: Fill Meringue Pie Shell with French vanilla ice cream and top with ⅓ cup crème de menthe syrup. Sprinkle with crushed peppermint candy.

EGGNOG PIE

Welcome the New Year with this light and elegant chiffon pie.

9-inch Baked Pie Shell (page 11)
3 egg yolks, slightly beaten
½ cup sugar
1 envelope (1 tablespoon) unflavored gelatin
½ teaspoon salt
1¼ cups milk
1 teaspoon light rum or ½ teaspoon rum flavoring
3 egg whites
¼ teaspoon cream of tartar
½ cup sugar
½ cup chilled whipping cream
Nutmeg

Bake pie shell. In saucepan blend egg yolks, ½ cup sugar, the gelatin, salt and milk. Cook over medium heat, stirring constantly, *just* until mixture boils. Place pan in bowl of ice and water or chill in refrigerator, stirring occasionally, until mixture mounds when dropped from a spoon (page 84). Stir in rum.

Beat egg whites and cream of tartar until frothy. Beat in ½ cup sugar, 1 tablespoon at a time; continue beating until stiff and glossy. *Do not underbeat.* In chilled bowl, beat cream until stiff; fold into gelatin mixture. Carefully fold mixture into meringue; pile into pie shell. Sprinkle top generously with nutmeg. Chill several hours until set.

Variation

Chocolate Eggnog Pie: Follow recipe above except—stir 1 square (1 ounce) unsweetened chocolate, melted, or 1 envelope (1 ounce) premelted unsweetened chocolate into the hot mixture; increase rum to 2 teaspoons and garnish top of pie with chocolate curls.

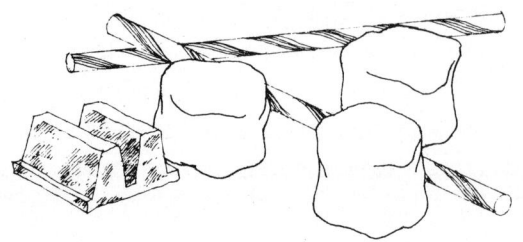

CHERRIES ON A CLOUD PIE

A beautiful valentine.

Meringue Pie Shell (page 19)
1 package (3 ounces) cream cheese, softened
½ cup sugar
½ teaspoon vanilla
1 cup chilled whipping cream
1 cup miniature marshmallows
Cherry Topping (below)

Prepare Meringue Pie Shell. Blend cream cheese, sugar and vanilla. In chilled bowl, beat cream until stiff. Gently fold cream and marshmallows into cheese mixture. Pile into meringue shell; cover and refrigerate 12 hours or overnight. Cut into wedges; top each with Cherry Topping.

Cherry Topping

Stir together 1 can (1 pound 5 ounces) cherry pie filling and 1 teaspoon lemon juice.

PINK PEPPERMINT PIE

A pink and puffy special Easter dessert.

Chocolate Coconut Crust (page 18)
24 large marshmallows
½ cup milk
1 teaspoon vanilla
⅛ teaspoon salt
6 drops peppermint extract
6 drops red food coloring
1 cup chilled whipping cream
2 tablespoons crushed peppermint stick candy

Prepare crust. In saucepan heat marshmallows and milk over medium heat, stirring constantly, *just* until marshmallows are melted. Remove from heat; stir in vanilla, salt, extract and food coloring. Chill until thickened. In chilled bowl beat cream until stiff. Stir marshmallow mixture until blended; fold in whipped cream. Pour into crust. Chill several hours until set. Just before serving, sprinkle with crushed candy.

HOLIDAY PIES

PARTY PETAL TARTS

Pretty, spring-like and perfect for Mother's Day.

Pastry for 8- or 9-inch One-crust Pie (page 8)
1 cup chilled whipping cream
¼ cup sugar
½ teaspoon vanilla
1 cup sliced fresh strawberries or 1 package (10 ounces) frozen raspberries, thawed and drained

Heat oven to 475°. Prepare pastry as directed except—after rolling, cut into 1¾-inch circles. Place one circle in bottom of each ungreased muffin cup. Press 5 circles, overlapping each slightly, around side of each muffin cup and onto bottom circle. Prick pastry. Bake 8 to 10 minutes or until lightly browned. Cool. Carefully remove from muffin cups. In chilled bowl, whip cream, sugar and vanilla until stiff. Fold in strawberries. Fill each shell with about 2 tablespoons whipped cream mixture. *Makes 9 tarts.*

No trick at all to treat family or friends with do-ahead Frosty Pumpkin Pie. Make it the day before Halloween and serve for a party on the 31st. No party planned? Serve to the family, then relax to greet young costumed invaders.

FROSTED APPLE-RAISIN PIE

Surprise Dad on Father's Day with this snow-capped pie made from convenience foods.

Pastry for 10-inch Two-crust Pie (page 8)
1 can (1 pound 4 ounces) pie-sliced apples, drained
1 can (1 pound 6 ounces) raisin pie filling
¼ cup brown sugar (packed)
2 tablespoons lemon juice
½ teaspoon salt
½ teaspoon cinnamon
½ teaspoon nutmeg
3 tablespoons butter or margarine
Vanilla Glaze (page 25)

Heat oven to 425°. Prepare pastry. Stir together apples, pie filling, brown sugar, lemon juice, salt, cinnamon and nutmeg. Pour into pastry-lined pie pan; dot with butter. Cover with top crust which has slits cut in it; seal and flute. Cover edge with 2- to 3-inch strip of aluminum foil to prevent excessive browning; remove foil last 15 minutes of baking. Bake 50 to 60 minutes or until crust is browned and juice begins to bubble through slits in crust. Cool slightly; frost with Vanilla Glaze.

FROSTY PUMPKIN PIE

Great for Halloween! Pumpkin-flavored ice cream in a nut pie shell adds up to enjoyment for pint-size spooks and full-size partyers alike.

Crunchy Nut Crust (page 19)
1 cup canned pumpkin
½ cup brown sugar (packed)
½ teaspoon salt
½ teaspoon cinnamon
½ teaspoon ginger
¼ teaspoon nutmeg
1 quart vanilla ice cream, slightly softened
Sweetened whipped cream
Walnut halves or candy corn

Bake pie shell. Beat pumpkin, brown sugar, salt and spices with rotary beater. Stir in ice cream. Pour into pie shell. Freeze overnight. Remove from freezer about 15 minutes before serving. Garnish with whipped cream and walnut halves.

Old-fashioned Pumpkin Pie

OLD-FASHIONED PUMPKIN PIE

Here's the most traditional of all holiday pies, smooth and mildly spiced to please most palates. This (and the remainder of the recipes in the chapter) are our festive Thanksgiving and Christmas representatives.

8-INCH PIE

Pastry for 8-inch
   One-crust Pie (page 8)
1 egg
1¼ cups canned pumpkin
⅔ cup sugar
¼ teaspoon salt
¾ teaspoon cinnamon
¼ teaspoon ginger
⅛ teaspoon cloves
1¼ cups evaporated milk or
   light cream

9-INCH PIE

Pastry for 9-inch
   One-crust Pie (page 8)
2 eggs
1 can (1 pound) pumpkin (2 cups)
¾ cup sugar
½ teaspoon salt
1 teaspoon cinnamon
½ teaspoon ginger
¼ teaspoon cloves
1⅔ cups evaporated milk or
   light cream

10-INCH PIE

Pastry for 10-inch
   One-crust Pie (page 8)
3 eggs
2¾ cups canned pumpkin
1 cup sugar
¾ teaspoon salt
1½ teaspoons cinnamon
¾ teaspoon ginger
½ teaspoon cloves
2¼ cups evaporated milk or
   light cream

Heat oven to 425°. Prepare pastry. In mixing bowl beat egg(s) slightly; mix in remaining ingredients and pour into pastry-lined pie pan. (To prevent spills, fill pie shell on oven rack or on open oven door.) Bake 15 minutes.

Reduce oven temperature to 350°. Bake 8-inch pie 35 minutes longer, 9-inch pie 45 minutes longer and 10-inch pie 55 minutes longer or until knife inserted in center comes out clean. Cool. If desired, serve with sweetened whipped cream.

PUMPKIN CHEESE PIE

Taste surprise—cheesecake with pumpkin. Mellow and good.

Pastry for 9-inch One-crust Pie (page 8)
1 package (8 ounces) cream cheese,
   softened
¾ cup sugar
2 tablespoons flour
1 teaspoon cinnamon
¼ teaspoon nutmeg
¼ teaspoon ginger
1 teaspoon grated lemon peel
1 teaspoon grated orange peel
¼ teaspoon vanilla
3 eggs
1 can (1 pound) pumpkin
Sour Cream Topping (right)

Heat oven to 350°. Prepare pastry. In large mixer bowl, blend cream cheese, sugar and flour. Add remaining ingredients except topping; beat at medium speed until smooth. Pour into pastry-lined pie pan. Cover edge with 2- to 3-inch strip of aluminum foil to prevent excessive browning; remove foil last 15 minutes of baking. Bake 50 to 55 minutes or until knife inserted in center of pie comes out clean. Immediately spread top of pie with Sour Cream Topping. Cool. Refrigerate at least 4 hours. Serve well chilled.

Sour Cream Topping

Blend ¾ cup dairy sour cream, 1 tablespoon sugar and ¼ teaspoon vanilla.

DARK AND SPICY PUMPKIN PIE

'Specially for spice lovers... dark, different and mellow.

Pastry for 9-inch One-crust Pie (page 8)
2 eggs
1 cup brown sugar (packed)
1 teaspoon pumpkin pie spice
½ teaspoon salt
½ teaspoon cinnamon
¼ teaspoon nutmeg
¼ cup maple syrup
1½ cups canned pumpkin
1 cup evaporated milk

Heat oven to 425°. Prepare pastry. In mixing bowl beat eggs slightly; mix in remaining ingredients and pour into pastry-lined pie pan. Cover edge with 2- to 3-inch strip of aluminum foil to prevent excessive browning. Bake 45 to 50 minutes or until knife inserted in center comes out clean. Cool.

CRUMBLE-TOPPED PUMPKIN PIE

1 package (11 ounces) pie crust mix
1 can (1 pound) pumpkin
1 can (14 ounces) sweetened condensed milk
1 egg
½ teaspoon salt
¾ teaspoon cinnamon
½ teaspoon nutmeg
½ teaspoon ginger
Orange Topping (below)

Heat oven to 375°. Prepare pastry for 9-inch One-crust Pie as directed on package. Beat pumpkin, milk, egg, salt and spices with rotary beater. Pour into pastry-lined pie pan. Sprinkle Orange Topping over pie. Cover edge with 2- to 3-inch strip of aluminum foil to prevent excessive browning; remove foil last 15 minutes of baking. Bake 50 to 55 minutes.

Orange Topping

Mix remaining pie crust mix (or 1 stick), 2 teaspoons grated orange peel and ½ cup brown sugar (packed) until crumbly.

PUMPKIN ICE-CREAM PIE

An attractive frozen pie with a ginger-flavored ice-cream layer and a spicy pumpkin layer.

9-inch Baked Pie Shell (page 11)
1 pint vanilla ice cream
2 to 3 tablespoons cut-up crystallized ginger
1 cup canned pumpkin
1 cup sugar
1 teaspoon pumpkin pie spice
½ teaspoon ginger
½ teaspoon salt
½ cup chopped walnuts
1 cup whipping cream, whipped

Bake pie shell. Stir ice cream to soften. Quickly fold in crystallized ginger and spread mixture in pie shell. Freeze until ice cream is solid. Stir together pumpkin, sugar, pumpkin pie spice, ginger, salt and walnuts. Fold in whipped cream. Pour over ice cream in pie shell. Freeze at least several hours. Remove from freezer about 15 minutes before serving.

PUMPKIN CHIFFON PIE

Light and luscious . . . perfect after a heavy meal.

8-inch Baked Pie Shell (page 11)
2 teaspoons unflavored gelatin
½ cup brown sugar (packed)
¼ teaspoon each salt, ginger, cinnamon and nutmeg
¾ cup canned pumpkin
2 egg yolks, slightly beaten
⅓ cup milk
2 egg whites
¼ teaspoon cream of tartar
⅓ cup granulated sugar

Bake pie shell. In saucepan blend gelatin, brown sugar, salt, spices, pumpkin, egg yolks and milk. Cook over medium heat, stirring constantly, *just* until mixture boils. Place pan in bowl of ice and water or chill in refrigerator, stirring occasionally, until mixture mounds when dropped from a spoon (page 84).

Beat egg whites and cream of tartar until frothy. Beat in granulated sugar, 1 tablespoon at a time; continue beating until stiff and glossy. *Do not underbeat.* Fold in pumpkin mixture; pile into pie shell. Chill several hours until set. If desired, garnish with whipped cream.

Variation

Surprise Pumpkin Chiffon Pie: Follow recipe above except—spread 1⅓ cups prepared mincemeat on bottom and side of 9-inch Baked Pie Shell (page 11).

WHITE CHRISTMAS PIE

A glamorous coconut chiffon pie, perfect for any festive holiday occasion.

9-inch Baked Pie Shell (page 11)
½ cup sugar
¼ cup all-purpose flour
1 envelope (1 tablespoon) unflavored gelatin
½ teaspoon salt
1¾ cups milk
¾ teaspoon vanilla
¼ teaspoon almond extract
3 egg whites
¼ teaspoon cream of tartar
½ cup sugar
½ cup whipping cream, whipped
1 cup shredded coconut

Bake pie shell. In saucepan blend ½ cup sugar, the flour, gelatin and salt. Stir in milk gradually. Cook over medium heat, stirring constantly, *just* until mixture boils. Place pan in bowl of ice and water or chill in refrigerator, stirring occasionally, until mixture mounds when dropped from a spoon (page 84). Stir in flavorings.

Beat egg whites and cream of tartar until frothy. Beat in ½ cup sugar, 1 tablespoon at a time; continue beating until stiff and glossy. *Do not underbeat.* Carefully fold gelatin mixture into meringue. Fold in whipped cream and coconut. Pile into pie shell. Chill several hours until set. If desired, serve with crushed strawberries or raspberries.

OLD-FASHIONED MINCE PIE

8-INCH PIE

Pastry for 8-inch
  Two-crust Pie (page 8)
1 jar (18 ounces) prepared
  mincemeat (2 cups)
1 cup diced pared tart apples

9-INCH PIE

Pastry for 9-inch
  Two-crust Pie (page 8)
1 jar (28 ounces) prepared
  mincemeat (3 cups)
1½ cups diced pared tart
  apples

10-INCH PIE

Pastry for 10-inch
  Two-crust Pie (page 8)
2 jars (18 ounces each)
  prepared mincemeat
  (4 cups)
2 cups diced pared tart
  apples

Heat oven to 425°. Prepare pastry. Mix mincemeat and apples; pour into pastry-lined pie pan. Cover with Lattice Top (page 15).

Cover edge with 2- to 3-inch strip of aluminum foil to prevent excessive browning; remove foil last 15 minutes of baking. Bake 8- and 9-inch pies 40 to 45 minutes and 10-inch pie 60 to 65 minutes. Serve warm. If desired, serve with Hard Sauce (page 24).

Variation

Flaming Mince Pie: Follow recipe for Old-fashioned Mince Pie (above) except—do not cut slits in top crust. Cut out 1¼-inch circles (one for center of each serving) about ½ inch from edge of pie. Bake as directed. Curl ½-inch-wide circular strips of orange peel to resemble blossoms; place in circles. Soak sugar cubes in lemon extract; insert one in each blossom. Ignite with match and serve blazing!

MINCE CREAM CHEESE PIE

Mincemeat and cream cheese give interesting texture and flavor contrast.

Pastry for 9-inch One-crust Pie (page 8)
1 jar (28 ounces) prepared mincemeat
  (3 cups)
2 packages (3 ounces each) cream cheese,
  softened
⅓ cup sugar
1 egg

Heat oven to 425°. Prepare pastry. Spread mincemeat in pastry-lined pie pan. Cover edge with 2- to 3-inch strip of aluminum foil to prevent excessive browning. Bake 20 minutes. In small mixer bowl, beat cream cheese, sugar and egg until creamy and smooth. Remove pie from oven; remove foil. Spread cream cheese mixture over mincemeat.

Reduce oven temperature to 350°. Bake 20 to 25 minutes longer or until knife inserted in center of topping comes out clean.

ORANGE–MINCE PIE

Pastry for 9-inch Two-crust Pie (page 8)
1 jar (28 ounces) prepared mincemeat
  (3 cups)
1 orange
Orange Glacé (below)

Heat oven to 425°. Prepare pastry. Spread mincemeat in pastry-lined pie pan. Peel orange and cut into sections. Cut sections into small pieces; sprinkle over mincemeat. Cover with top crust which has slits cut in it; seal and flute. Cover edge with 2- to 3-inch strip of aluminum foil to prevent excessive browning; remove foil last 15 minutes of baking. Bake 35 to 40 minutes or until crust is browned. While warm, spread top with Orange Glacé.

Orange Glacé

Mix 1 cup confectioners' sugar, 2 teaspoons grated orange peel and 2 tablespoons orange juice until smooth.

Orange-Mince Pie

Partridge-in-a-Pear-Tree Pie

PARTRIDGE-IN-A-PEAR-TREE PIE

Rosy red cranberries make this a festive holiday pie.

2½ cups cranberries
1½ cups sugar
1 can (8¾ ounces) crushed pineapple, drained (reserve ¼ cup syrup)
Pastry for 9-inch Two-crust Pie (page 8)
3 tablespoons flour
¼ teaspoon salt
¼ teaspoon cinnamon
1 can (8 ounces) pear halves, drained and cut in half
Sugar

In saucepan cook cranberries, 1½ cups sugar, the pineapple and reserved syrup, stirring constantly, until cranberries pop, about 5 minutes. Cool.

Heat oven to 400°. Prepare pastry. Mix flour, salt and cinnamon; stir into cranberry mixture. Pour into pastry-lined pie pan. Gently press pear slices spoke-fashion onto cranberry mixture. Roll remaining pastry as directed for top crust except—do not cut slits in pastry. Make partridge-in-a-pear-tree design cutouts to top pie. For a tree trunk, cut a strip about 8 inches long, 2 inches wide at one end and tapered to about 1 inch at other end. Sprinkle with sugar; place on center of pie.

Cut 4 to 6 tapered narrow "branches"; sprinkle with sugar and place alongside trunk of tree. Cut 6 partridge shapes; sprinkle with sugar and place between branches of tree. Cover edge of pie with 2- to 3-inch strip of aluminum foil to prevent excessive browning; remove foil last 15 minutes of baking. Bake about 40 minutes.

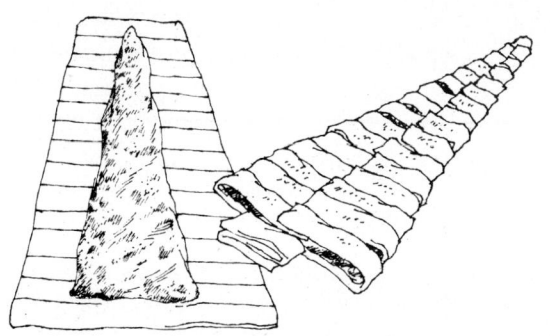

CREAMY MINCE-PECAN PIE

Pastry for 10-inch Two-crust Pie (page 8)
1 cup chilled whipping cream
1 jar (28 ounces) prepared mincemeat (3 cups)
3 tablespoons brown sugar
2 tablespoons flour
½ cup pecan halves

Heat oven to 425°. Prepare pastry. In chilled bowl, whip cream until stiff. Fold mincemeat into cream; pour into pastry-lined pie pan. Stir together sugar and flour; sprinkle over mincemeat. Arrange pecan halves on top. Cover with top crust which has slits cut in it; seal and flute. Cover edge with 2- to 3-inch strip of aluminum foil to prevent excessive browning; remove foil last 15 minutes of baking. Bake 40 to 45 minutes. Cool slightly before serving.

MINCEMEAT CHRISTMAS TREE

Festive and fun to make for the holiday season—a surprise treat for mincemeat lovers.

1 package pie crust mix
1 jar (28 ounces) prepared mincemeat, well drained
2 tablespoons soft butter or margarine
Green decorators' sugar

Heat oven to 425°. Prepare pastry for Two-crust Pie as directed on package. Divide dough in half. Roll each half into a triangle with 13-inch base and 15-inch sides. Place each triangle on a baking sheet. On each triangle, spread half of mincemeat 1 inch from top and bottom, forming a triangle with a 6-inch base. Make cuts at 1-inch intervals from outer edge of dough triangle in to edge of mincemeat triangle. Bring opposite strips up over filling, overlapping slightly to form Christmas tree. Form base with bottom strip. Brush top with soft butter; sprinkle with green decorators' sugar. Bake about 25 minutes. Serve warm or cool.

Makes 2 Christmas trees.

SANTA CLAUS PIE

A jolly holiday pie layered with mincemeat and tart apple slices.

Pastry for 9-inch One-crust Pie (page 8)
¼ cup all-purpose flour
⅓ cup sugar
⅛ teaspoon salt
1 tablespoon butter or margarine
¼ cup water
2 tablespoons red cinnamon candies
1 jar (18 ounces) prepared mincemeat (2 cups)
3 medium tart apples

Heat oven to 425°. Prepare pastry. Sprinkle 2 tablespoons of the flour in pastry-lined pie pan. Combine remaining flour, the sugar and salt in small bowl. Cut in butter until mixture looks like coarse meal. Heat water and cinnamon candies, stirring until candies are dissolved; set aside. Spread mincemeat in pie pan.

Pare apples and cut into quarters. Cut quarters into wedges, ½ inch thick at outer side. Cover mincemeat with 2 circles of overlapping apple wedges. Sprinkle sugar mixture over apples. Spoon cinnamon candy syrup over top, moistening as much of sugar mixture as possible. Cover edge of pastry with 2- to 3-inch strip of aluminum foil to prevent excessive browning; remove foil last 15 minutes of baking. Bake 40 to 50 minutes.

DELLA ROBBIA PIE

A happy combination of apples, dates, cherries and nuts ... inspired by Italy's beautiful fifteenth century Della Robbia wreaths.

Pastry for 9-inch Two-crust Pie (page 8)
4 cups diced pared tart apples
¼ cup lemon juice
½ cup dates, cut up
½ cup maraschino cherries, quartered
½ cup coarsely chopped walnuts
½ cup sugar
¼ cup all-purpose flour
¼ teaspoon salt
¼ cup light cream
Della Robbia Wreath (below)

Heat oven to 425°. Prepare pastry. Mix apples and lemon juice. Stir in remaining ingredients except Della Robbia Wreath. Pour into pastry-lined pie pan. Cover with top crust which has slits cut in it; seal and flute. Cover edge with 2- to 3-inch strip of aluminum foil to prevent excessive browning; remove foil last 15 minutes of baking. Bake 50 to 60 minutes. Cool. Serve garnished with Della Robbia Wreath.

Della Robbia Wreath

Mold process cheese into shapes of small apples and pears and "blush" tops with red decorators' sugar. Form a wreath on top of pie with cheese fruits, green and red maraschino cherries and dates.

Spectaculars

The spectaculars in this section run the full gamut of pastry possibilities. There are conventional one- and two-crust pies, of course. But in addition we've borrowed every delicious pastry trick in the book for these pie extravaganzas.

Our Thousand Leaves Torte, for instance, is a layered structure with creamy filling sandwiched between rounds of pastry.

The Chocolate Mocha Pastry Torte mixes chocolate syrup, coffee and cinnamon with the pastry itself for a rich refrigerator-cake consistency.

Sundae Bubble Crown consists of tiny cream puffs mingled marvelously with ice cream and chocolate sauce.

And finally there are tartlets, Napoleons, fans, leaves and horns all made from puff pastry prepared by a new super streamlined method which we spell out step by step for you.

SILHOUETTE PARFAIT PIE

Two kinds of crust line this ice-cream party pie.

Prepare 9-inch Baked Pie Shell (page 11). *Heat oven to 325°.* Prepare Meringue for 9-inch Pie (page 82) as directed except—increase sugar to ¾ cup and after beating in sugar, sift 3 tablespoons cocoa over meringue; fold in carefully with a flexible spatula. Spread mixture evenly in baked pie shell, sealing meringue over fluted edge. Bake 25 minutes. (Meringue will be soft.) Cool thoroughly. Just before serving, fill with 1 quart vanilla ice cream; top with Fudge Sauce (page 24). If desired, other ice cream and sauce combinations can be substituted (see page 115).

BAKED ALASKA COOKIE PIE

Choose a colorful ice cream or mix more than one flavor to make this a sensational dessert.

Bake 9-inch Cookie Crust (page 18). Cool; chill. Working quickly, pack 1 quart of your favorite ice cream into pie shell. Freeze overnight.

Just before serving, heat oven to 500°. Prepare Meringue for 9-inch Pie (page 82). Quickly cover ice cream with meringue, carefully sealing meringue onto edge of crust. (If desired, pie with unbaked meringue can be frozen up to 24 hours.) Place pie on a dampened board; bake 2 to 3 minutes or until meringue is golden brown. Serve immediately. *8 to 10 servings.*

CREAM PUFF BOWL

Dessert with drama! Tiny ice-cream-filled puffs enfolded in whipped cream and swirled with rich chocolate sauce. Serve from a glittering punch bowl.

Miniature Cream Puffs (page 132)
1 quart vanilla ice cream
Chocolate Sauce (below)
2 cups chilled whipping cream
½ cup confectioners' sugar

Bake Miniature Cream Puffs. Cut off tops with sharp knife. Scoop out any filaments of soft dough; fill each generously with ice cream. Place in freezer at least 1 hour. Prepare Chocolate Sauce. Just before serving whip cream and confectioners' sugar in chilled bowl until stiff. Remove puffs from freezer; place half of puffs in 4-quart bowl. Spoon half of whipped cream over puffs; fold gently to combine puffs and cream. Repeat with remaining puffs and cream. Pour puff-cream mixture into 3-quart serving dish or punch bowl. Drizzle Chocolate Sauce over top; swirl to give marbled effect. Serve remaining sauce with the puffs.

12 to 14 servings.

Chocolate Sauce

Heat ½ cup light cream and 1½ bars (6 ounces) sweet cooking chocolate in top of double boiler over boiling water until chocolate melts. Beat until smooth; cool.

CHOCOLATE-MOCHA PASTRY TORTE

A chocolate pastry torte that's filled with chocolate—easy to cut and serve after it has mellowed in the refrigerator.

1½ cups chocolate syrup
2 teaspoons instant coffee
1 teaspoon cinnamon
1 package (11 ounces) pie crust mix
2 teaspoons vanilla
2 cups chilled whipping cream

Heat oven to 425°. Combine syrup, coffee and cinnamon. Add ½ cup of this mixture to pastry mix (enough dry mix for Two-crust Pie). Mix thoroughly; divide into 6 equal parts. Press each part over bottom of an inverted 8x1½-inch layer pan to within ½ inch of edge. (If you do not have 6 pans, let remaining pastry stand at room temperature while first layer bakes.) Bake 6 to 8 minutes or until almost firm. Cool slightly; while warm loosen with wide spatula. (Remove pastry from pans before it is completely cool to prevent cracking.) Turn out onto cake racks to cool.

In chilled bowl whip remaining chocolate mixture, the vanilla and whipping cream until mixture holds soft peaks. Stack pastry, spreading chocolate cream between layers and over top. Chill at least 8 hours or overnight.   *9 to 12 servings.*

STRAWBERRY CHANTILLY TORTE

1 package pie crust mix
Granulated sugar
1 pint fresh strawberries,
  washed and hulled
2 cups chilled whipping cream
½ cup confectioners' sugar
½ teaspoon vanilla
Confectioners' sugar

Heat oven to 450°. Prepare pastry for Two-crust Pie as directed on package except—divide dough into 6 equal parts. Roll each into a 7-inch circle; place on ungreased baking sheets. Prick circles with fork; sprinkle each with granulated sugar. Bake 6 to 8 minutes. Cool on wire racks.

Reserve 3 strawberries for garnish; chop remaining berries. In chilled bowl, beat cream, ½ cup confectioners' sugar and the vanilla until stiff. Fold in chopped strawberries. Stack circles, spreading about ¾ cup cream mixture between each layer. Frost top with remaining cream mixture and garnish with reserved strawberries. Refrigerate at least 2 hours before serving. Sprinkle with confectioners' sugar.

8 servings.

CHERRY HEERING PIE

1 package (7.2 ounces) fluffy white frosting mix
2 cups whipping cream
1½ cups chocolate wafer crumbs
¼ cup butter or margarine, melted
¼ cup Cherry Heering
5 or 6 drops red food coloring
12 maraschino cherries,
  chopped and drained

In small mixer bowl, chill frosting mix (dry) and whipping cream 1 hour.

Mix wafer crumbs and butter; press mixture evenly and firmly on bottom and side of 9-inch pie pan. Beat frosting-cream mixture until stiff. Gradually beat in Cherry Heering. Blend in food coloring. Fold in cherries; mound mixture in crumb crust. Freeze until firm, about 12 hours. If desired, sprinkle 2 tablespoons chocolate wafer crumbs over top.

Strawberry Chantilly Torte

Baked Alaska Spumoni Pie

BAKED ALASKA SPUMONI PIE

Strawberry, pistachio and chocolate ice cream are used to make this "mock" spumoni ice-cream pie.

Bake 9-inch pie shell (page 11). Cool; chill. Working quickly, pack scoops, alternating flavors, of 1 pint *each* slightly softened strawberry, pistachio and chocolate ice cream into pie shell. Freeze overnight.

Just before serving, heat oven to 500°. Prepare Meringue for 9-inch Pie (page 82). Quickly cover ice cream with meringue, carefully sealing meringue to edge of crust. (If desired, pie with unbaked meringue can be frozen up to 24 hours.) Place pie on a dampened board; bake 3 to 5 minutes or until meringue is golden brown. Serve immediately. *8 to 10 servings.*

BAKED ALASKA PUMPKIN PIE

Pastry for 9-inch One-crust Pie (page 8)
3 egg yolks, slightly beaten
1 can (1 pound) pumpkin
¾ cup sugar
1 teaspoon cinnamon
½ teaspoon salt
½ teaspoon ginger
¼ teaspoon cloves
1⅔ cups evaporated milk
1 pint vanilla or butter pecan ice cream
Brown Sugar Meringue for 9-inch Pie (page 82)

Heat oven to 425°. Prepare pastry. Mix remaining ingredients except ice cream and Brown Sugar Meringue. Pour into pastry-lined pie pan. Bake 15 minutes. *Reduce oven temperature to 350°;* bake pie 45 minutes longer or until knife inserted in center comes out clean.

Soften ice cream slightly. Line an 8-inch pie pan with waxed paper; press ice cream into pan. Freeze solid. Refrigerate baked pie at least 1 hour.

Just before serving, heat oven to 500°. Prepare Brown Sugar Meringue. Unmold ice cream onto pie; remove waxed paper. Pile meringue onto pie, covering ice cream completely and sealing meringue onto edge of crust. Bake 2 to 3 minutes or until meringue is golden brown; serve immediately.

DANISH PUFF

A layer of flaky pastry topped by a layer of cream puff pastry forms this delectable dessert.

½ cup butter
1 cup all-purpose flour
2 tablespoons water
½ cup butter
1 cup water
1 teaspoon almond extract
1 cup all-purpose flour
3 eggs
Confectioners' Sugar Glaze (below)
Chopped nuts

Heat oven to 350°. Cut ½ cup butter into 1 cup flour. Sprinkle 2 tablespoons water over mixture; mix with fork. Round into ball; divide in half. On ungreased baking sheet, pat each half with hands into a strip, 12x3 inches. Strips should be about 3 inches apart.

In saucepan heat ½ cup butter and 1 cup water to a rolling boil. Remove from heat and quickly stir in almond extract and 1 cup flour. Stir vigorously over low heat until mixture forms a ball, about 1 minute. Remove from heat. Add eggs; beat until smooth. Divide in half; spread each half evenly over strips. Bake about 60 minutes, until topping is crisp and nicely browned. Cool. Frost with Confectioners' Sugar Glaze and sprinkle generously with nuts. *10 to 12 servings.*

Confectioners' Sugar Glaze

Mix 1½ cups confectioners' sugar, 2 tablespoons soft butter, 1½ teaspoons vanilla and 1 to 2 tablespoons warm water until smooth.

Variation

Individual Danish Puffs: Follow recipe for Danish Puff (above) except—pat dough into 3-inch circles, using a rounded teaspoonful (1½ teaspoons) for each. Spread rounded tablespoonful (1½ tablespoons) batter over each circle, extending it just beyond edge of circle. (Topping will shrink slightly when baked.) Bake 30 minutes. *Makes 2 dozen puffs.*

THOUSAND LEAVES TORTE

1 cup butter, softened
1⅔ cups all-purpose flour*
4 tablespoons water
7 tablespoons sugar
¾ cup applesauce
Custard Filling (below)
½ cup chilled whipping cream

Cut butter into flour. Sprinkle with water, 1 tablespoon at a time, mixing with wooden spoon until smooth. Cover dough and chill at least ½ hour.

Heat oven to 450°. Divide dough into 7 equal parts. With slightly dampened hands, pat each part into an 8-inch circle on ungreased baking sheets. (Dough will be quite thin.) Prick circles with fork; sprinkle each with 1 tablespoon sugar. Bake 6 to 8 minutes. Cool on wire racks. Stack pastry circles, spreading alternately with ¼ cup applesauce and ¼ cup Custard Filling. (You will have about ¼ cup filling left.) In chilled bowl beat cream until stiff. Fold remaining Custard Filling into cream; spread over top of torte. If desired, garnish with toasted slivered almonds. Refrigerate any leftover torte.

6 to 8 servings.

*Do not use self-rising flour in this recipe.

Custard Filling

¼ cup sugar
1 tablespoon cornstarch
¼ teaspoon salt
1 cup milk
1 egg yolk, slightly beaten
1 tablespoon butter or margarine
1 teaspoon vanilla

In small saucepan, blend sugar, cornstarch, salt, milk and egg yolk. Cook, stirring constantly, until mixture thickens and boils. Boil and stir 1 minute. Remove from heat; stir in butter and vanilla. Press plastic wrap onto filling; cool.

SUNDAE BUBBLE CROWN

An impressive dessert that's easy on the hostess—it can be completed a day before it's needed.

Bake Miniature Cream Puffs (below). Cool. Prepare Fudge Sauce (page 24); cool. When ready to assemble Sundae Bubble Crown, soften 2 quarts vanilla ice cream. If desired, other ice cream and sauce combinations (page 115) can be substituted.

In 10-inch tube pan with removable bottom, place a layer of cream puffs. Spread 1 quart of the ice cream over puffs. Repeat with a layer of puffs, ice cream and puffs. With a teaspoon, drizzle about ½ cup of the Fudge Sauce over top layer of puffs. Freeze overnight or until firm.

Remove from freezer about 15 minutes before serving. To remove crown from pan, loosen around edge with spatula and push bottom up and out of pan. With two broad spatulas, lift crown from bottom of pan and place on serving plate. Cut into slices and serve with remaining Fudge Sauce.   *16 servings.*

Miniature Cream Puffs

1 cup water
½ cup butter
1 cup all-purpose flour
4 eggs

Heat oven to 400°. In small saucepan heat water and butter to a rolling boil. Stir in flour. Stir vigorously over low heat until mixture forms a ball, about 1 minute. Remove from heat; beat in eggs, all at one time; continue beating until mixture is smooth. Drop dough by slightly rounded teaspoonfuls onto ungreased baking sheet. Bake 25 to 30 minutes or until puffed and golden. Allow to cool away from draft.

Makes about 60 puffs.

For a spectacular color and flavor treat, try layers of pistachio and black cherry ice cream instead of vanilla. Or substitute Butter Brickle and vanilla-almond for the vanilla ice cream.

CHOCOLATE NESSELRODE PIE

9-inch Baked Pie Shell (page 11)
4 teaspoons unflavored gelatin
½ cup sugar
¼ cup cornstarch
½ teaspoon salt
2 cups milk
6 egg yolks, slightly beaten
1 bar (4 ounces) sweet cooking chocolate, grated
1 teaspoon vanilla
½ teaspoon rum flavoring
1 jar (10 ounces) Nesselrode
3 cups chilled whipping cream

Bake pie shell. In saucepan blend gelatin, sugar, cornstarch, salt, milk and egg yolks. Cook over medium heat, stirring constantly, until mixture thickens and boils. Boil and stir 1 minute. Pour 1½ cups of the hot mixture into a bowl; set aside and cool. Reserving 2 tablespoons of the chocolate for topping, blend remaining chocolate and the vanilla into hot mixture in saucepan. Cool mixture completely.

Line bottom of another 9-inch pie pan with waxed paper; set aside. Stir rum flavoring and Nesselrode into plain mixture. In chilled bowl whip 2 cups of the cream until stiff; fold one half into each mixture. Pour chocolate mixture into baked pie shell. Pour Nesselrode mixture into pan lined with waxed paper. Chill mixture in each pan until firm. About 1 hour before serving, assemble pie. Loosen edge of Nesselrode layer with spatula; invert layer on chocolate filling and remove waxed paper.

In chilled bowl whip remaining cream until stiff; spread over pie, covering surface completely. Sprinkle with reserved chocolate. Serve immediately or refrigerate until serving time. *9 servings.*

Nesselrode, a mixture of preserved fruits and nuts, is layered between chocolate and whipped cream to make this pie a tower of good eating.

Top: Cream Horn; Napoleon (page 137)

Center: Cream-filled Leaf; Flaky Pastry Fan (page 136)

Bottom: Jam Tartlet (page 136); Fruited Cheese Tartlet (page 137)

STREAMLINED PUFF PASTRY DOUGH

Here's our new, simplified version of puff pastry—so easy that even beginners can make it. One easy dough is used to make any of the special shapes pictured.

1 cup butter
1½ cups all-purpose flour*
½ cup dairy sour cream

With pastry blender cut butter into flour until completely mixed. Stir in sour cream until thoroughly blended. Divide dough into 2 parts; wrap each and refrigerate 8 hours or overnight.

Heat oven to 350°. Roll pastry on *well-floured* cloth-covered board as directed in individual recipe. Refrigerate scraps before rerolling.

*Self-rising flour can be used in this recipe. Baking time may be shorter.

CREAM-FILLED LEAVES

Prepare Streamlined Puff Pastry Dough (left). Roll each part pastry to 1/16 inch; cut with 3 1/2-inch fluted leaf cutter. Brush with Sugar Glaze (left). Bake on ungreased baking sheet 15 to 20 minutes. Cool. Top half of leaves with Rum-flavored Whipped Cream (below); place remaining leaves on top. If desired, decorate each with a dot of whipped cream and a maraschino cherry. *Makes 12 double leaves.*

Rum-flavored Whipped Cream

In chilled bowl beat 1 cup chilled whipping cream, ¼ cup confectioners' sugar and ½ teaspoon rum flavoring until stiff.

CREAM HORNS

Prepare Streamlined Puff Pastry Dough (above). Use cream horn molds or cut doubled heavy-duty aluminum foil into 8-inch squares. Fold each square into a triangle; roll into cone shape, folding the top over at wide end to make cone firm. Roll one part pastry into rectangle, 16x12 inches. Brush with Sugar Glaze (below). Cut into twelve 1-inch strips.

Spiral dough (glazed side out), 2 strips around each foil cone, overlapping ½ inch with each turn. (Be careful not to stretch dough while forming horns.) Place on side on ungreased baking sheet. Bake 20 to 25 minutes. Cool slightly before removing from foil cones. Repeat with second part of pastry. Fill with Cream-Fruit Filling (below). *Makes 12 horns.*

Cream-Fruit Filling

In chilled bowl beat 1½ cups chilled whipping cream and ¼ cup plus 2 tablespoons confectioners' sugar until stiff. Fold in ¾ cup fruit glacé or drained fruit cocktail.

Sugar Glaze

Mix 3 tablespoons sugar and 1 tablespoon water.

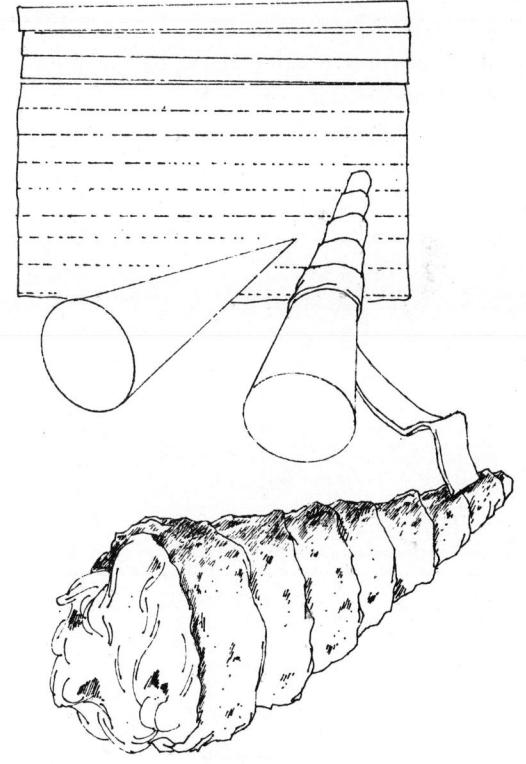

CONTINENTAL PASTRIES

Prepare Streamlined Puff Pastry Dough (page 135). Divide each part pastry into thirds. Roll out into 7-inch circles and place on ungreased baking sheet. Flute edge of each; prick with fork. Brush with Sugar Glaze (page 135). Bake 25 to 30 minutes. Cool. Spread each round with about 3 tablespoons Cheese-Marron Topping (below). Garnish with halved grapes or other fruits. *Makes 6 pastries.*

Cheese-Marron Topping

Soften 1 package (8 ounces) cream cheese in small mixing bowl. Beat in 6 whole marrons (half of a 9½-ounce jar) and 1 tablespoon marron syrup about 2 minutes.

JAM TARTLETS

Prepare Streamlined Puff Pastry Dough (page 135). Roll one part pastry to 1/16 inch; cut into 2-inch shapes. Cut small hole in center of half of the shapes. Brush with Sugar Glaze (page 135) and place on top of plain shapes. Fill holes with jam (about ½ teaspoon for each). Bake on ungreased baking sheet about 20 minutes. *Makes about 20 tartlets.*

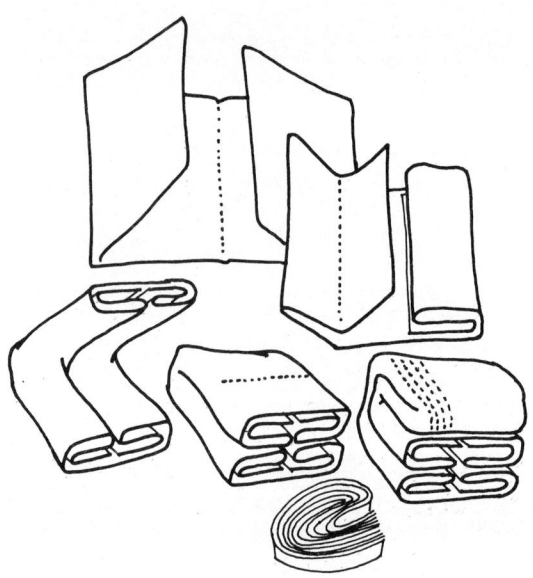

PUDDING-FILLED NAPOLEONS

1 package (about 3½ ounces) vanilla pudding and pie filling
1 package pie crust mix
Confectioners' Glaze (page 137)
Chocolate syrup

Cook pudding and pie filling as directed on package except—decrease milk to 1¾ cups. Press plastic wrap onto pudding; cool.

Heat oven to 475°. Prepare pastry for Two-crust Pie as directed on package except—roll pastry into rectangle, 14x12 inches. Cut rectangle into 4 strips, each 14x3 inches. Prick strips; place on ungreased baking sheet. Bake 8 to 10 minutes or until lightly browned. Cool.

Spread cooled pudding on 2 of the pastry strips. Spread the 2 remaining strips with Confectioners' Glaze; drizzle chocolate syrup from teaspoon in straight lines and immediately draw knife or spatula across lines for a feathery effect. Carefully place glazed pastry strip on top of each pudding-spread strip. Refrigerate until serving time. Cut each strip into nine 1½-inch bars. *Makes 18 Napoleons.*

FLAKY PASTRY FANS

Pictured on page 134.

Prepare Streamlined Puff Pastry Dough (page 135). Roll one part pastry into rectangle, 16x8 inches, on *sugared* cloth-covered board. Fold ends to meet in middle, forming a square. Sprinkle with sugar. Fold in folded edges to meet in the center and pinch these edges together to make a center seam. Fold in half to form a square (as if you were closing a book). Flatten lightly; fold again in the same way. Cutting perpendicularly to folded edge, cut into ¼-inch slices; place on ungreased baking sheet, fanning out each slice. Sprinkle with sugar. Bake 20 to 25 minutes. *Makes about 12 fans.*

FRUITED CHEESE TARTLETS

Pictured on page 134.

Prepare Streamlined Puff Pastry Dough (page 135). Roll one part pastry to 1/16 inch; cut into 2½-inch rounds with a plain or scalloped cutter. In ⅔ of the rounds, cut out 1-inch circles. Place plain rounds on ungreased baking sheet. Brush with Sugar Glaze (page 135); top each with a round with center removed. Brush with glaze and top with another round with center removed (you will have 3 layers—one plain, 2 with centers removed). Repeat with second part of pastry. Bake about 25 minutes or until lightly browned. Cool.

Soften 2 packages (3 ounces each) cream cheese in bowl; beat in 1 cup dairy sour cream, 1 tablespoon sugar and about ¼ teaspoon pumpkin pie spice. Spoon into shells; top each with fresh fruit dipped in sugar or dot with jam. *Makes about 3 dozen tartlets.*

NAPOLEONS

Pictured on page 134.

Prepare Streamlined Puff Pastry Dough (page 135). Roll one part pastry into rectangle, 12x10 inches. Cut into 15 rectangles, each 4x2 inches. Brush with Sugar Glaze (page 135). Bake on ungreased baking sheet 15 to 18 minutes until lightly browned. Repeat with second part of pastry. Cool.

Mix 1 cup sifted confectioners' sugar with 1 tablespoon milk. Spread on 10 of the rectangles. Drizzle 1 square (1 ounce) melted semisweet chocolate on frosted rectangles.

Prepare 1 package (about 4½ ounces) chocolate instant pudding as directed on package except—substitute ½ cup sour cream for ½ cup of the milk. Put 3 rectangles together with 1 tablespoon pudding between each. Use frosted rectangle for top layer of each. Repeat until all rectangles are used.

Makes 10 Napoleons.

SHORTCUT NAPOLEONS

1 package pie crust mix
¾ cup chilled whipping cream
3 tablespoons confectioners' sugar
¼ teaspoon maple flavoring
Confectioners' Glaze (below)
4 tablespoons toasted sliced almonds

Heat oven to 475°. Prepare pastry for Two-crust Pie as directed on package except—roll pastry into rectangle, 14x12 inches. Cut rectangle into 4 strips, each 14x3 inches. Prick strips; place on ungreased baking sheet. Bake 8 to 10 minutes or until lightly browned. Cool.

In chilled bowl whip cream, confectioners' sugar and flavoring until stiff; spread on 2 of the pastry strips. Spread the 2 remaining strips with Confectioners' Glaze; garnish with almonds. Carefully place glazed pastry strip on top of each cream-spread strip. Refrigerate until serving time. Cut each strip into nine 1½-inch bars. *Makes 18 Napoleons.*

Confectioners' Glaze

Blend 1 cup confectioners' sugar and 2 tablespoons light cream.

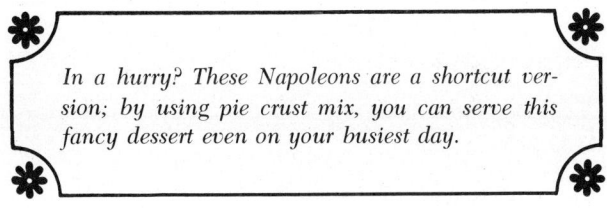

In a hurry? These Napoleons are a shortcut version; by using pie crust mix, you can serve this fancy dessert even on your busiest day.

CHEESECAKE SUPREME

This famous cheesecake is fit for a king—it's very big and very rich. Make it a day ahead when you're expecting a crowd.

Cheesecake Pastry (below)
5 packages (8 ounces each) cream cheese, softened
1¾ cups sugar
3 tablespoons flour
1½ teaspoons each grated orange and lemon peel
½ teaspoon vanilla
5 eggs
2 egg yolks
¼ cup whipping cream

Prepare Cheesecake Pastry. Heat oven to 500°. In large mixer bowl, beat cream cheese, sugar, flour, orange and lemon peel, vanilla and 2 of the eggs until smooth. Continue beating, adding remaining eggs and the yolks one at a time, until blended. On low speed, blend in cream. Pour into pastry-lined pan. Bake 12 to 15 minutes.

Reduce oven temperature to 200°; bake 1 hour longer. Cool. Refrigerate overnight or 12 to 24 hours. Loosen cake from side of pan; remove side, leaving cake on bottom of pan. *20 to 22 servings.*

Cheesecake Pastry

1 cup all-purpose flour*
1 egg yolk
¼ cup sugar
¼ cup soft butter
1 teaspoon grated lemon peel
⅛ teaspoon salt

Heat oven to 400°. Lightly grease 9-inch springform pan; remove bottom. In small bowl, combine all ingredients; work with hands until blended. Press ¼ of mixture evenly on bottom of pan. Place on baking sheet; bake 8 to 10 minutes or until golden. Cool. Press remaining mixture ⅔ of the way up on side of pan. Assemble bottom and side of pan; secure side.

°If using self-rising flour, omit salt.

MAZARINE TORTE

1⅓ cups all-purpose flour*
1 teaspoon baking powder
⅓ cup sugar
½ cup butter or margarine, softened
1 egg
½ cup raspberry jam
Almond Filling (below)
Mazarine Frosting (below)

Heat oven to 350°. Grease layer pan, 9x1½ inches. (For ease in removing torte from pan, use pan with removable bottom.) Stir dry ingredients together. Mix in butter and egg until all flour is moistened. Press dough evenly on bottom and side of pan. Spread ¼ cup of the jam over dough. Chill while preparing Almond Filling.

Spoon filling over jam. Bake about 50 minutes. Cool torte in pan. Carefully remove from pan; spread remaining jam over top. Drizzle with Mazarine Frosting. *10 servings.*

°If using self-rising flour, omit baking powder.

Almond Filling

½ cup butter or margarine, softened
⅔ cup sugar
1 cup ground or very finely chopped blanched almonds
½ teaspoon almond extract
2 eggs

Cream butter and sugar; stir in almonds and extract. Add eggs, one at a time, beating well after each addition.

Mazarine Frosting

Mix 1 cup sifted confectioners' sugar, 1 tablespoon lemon juice and 1 teaspoon water until smooth.

SPECTACULARS 139

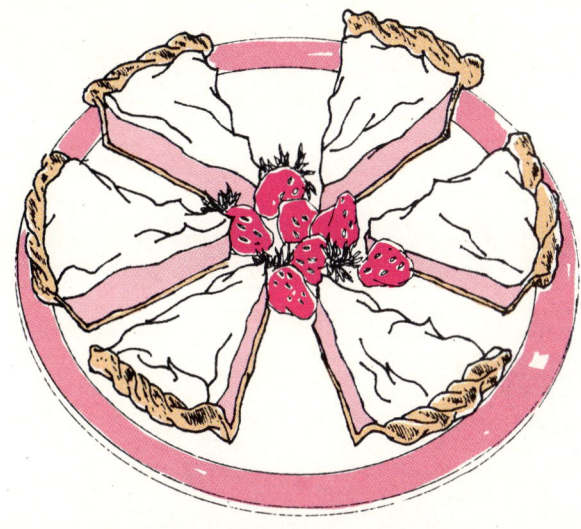

STRAWBERRY SNOWCAP PIE

This frosty pie is especially elegant when topped with warm sauce. For convenience, make the sauce ahead and reheat it at serving time.

9-inch Baked Pie Shell (page 11)
3 pints strawberry ice cream, slightly softened
Meringue for 9-inch Pie (page 82)
Strawberry Sauce (below)

Bake pie shell. Cool; chill. Working quickly, pack ice cream into pie shell. Freeze overnight.

Just before serving, heat oven to 500°. Prepare meringue. Quickly cover ice cream with meringue, carefully sealing meringue onto edge of crust. (If desired, pie with unbaked meringue can be frozen up to 24 hours.) Place pie on a dampened board; bake 2 to 3 minutes or until meringue is golden brown. Serve immediately with warm Strawberry Sauce.

Strawberry Sauce

1 package (10 ounces) frozen strawberries, thawed and drained (reserve syrup)
2 teaspoons cornstarch
1 teaspoon lemon juice
1 teaspoon grated orange peel, if desired
½ cup fresh strawberries, washed and hulled

In saucepan mix strawberry syrup and cornstarch. Stir in lemon juice and orange peel. Cook over medium heat, stirring constantly, until mixture thickens and boils. Boil and stir 1 minute. Stir in thawed and fresh strawberries; heat through.

NEAPOLITAN PIE

9-inch Baked Pie Shell (page 11)
⅔ cup sugar
¼ cup cornstarch
½ teaspoon salt
3 cups milk
4 egg yolks, slightly beaten
2 tablespoons soft butter
4 teaspoons vanilla
1 square (1 ounce) unsweetened chocolate, melted, or 1 envelope (1 ounce) premelted unsweetened chocolate
Red food coloring
1 teaspoon almond extract
1 cup chilled whipping cream
¼ cup confectioners' sugar
1 tablespoon pistachio nuts, chopped

Bake pie shell. In saucepan, blend sugar, cornstarch, salt, milk and egg yolks. Cook, stirring constantly, over medium heat until mixture thickens and boils. Boil and stir 1 minute. Remove from heat; blend in butter and vanilla. Divide mixture among 3 bowls. Blend chocolate thoroughly into one portion. Stir in about 6 drops food coloring to second portion. Stir almond extract into third portion.

Pour chocolate mixture into baked pie shell; refrigerate about 10 minutes or until firm. Spread pink mixture over chocolate layer; refrigerate 10 minutes or until firm. Spread almond mixture over pink layer; refrigerate until firm. Just before serving whip cream and confectioners' sugar in chilled bowl until stiff. Place in a ring on pie and sprinkle with pistachio nuts.

When time is short (probably always, if you're a typical homemaker), try our quickie version of Neapolitan Pie. Simply substitute 1 package (about 6 ounces) vanilla pudding and pie filling, made as directed on the package, for the cream filling. Divide filling and complete as directed in the recipe.

Pies in Disguise

Sometimes the very same kinds of filling and pastry used in conventional pies are formed into different shapes and called by different names. These pies in disguise are often, though not always, delicious one-to-a-customer deals, each constituting an individual serving. Take tarts for example. They are little pastry cups, in most cases baked and then filled with practically anything sweet—fresh fruit or fruit pie filling, ice cream, pudding or berries and whipped cream. You won't even need any special equipment for forming the tart shells—just follow our instructions for making them on the back of your muffin tin or on aluminum foil.

But tarts are only the beginning. After them come turnovers—rounds of pastry, individual- or family-size, half-covered with filling such as strawberries, apples, dates or mincemeat, then folded over and sealed. Turnovers can be baked or deep fried, in which case they're called fried pies. If you like you can add a frosting or glaze for added embellishment.

Then there are cobblers, a kind of pseudo-pie, made by dropping biscuit dough on top of warm fruit and baking. We've given recipes for traditional cobblers with fresh fruit, but also added a few quick and easy variations that use canned pie fillings.

And still another combination of fruit and crust is called a dumpling. Dumplings can be cored apples filled with raisins and nuts or with chopped apricots. Or they could be peaches, halved, pitted and put together with cranberry relish in the middle. The filled fruit is then encased in pastry and baked until golden brown on the outside, hot and bubbly on the inside.

Special favorites of the young are "pies" you can eat with your fingers—little cinnamon-filled sugar crisps, tiny turn-ups of crust folded over jam, and pastry wafers put together with a cream filling between. So whenever you'd like to give the family something a little different, try one of these surprise pies. Expect a delighted reaction from one and all!

APPLE TURNOVERS

Pastry for 9-inch Two-crust Pie (page 8)
1 can (1 pound 4 ounces) pie-sliced apples, drained
¼ cup sugar
1 teaspoon cinnamon
½ teaspoon nutmeg
2 tablespoons butter or margarine

Heat oven to 450°. Prepare pastry as directed except—after rolling pastry, cut each circle into eight 4½-inch rounds. Stir together apples, sugar, cinnamon and nutmeg. Place about 1 tablespoon apple mixture on half of each round and dot with butter. Moisten lower edge of round; fold pastry over. Press edges firmly with fork to seal securely. Prick tops; place on ungreased baking sheet. Bake 15 to 20 minutes or until lightly browned.

Makes 16 turnovers.

DATE TURNOVERS

1 package (8 ounces) dates, cut up
½ cup chopped pared apple
¼ cup chopped walnuts
⅛ teaspoon salt
1 teaspoon grated orange peel
⅓ cup orange juice
Pastry for 9-inch Two-crust Pie (page 8)
Fresh Orange Glaze (below)

Heat oven to 450°. Stir together dates, apple, walnuts, salt, orange peel and juice; set aside. Prepare pastry as directed except—after rolling pastry, cut each circle into eight 4½-inch rounds. Place about 1 tablespoon date mixture on half of each round. Moisten lower edge of round; fold pastry over. Press edges firmly with fork to seal securely. Prick tops; place on ungreased baking sheet. Bake 15 to 20 minutes or until lightly browned. Cool slightly; spread Fresh Orange Glaze over tops. Serve warm or cool.

Makes 16 turnovers.

Fresh Orange Glaze

Blend 1 cup confectioners' sugar, 1 tablespoon soft butter and 1 tablespoon orange juice.

BLUSHING PEACH FRIED PIES

Golden peaches with a blush of red from cinnamon candies fill these tender turnovers.

Pastry for 9-inch Two-crust Pie (page 8)
1 can (1 pound 13 ounces) peach slices, drained
1 tablespoon red cinnamon candies
3 tablespoons granulated sugar
1½ tablespoons cornstarch
Confectioners' sugar

In heavy kettle or deep fat fryer, heat fat or oil (3 to 4 inches) to 375°. (If desired, an electric skillet can be used; use about 1 inch of fat or oil.) Prepare pastry as directed except—after rolling pastry, cut each circle into eight 4½-inch rounds. Stir together peach slices, candies, granulated sugar and cornstarch. Place about 1 tablespoon peach mixture on half of each round. Moisten lower edge of round; fold pastry over. Press edges firmly with fork to seal securely. Fry in hot fat, turning once, until golden brown, about 5 minutes. Drain pies on paper towels; sprinkle with confectioners' sugar. Serve warm or cool. *Makes 16 fried pies.*

MINCEMEAT FRIED PIES

Pastry that is fried takes on a delightful new eating sensation . . . one of extreme flakiness and tenderness.

Pastry for 9-inch Two-crust Pie (page 8)
1⅓ cups prepared mincemeat
½ cup shredded sharp natural Cheddar cheese
Confectioners' sugar

In heavy kettle or deep fat fryer, heat fat or oil (3 to 4 inches) to 375°. (If desired, an electric skillet can be used; use about 1 inch of fat or oil.) Prepare pastry as directed except—after rolling pastry, cut each circle into eight 4½-inch rounds. Place about 1 tablespoon mincemeat and 1 teaspoon cheese on half of each round. Moisten lower edge of round; fold pastry over. Press edges firmly with fork to seal securely. Fry in hot fat, turning once, until golden brown, about 5 minutes. Drain pies on paper towels; sprinkle with confectioners' sugar. Serve warm or cool. *Makes 16 fried pies.*

Blushing Peach Fried Pies

144 PIES IN DISGUISE

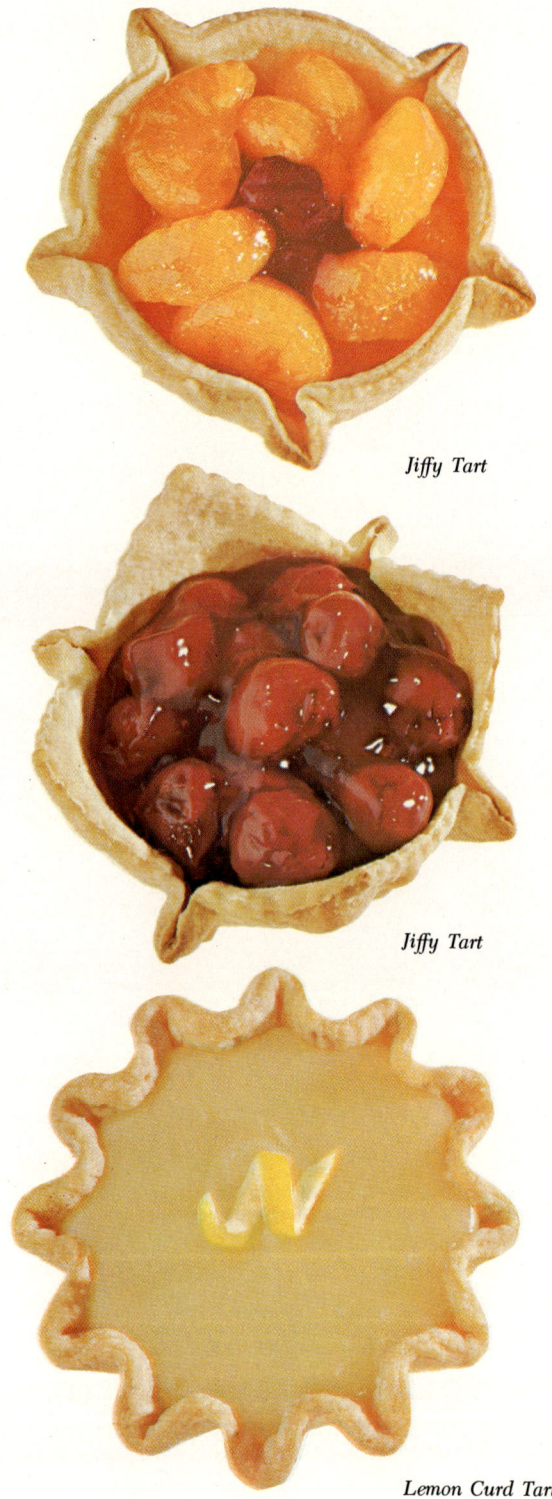

Jiffy Tart

Jiffy Tart

Lemon Curd Tart

JIFFY TARTS

Bake tart shells (page 146). Select one of the following fillings:

1. Spoon canned fruit pie filling into tart shells. If desired, garnish with whipped cream.
2. Prepare pudding mix as directed on package. Spoon into tart shells; if desired, garnish with nuts.
3. Fill each shell with a scoop of ice cream and top with favorite dessert sauce (pages 23–24).
4. Fill each shell with a scoop of ice cream and top with fresh or thawed frozen fruit.
5. Fill with sweetened fresh or well-drained canned fruit. Dot with jelly for color and flavor.
6. Fold 1 package (10 ounces) frozen raspberries or strawberries, thawed and drained, into 2 cups sweetened whipped cream.

LEMON CURD TARTS

This tangy lemon filling of British origin makes a perfect teatime treat.

Baked Tart Shells (page 146)
3 eggs
1 cup sugar
¾ cup butter or margarine, softened
1 tablespoon grated lemon peel
½ cup lemon juice

Bake tart shells. In top of double boiler, beat eggs slightly. Add remaining ingredients. Place over hot water; cook, stirring constantly, 8 to 10 minutes until mixture coats a metal spoon. Cool. Divide mixture among tart shells. Chill tarts. If desired, garnish with whipped cream. *Makes 8 tarts.*

PRUNE-ORANGE TARTS

Baked Tart Shells (page 146)
2 jars (1 pound each) stewed prunes, pitted
½ cup brown sugar (packed)
2 tablespoons cornstarch
½ teaspoon salt
1 orange, peeled and diced
2 tablespoons butter or margarine

Bake tart shells. Drain prunes, reserving 1 cup syrup. In saucepan mix sugar, cornstarch and salt. Stir in reserved syrup. Cook over medium heat, stirring constantly, until mixture thickens and boils. Boil and stir 1 minute. Stir in prunes, orange and butter; cook, stirring frequently, 10 minutes. Cool. Divide mixture among tart shells. Chill until very thick. If desired, garnish tarts with whipped cream. *Makes 8 tarts.*

STRAWBERRY MALLOW TARTS

Baked Tart Shells (page 146)
32 large marshmallows
1 can (8¾ ounces) crushed pineapple
1 teaspoon almond extract
1½ cups chilled whipping cream
2 cups sliced fresh strawberries
4 whole strawberries, cut into halves

Bake tart shells. In saucepan heat marshmallows, pineapple (with syrup) and almond extract over medium heat, stirring constantly, *just* until marshmallows melt. Chill until thickened. In chilled bowl beat cream until stiff. Stir marshmallow mixture until blended; fold in whipped cream and sliced strawberries. Divide mixture among tart shells; garnish each tart with a strawberry half. Chill several hours until set. *Makes 8 tarts.*

Jiffy Tart

Prune-Orange Tart

Strawberry Mallow Tart

  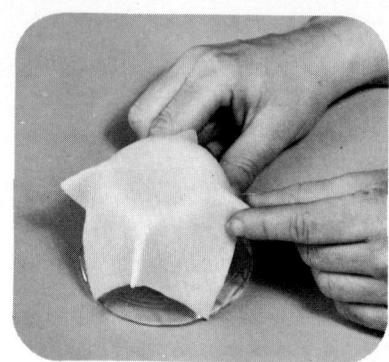

Baked Tart Shells *Easy Foil Tarts* *Jiffy Petal Tart Shells*

BAKED TART SHELLS

For more detailed directions on mixing dough and rolling pastry, refer to our step-by-step photographs on pages 9–11.

1 cup all-purpose flour*
½ teaspoon salt
⅓ cup plus 1 tablespoon shortening or
　⅓ cup lard
2 tablespoons cold water

Heat oven to 475°. Measure flour and salt into mixing bowl. Cut in shortening thoroughly. Sprinkle in water, *1 tablespoon* at a time, mixing with fork until all flour is moistened and dough almost cleans side of bowl (1 to 2 teaspoons water may be added if needed). Gather dough into a ball; shape into flattened round. With floured stockinet-covered rolling pin, roll on lightly floured cloth-covered board into 13-inch circle (about ⅛ inch thick).

Cut circle into 4½-inch rounds. (If using individual pie pans or tart pans, cut pastry rounds 1 inch larger than inverted pans; fit into pans.) Fit over backs of muffin cups or small custard cups, making pleats so pastry will fit closely. Prick with fork; place on baking sheet. Bake 8 to 10 minutes. Cool.

Makes 8 tart shells.

*If using self-rising flour, omit salt.

EASY FOIL TARTS

Follow recipe for Baked Tart Shells (left) except—divide pastry into 6 equal parts. Place each part on 6-inch square of heavy-duty aluminum foil; roll each into 6-inch circle. Trim edges to make even. Shape foil and pastry together into tart by turning up 1½-inch edge; flute. Prick bottoms of tarts with fork. Place on baking sheet; bake 8 to 10 minutes. Cool. Fill with your favorite filling. *Makes 6 tart shells.*

JIFFY PETAL TART SHELLS

Follow recipe for Baked Tart Shells (left) except—roll pastry into rectangle, about 14x10 inches; cut into six 4½-inch squares; prick with fork and place squares over backs of small custard cups, making a pleat between each 2 points so pastry will fit closely.

Makes 6 tart shells.

MINCEMEAT TARTS

An easy-to-serve dessert—perfect for holiday buffets.

Prepare tart shells as directed at left except—when mixing pastry, add 1 teaspoon grated orange peel and ½ teaspoon orange extract with the water. Bake as directed; cool. Just before serving, heat 1 jar (28 ounces) prepared mincemeat. Divide warm mincemeat among tart shells; serve with Hard Sauce (page 24).

CHESS TARTS

Merry old England claims authorship of this rich date-nut custard filling.

Pastry for 9-inch One-crust Pie (page 8)
2 egg yolks
⅓ cup sugar
1 tablespoon flour
¼ teaspoon salt
⅔ cup whipping cream
½ teaspoon vanilla
½ cup cut-up dates
½ cup chopped walnuts

Heat oven to 350°. Prepare pastry as directed except—after rolling pastry, cut circle into eight 4½-inch rounds. Fit rounds into muffin cups or custard cups, making pleats so pastry will fit. (Do not prick.) In small mixer bowl, beat egg yolks, sugar, flour and salt on medium speed until thick and lemon colored. On low speed, blend in whipping cream and vanilla. Stir in dates and walnuts. Pour about ¼ cup of mixture into each tart shell. Bake 25 to 30 minutes or until top is golden and pastry is nicely browned. Cool.
Makes 8 tarts.

SUMMER JEWEL TARTS

Baked Tart Shells (page 146)
Orange Glacé (below)
2 cups seedless green grapes
1 cup raspberries
1 cup blueberries
1½ cups sliced fresh peaches (2 medium)
½ cup sliced banana
Whole strawberries

Bake tart shells. Prepare Orange Glacé; cool. Place fruits (except strawberries) in bowl; toss lightly with Orange Glacé. Fill tarts with fruit mixture. Garnish with strawberries. Chill. *Makes 8 tarts.*

Orange Glacé

In saucepan blend ½ cup sugar, 2 tablespoons cornstarch and ⅛ teaspoon salt. Stir in ⅔ cup orange juice and ⅓ cup water. Cook over medium heat, stirring constantly, until mixture thickens and boils. Boil and stir 1 minute.

BAKED ALASKA TARTS

Be sure to bake these tarts on a dampened board; this allows the heat to brown the meringue without melting the ice cream.

Baked Tart Shells (page 146)
1 quart of your favorite ice cream
Meringue for 8-inch Pie (page 82)

Bake tart shells. Fill each shell with a scoop of ice cream. Place in freezer. Prepare meringue. Working quickly, pile meringue onto each tart, being careful to seal meringue onto edge of crust to prevent shrinking. Freeze overnight.

Heat oven to 500°. Place tarts on dampened cutting board; bake 3 minutes. Serve immediately.
Makes 8 tarts.

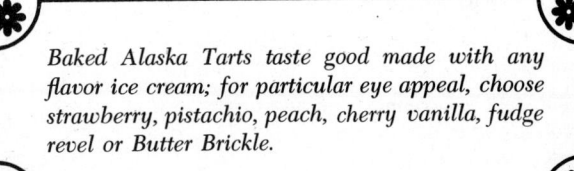

Baked Alaska Tarts taste good made with any flavor ice cream; for particular eye appeal, choose strawberry, pistachio, peach, cherry vanilla, fudge revel or Butter Brickle.

PEACH MELBA TARTS

Baked Tart Shells (page 146)
1 package (10 ounces) frozen red raspberries, thawed
Melba Sauce (below)
1½ cups sliced fresh peaches (2 medium)
Vanilla ice cream

Bake tart shells. Drain raspberries, reserving syrup. Prepare Melba Sauce. Just before serving, combine raspberries and peach slices. Divide fruit mixture among tarts; top each tart with ice cream and Melba Sauce. *Makes 8 tarts.*

Melba Sauce

In small saucepan mix 2 teaspoons cornstarch, ¼ cup currant jelly and ½ cup reserved raspberry syrup. Cook over medium heat, stirring constantly, until mixture thickens and boils. Boil and stir 1 minute. Cool.

PECAN TARTS

1 package pie crust mix
1 egg
¼ cup sugar
⅛ teaspoon salt
2 tablespoons butter or margarine, melted
⅓ cup dark or light corn syrup
⅓ cup pecan halves or pieces

Heat oven to 375°. Prepare pastry for One-crust Pie as directed on package except—divide pastry into 6 equal portions. Form each into a ball and roll to 4-inch circle. Ease into muffin cups, making pleats so pastry will fit. (Do not prick.) In small mixer bowl beat egg, sugar, salt, butter and syrup thoroughly. Stir in nuts. Pour filling into pastry-lined muffin cups. Bake about 40 minutes, until filling is set and pastry is lightly browned. Cool. Serve with whipped cream.
Makes 6 tarts.

CREAM WAFERS

1 package (11 ounces) pie crust mix
2 tablespoons soft butter
¼ cup whipping cream
Sugar
Creamy Butter Filling (below)

Thoroughly blend pie crust mix (2 sticks), butter and cream with fork. Chill at least 1 hour.

Heat oven to 375°. On floured surface, roll half of dough at a time into a 12-inch circle. (If dough is hard after chilling, allow to soften slightly before rolling, but work with dough while it is still cool.) Cut into 1½-inch rounds. Sprinkle shallow pan or sheet of waxed paper heavily with sugar. Place rounds on sugar, turning each to coat both sides. Place on ungreased baking sheet; prick with fork. Bake 6 to 8 minutes or until slightly puffy but not brown. Cool. Put each 2 rounds together with Creamy Butter Filling.
Makes about 3 dozen cream wafers.

Creamy Butter Filling

Blend ¾ cup confectioners' sugar, ¼ cup butter or margarine, softened, 1 teaspoon vanilla and about 2 teaspoons cream until smooth and creamy. Tint with food coloring as desired.

STRAWBERRY TURNOVER

One big, tempting turnover—bubbling with freshly baked strawberries.

¼ cup sugar
1½ tablespoons cornstarch
2 cups sliced fresh strawberries
Pastry for 10-inch One-crust Pie (page 8)
Frosty Glaze (below)

In saucepan combine sugar, cornstarch and strawberries. Cook over medium heat, stirring constantly, until mixture thickens. Cool.

Heat oven to 425°. Prepare pastry as directed except—place pastry circle on ungreased baking sheet so that one half of circle is centered on sheet. Spread filling over centered half of circle; fold pastry over filling. Seal edges; turn up ½ inch of edge and flute. Cut slits in top. Bake 35 minutes. While warm, frost with Frosty Glaze. Serve warm, cut into wedges. *6 servings.*

Frosty Glaze

Blend ½ cup confectioners' sugar, 1 tablespoon soft butter and 1 tablespoon light cream.

APPLE DELIGHTS

Pastry sandwiches filled with apples and raisins.

1 package pie crust mix
1 can (1 pound 5 ounces) apple pie filling
½ cup raisins
1 cup confectioners' sugar
1 to 2 tablespoons milk

Heat oven to 450°. Prepare pastry for 9-inch Two-crust Pie as directed on package except—roll half of dough into 13x9-inch rectangle; place on ungreased baking sheet. Stir together pie filling and raisins; spread evenly over pastry to within ¾ inch of edge. Roll out remaining dough for top crust; place over filling. Pinch edges together securely; cut slits in top to allow steam to escape. Bake about 20 minutes or until golden brown. Mix confectioners' sugar and milk until smooth; spread over top. Cool; cut into squares or strips.
About 15 servings.

Strawberry Turnover

Fresh Blueberry Cobbler

FRESH BLUEBERRY COBBLER

½ cup sugar
1 tablespoon cornstarch
4 cups fresh blueberries
1 teaspoon lemon juice
1 cup all-purpose flour*
1 tablespoon sugar
1½ teaspoons baking powder
½ teaspoon salt
3 tablespoons shortening
½ cup milk

Blend ½ cup sugar and the cornstarch in small saucepan. Stir in blueberries and lemon juice. Cook, stirring constantly, until mixture thickens and boils. Boil and stir 1 minute. Pour mixture into 2-quart casserole.

Heat oven to 400°. Stir together flour, 1 tablespoon sugar, the baking powder and salt. Add shortening and milk. Cut through shortening with fork 6 times; mix until dough forms a ball. Drop mixture by spoonfuls onto hot fruit. Bake 25 to 30 minutes or until biscuit topping is golden brown. Serve warm and, if desired, with cream.   *6 to 8 servings.*

*If using self-rising flour, omit baking powder and salt.

Variation

Fresh Peach Cobbler: Follow recipe above except—substitute 4 cups fresh peach slices for the blueberries and add ¼ teaspoon cinnamon to sugar-cornstarch mixture.

> *"Cobble up" means to put together in a hurry. Cobblers are quick and easy-to-make hearty desserts; the fruit filling is usually topped with a rich biscuit dough.*

FRESH CHERRY COBBLER

1¼ cups sugar
3 tablespoons cornstarch
4 cups fresh red tart cherries, pitted
¼ teaspoon almond extract
1 cup all-purpose flour*
1 tablespoon sugar
1½ teaspoons baking powder
½ teaspoon salt
3 tablespoons shortening
½ cup milk

Heat oven to 400°. Blend 1¼ cups sugar and the cornstarch in small saucepan. Stir in cherries and extract. Cook, stirring constantly, until mixture thickens and boils. Boil and stir 1 minute. Pour mixture into 2-quart casserole.

Stir together flour, 1 tablespoon sugar, the baking powder and salt. Add shortening and milk. Cut through shortening with fork 6 times; mix until dough forms a ball. Drop mixture by spoonfuls onto hot fruit. Bake 25 to 30 minutes or until biscuit topping is golden brown. Serve warm and, if desired, with cream.
    6 to 8 servings.

*If using self-rising flour, omit baking powder and salt.

Variation

Fresh Plum Cobbler: Follow recipe above except—substitute 4 cups unpeeled fresh plum slices for the cherries; decrease sugar in fruit mixture to ¾ cup and add ½ teaspoon cinnamon to sugar-cornstarch mixture. Substitute 1 teaspoon lemon juice for the extract.

QUICK CHERRY COBBLER

Made in minutes with canned pie filling.

1 can (1 pound 5 ounces) cherry pie filling
½ teaspoon almond extract
1 cup all-purpose flour*
1 tablespoon sugar
1½ teaspoons baking powder
½ teaspoon salt
3 tablespoons shortening
½ cup milk
2 tablespoons toasted slivered blanched almonds

Heat oven to 400°. In 1½-quart casserole, combine pie filling and almond extract. Place in oven 10 to 15 minutes until hot and bubbly. Stir together flour, sugar, baking powder and salt. Add shortening and milk. Cut through shortening with fork 6 times. Stir in almonds. Mix until dough forms a ball. Drop dough by 6 spoonfuls onto hot mixture. Bake 25 to 30 minutes or until biscuit topping is golden brown.

6 servings.

*If using self-rising flour, omit baking powder and salt.

Variation

Quick Blueberry Cobbler: Follow recipe above except—substitute 1 can (1 pound 5 ounces) blueberry pie filling and ½ teaspoon grated orange peel for the cherry pie filling and almond extract; substitute ½ cup orange juice for the milk in the biscuits and omit the almonds.

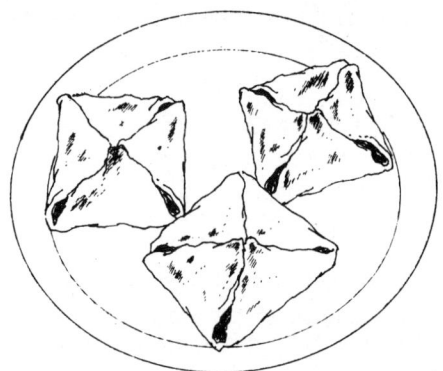

QUICK PEACH COBBLER

1 can (1 pound 13 ounces) sliced peaches
½ teaspoon cinnamon
3 tablespoons cornstarch
1 cup all-purpose flour*
1 tablespoon sugar
1½ teaspoons baking powder
½ teaspoon salt
3 tablespoons shortening
½ cup milk

Heat oven to 400°. In saucepan combine peaches (with syrup), cinnamon and cornstarch. Cook, stirring constantly, until mixture thickens and boils. Boil and stir 1 minute. Pour into 1½-quart casserole. Stir together flour, sugar, baking powder and salt. Add shortening and milk. Cut through shortening with fork 6 times; mix until dough forms a ball. Drop dough by 6 spoonfuls onto hot fruit. Bake 25 to 30 minutes or until biscuit topping is golden brown. *6 servings.*

*If using self-rising flour, omit baking powder and salt.

Variation

Quick Pear Cobbler: Follow recipe above except—substitute 1 can (1 pound 13 ounces) pears and ¼ teaspoon nutmeg for the peaches and cinnamon; stir ⅓ cup shredded sharp natural Cheddar cheese in with the flour when making biscuit topping.

APRICOT TURN-UPS

Heat oven to 450°. Prepare pastry for Two-crust Pie as directed on the pie crust mix package except—on sugared surface, roll half of dough at a time into a 12x9-inch rectangle. Place rectangle on ungreased baking sheet; cut into twelve 3-inch squares. Stir ⅓ cup raisins into ⅔ cup apricot jam. Place about 1 teaspoon jam mixture in center of each square. Bring corners of each square together and pinch securely. Bake 8 to 10 minutes. Immediately remove from baking sheet. Cool on rack. *Makes 24 turn-ups.*

APPLE DUMPLINGS

Baked apples enclosed in tender, golden pastry.

Pastry for 9-inch Two-crust Pie (page 8)
6 baking apples (each about 3 inches in diameter), pared and cored
3 tablespoons raisins
3 tablespoons chopped nuts
2 cups brown sugar (packed)
1 cup water
Sweetened whipped cream

Heat oven to 425°. Prepare pastry as directed except—roll ⅔ of dough into a 14-inch square and cut into 4 squares; roll remaining dough into a rectangle, 14x7 inches, and cut into 2 squares. Place an apple on each square. Stir together raisins and nuts; fill center of each apple. Moisten corners of squares; bring 2 opposite corners of pastry up over apple and press corners together. Fold in sides of remaining corners (as if wrapping a package); bring corners up over apple and press together. Place dumplings in baking dish, 11½x7½x1½ inches.

Heat sugar and water to boiling; carefully pour around dumplings. Spoon syrup over apples 2 or 3 times during baking. Bake about 40 minutes or until crust is nicely browned and apples are tender when pricked with a fork. Serve warm or cool with whipped cream. *6 servings.*

Variations

Company-best Apple Dumplings: Follow recipe for Apple Dumplings (above) except—substitute 6 tablespoons chopped dried apricots for the raisins and chopped nuts.

Peach Dumplings: Follow recipe for Apple Dumplings (above) except—substitute 6 peaches, peeled, halved and pitted, for the apples and ¼ cup cranberry relish for the raisins and chopped nuts.

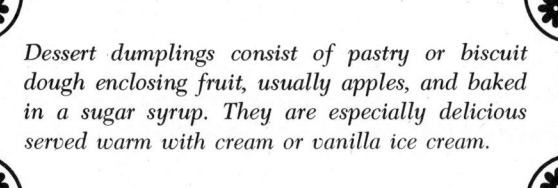

Dessert dumplings consist of pastry or biscuit dough enclosing fruit, usually apples, and baked in a sugar syrup. They are especially delicious served warm with cream or vanilla ice cream.

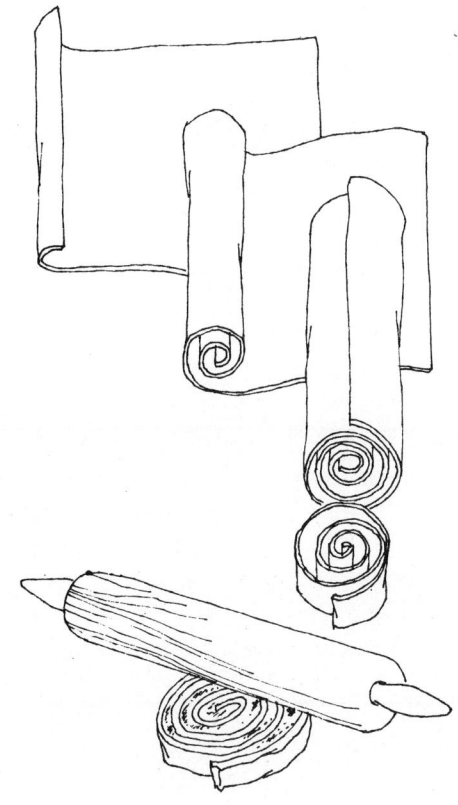

MOCK SUGAR CRISPS

A crisp imitation of a popular yeast roll known by such names as sugar crisps or elephant ears.

Prepare pastry for Two-crust Pie as directed on the pie crust mix package except—roll dough into rectangle, 13x8 inches and about ¼ inch thick. Brush with 1 tablespoon melted butter or margarine and sprinkle with mixture of 2 tablespoons sugar and ¼ teaspoon cinnamon. Roll up from long side as for jelly roll; refrigerate several hours or overnight.

Heat oven to 425°. Cut roll into ½-inch slices. On sugared surface and with sugared stockinet-covered rolling pin, flatten and roll each slice into a 3½-inch circle. (If end of dough begins to unroll while being flattened, pinch to rest of circle.) Bake on lightly greased baking sheet 6 to 8 minutes. Immediately remove from baking sheet. Cool on rack.

Makes about 2 dozen crisps.

Index

A

Alexander pie, 96
Almond
  daisy, 27
  filling, 138
Almond-crunch pineapple pie, 61
Anchovy pizza, 51
Appetizers. *See also* Snack(s)
  bambinos, 36
  canapés, liver pâté, 36
  cheese
    pennies, 35
    puff pastry, streamlined, 37
    puffs, Italian, 31
    sticks, 35
    straws, 30
  circles, 33
  cocktail kabobs, 30
  cornucopias, 32–33
  crabmeat puffs, 31
  empanaditas, 35
  kabobs, cocktail, 30
  liver pâté canapés, 36
  Mexicali puffs, 30
  olive-cheese balls, 31
  penny surprises, 35
  pocketbooks, 33
  puffs
    crabmeat, 31
    Italian cheese, 31
    Mexicali, 30
  quick Lorraine tarts, 36
  sandwiches, 33
  savory surprises, 31
  tarts, quick Lorraine, 36
  triple-cheese appetizer wheel, 34
  twists, 33
Apple
  chart, 69
  cider pie, 71
  delights, 148
  dumplings, 153
    company-best, 153
  pandowdy, 106
    molasses, 106

Apple *(cont.)*
  seasonal chart, 63
  turnovers, 142
  varieties, 69
Apple pie, 68
  applescotch, 72
  butterscotch, crumble, 71
  canned, 68
    deep dish, 108
  cheese surprise, 68
  cider, 71
  coconut, 71
  cranberry, 72
  crumble pizza, 108
  deep dish, 108
    canned, 108
    frozen, 108
  Dutch, 68
  French, 68
  frozen, 68
  green apple, 68
  green apple-peach, 65
  meringue, 71
  pandowdy, 106
    molasses, 106
  peach-green apple, 65
  pecan, 68
    upside-down, 72
  raisin, frosted, 117
  schnitz, 105
  toppings. *See* Topping(s)
Applesauce pie (Marlborough pie), 106
Applescotch pie, 72
Apricot
  pie, 65
    prune, 67
  turn-ups, 152

B

Bacon bit dip, 37
Baked Alaska
  pie(s)
    cookie, 127
    freezing, 20
    pumpkin, 131
    spumoni, 131
  tarts, 147

Baked shell(s)
  pie, 11
  tart, 146
Bambinos, 36
Banana pie
  cherry, 58
  cream, 77
  sour cream, 79
Beef. *See* Main dish(es); Meat pies and turnovers
Beef Burgundy pie, 50
Black bottom pie, 109
Blackberry pie, 57
Blueberry
  cinnamon sauce, 23
  cobbler
    fresh, 151
    quick, 152
  pie, 56
    canned, 56
    frozen, 56
    peach, 66
Blushing peach fried pies, 142
Boston cream pie, 104
Boysenberry pie, 57
Brandied hard sauce, 24
Brown sugar
  meringue, 82
  peach pie, 65
Browned butter-rum sauce, 24
Butter
  crunch crust, 18
  rum sauce, browned, 24
Butterscotch
  pie
    apple crumble, 71
    cream, 77
  sauce, 24

C

Cake pie(s)
  Boston cream, 104
  colonial innkeeper's, 103
  lemon, 105
  shoo-fly, 106
  Washington, 104

Canapés, liver pâté, 36. *See also* Appetizers
Candy-mallow pie, 97
Canned
  apple pie, 68
    deep dish, 108
  blueberry pie, 56
  peach pie, 65
  pear pie, 61
Caramel
  fluff, 26
  nut chiffon pie, 89
Celery seed pastry, 17
Cheddar cheese pie, 49
Cheese
  appetizer wheel, triple, 34
  cream. *See* Cream cheese
  cutouts, 27
  filling, 34
  olive balls, 31
  pastry, 17
  pennies, 35
  pie
    apple-cheese surprise, 68
    Cheddar, 49
    pumpkin, 119
  puff pastry appetizers, streamlined, 37
  puffs, Italian, 31
  pumpkins, 27
  savory surprises, 31
  sticks, 35
  straws, 30
  tartlets, fruited, 137
  topping, 42
    marron, 136
Cheeseburger pie, 42
Cheesecake
  pastry, 138
  pie, creamy, 96
  supreme, 138
  topping, 96
Cherries on a cloud pie, 116
Cherry cobbler
  fresh, 151
  quick, 152
Cherry Heering pie, 128

INDEX

Cherry pie, 58
  banana, 58
  chocolate pudding, 79
  cream, imperial, 97
  fresh, 58
  frozen, 58
  jubilee chiffon, 89
  orange-glazed, 58
  pineapple, 62
Cherry sauce, dark sweet, 23
Cherry topping, 116
Chess
  pie, 103
  tarts, 147
Chicken
  empanaditas, 35
  Henny Penny cass-a-rolls, 45
  pie
    dinner, 46
    party, 45
    plantation ham 'n, 45
Chiffon pie(s)
  black bottom, 109
  caramel nut, 89
  cherry jubilee, 89
  chocolate, 87
    marvel, 88
  coffee, 84
  freezing, 20
  lemon, 83
    lime, 88
    mile high, 85
  lime, 83
  mincemeat, 89
  mixtures, 84
  Nesselrode, 88
  orange, 83
  pumpkin, 121
    surprise, 121
  raspberry, 87
  strawberry, 87
    frozen, 87
  tutti-frutti, 84
  weight watcher's, 94
  white Christmas, 121
Chocolate
  coconut crust, 18
  curls, 27
  glaze, 104
  mocha pastry torte, 128
  sauce, 127
    fudge, 24
  toffee whipped topping, 26
Chocolate pie
  angel, 93
  black bottom, 109
  cherry-chocolate pudding, 79
  chiffon, 87

Chocolate pie (cont.)
  cream, 77
  deluxe, 93
  eggnog, 116
  frozen, 92
  marvel, 88
  Neapolitan, 139
  Nesselrode, 133
  pecan, 100
  pudding, 78
  sour cream, 79
Christmas pies
  Della Robbia, 126
  meringue parfait, 115
  mince
    cream cheese, 122
    creamy pecan, 125
    flaming, 122
    old-fashioned, 122
    orange, 122
    Santa Claus, 126
  mincemeat Christmas tree, 125
  partridge-in-a-pear-tree, 125
  Santa Claus, 126
  white Christmas, 121
Cinnamon
  blueberry sauce, 23
  pastry, 17
Circles (appetizers), 33
Clear orange sauce, 110
Cobbler(s)
  blueberry
    fresh, 151
    quick, 152
  cherry
    fresh, 151
    quick, 152
  freezing, 22
  peach
    fresh, 151
    quick, 152
  pear, quick, 152
  plum, fresh, 151
Cocktail kabobs, 30
Coconut crust
  chocolate, 18
  toasted, 18
Coconut pie
  apple, 71
  cream, 77
Coffee chiffon pie, 84
Colonial innkeeper's pie, 103
Colored pastry, 17
Company-best apple dumplings, 153
Concord grape pie, 57
Confectioners' glaze, 137
  sugar, 131

Continental pastries, 136
Cookie crust, 18
  crumb, 19
Corn syrup glaze, 61
Cornish pasties, 48
Cornmeal pastry, 17
Cornucopias, and variations, 32–33
Crab rémoulade pie, 40
Crabmeat puffs, 31
Cranberry
  apple pie, 72
  fluff pie, 93
Cream
  filled leaves, 135
  filling, 104
    fruit, 135
  horns, 135
  sour cream. See Sour cream
  topping. See also Whipped cream
    honey-ginger, 26
    spiced orange, 25
  wafers, 148
  whipped. See Whipped cream
Cream cheese
  pastry, 45
  pie, mince, 122
  topping, whipped, 25
  whipped, 25
Cream pie(s)
  banana, 77
  Boston, 104
  butterscotch, 77
  chocolate, 77
  coconut, 77
  freezing, 21
  fruit, 79
  strawberry glacé, 79
  vanilla, 77
Cream puff(s)
  bowl, 127
  defrosting, 21
  freezing, 21
  miniature, 132
Creamy
  butter filling, 148
  cheesecake pie, 96
  lemon pie, 97
  mince-pecan pie, 125
Crisps, mock sugar, 153
Crumb
  crusts, 19
  topping, 68
Crumble-topped pies
  pear, 61
  pumpkin, 120
Crumble topping, 108

Crunchy
  nut crust, 19
  pecan glaze, 25
Crust(s). See also Pastry
  chocolate coconut, 18
  cookie, 18
  crumb, 19
    cookie, 19
  crunchy nut, 19
  freezing, 20
  graham cracker crumb, 19
  meringue pie shell, 19
  mixes, shortcuts with, 22
  nut, 18
    butter-crunch, 18
    crunchy, 19
    peanut butter, 19
  short pie, 18
  toasted coconut, 18
Cucumber sauce, 41
Curls, chocolate, 27
Custard filling, 132
Custard pie, 74
  freezing, 21
  Marlborough, 106
  perfect pineapple, 75
  rhubarb, 109
  slip-slide, 74
  spicy walnut raisin, 75
Cutouts
  cheese, 27
  pastry, 16

D

Daisy, almond, 27
Danish puff(s), 131
  individual, 131
Dark
  and spicy pumpkin pie, 120
  sweet cherry sauce, 23
Date
  ice-cream pie, 110
  turnovers, 142
Deep dish apple pie, 108
  canned, 108
  frozen, 108
Defrosting pastries, 20–21
Della Robbia pie, 126
Deluxe
  chocolate pie, 93
  pecan pie, 100
Dessert pies. See names of pies
Diamond lattice top, 15
Dill pastry, 17
Dip
  bacon bit, 37
  harlequin, 37
  shrimp, 37

INDEX

Double-crust lemon pie, 109
Double meat pie, 48
Dumplings
 apple, 153
  company-best, 153
 freezing, 21
 peach, 153
Dutch apple pie, 68

E

Easter pies
 meringue parfait, 115
 pink peppermint, 116
Easy
 foil tarts, 146
 mushroom sauce, 40
 peach pie, 78
Edges, 14
 pastry wheel for edges, 7
Egg(s)
 pastry, 18
 sauce, 40
 scrambled, in puffy bowl, 46
Egg yolk paint, 16
Eggnog pie, 116
 chocolate, 116
Empanaditas, 35
Equipment, 7

F

Fans, flaky pastry, 136
Father's Day pies
 frosted apple-raisin, 117
 meringue parfait, 115
Filling(s)
 almond, 138
 cream, 104
 cream-fruit, 135
 custard, 132
 defrosting, 21
 freezing, 21
 low-calorie whipped, 94
Flaky pastry fans, 136
Flaming
 mince pie, 122
 orange sauce, 23
Fluff, caramel, 26
Fluffy hard sauce, 24
Fourth of July pie, 115
Freezing, 20–22
 baked Alaska, 20
 chiffon, 20
 cobblers, 22
 cream and custard, 21
 cream puffs, 21
 dough, 20
 dumplings, 21

Freezing (cont.)
 fillings, 21
 fruit pies, two-crust, 21
 main dish, 22
 puff pastry, streamlined, 21
 pumpkin, 20
 shells, 20
French apple pie, 68
Fresh
 apricot pie, 65
 berry pie, 57
 blueberry cobbler, 151
 cherry
  cobbler, 151
  pie, 58
 fruit chart, 63
 Italian prune pie, 110
 orange glaze, 142
 peach
  cobbler, 151
  pie, 64
 pineapple pie, 62
 plum cobbler, 151
 raspberry pie, 57
 rhubarb pie, 73
Fried pies, mincemeat, 142
Frosted apple-raisin pie, 117
Frosting, mazarine, 138
Frosty pumpkin pie, 117
Frozen
 apple pie, 68
  deep dish, 108
 blueberry pie, 56
 cherry pie, 58
 chocolate pie, 92
 lemon pie, 97
 peach pie, 65
 rhubarb pie, 73
 strawberry chiffon pie, 87
 whipped cream, 27
Fruit. See also names of fruits
 chart, 63
  apple, 69
 cream filling, 135
 pie(s). See also names of
  fruits
  cream, 79
  freezing, 21
  platter, 110
  salad, 62
  summer jewel, 66
Fruited cheese tartlets, 137
Fudge sauce, 24

G

Garnishes, 27
 almond daisy, 27
 cheese cutouts, 27

Garnishes (cont.)
 cheese pumpkins, 27
 chocolate curls, 27
 frozen whipped cream, 27
 gumdrop cat, 27
 lemon roses, 27
 orange or lemon windmills, 27
 toasted marshmallow treat, 27
Glacé
 orange, 66, 147
 strawberry, 79
Glacé pie
 peach, 90
 raspberry, 90
 strawberry, 90
 cream, 79
Glaze
 chocolate, 104
 confectioners', 137
  sugar, 131
 corn syrup, 61
 crunchy pecan, 25
 lemon, 25
 orange, 25
  fresh, 142
 pecan, crunchy, 25
 sugar, 135
 vanilla, 25
Gooseberry pie, 56
Graham cracker crumb crust, 19
Grape
 and raspberry pie, 57
 jam pie, 57
 pie, Concord, 57
Grasshopper pie, 96
Green apple pie, 68
 peach, 65
Ground beef pizza, 51
Guacamole, 30
Gumdrop cat, 27

H

Halloween pies
 frosty pumpkin, 117
 meringue parfait, 115
Ham
 plantation ham 'n chicken
  pie, 45
 stacks, 41
Hard sauce and variations, 24
Harlequin dip, 37
Heavenly topping, 26
Henny Penny cass-a-rolls, 45
Holiday pies, 115–26
Homespun sausage pie, 42

Honey-ginger cream topping, 26
Horns, cream, 135

I

Ice cream
 cream puff bowl, 127
 sundae bubble crown, 132
 tarts, 147
Ice-cream pies
 baked Alaska
  cookie, 127
  pumpkin, 131
  spumoni, 131
 date, 110
 frosty pumpkin, 117
 meringue parfait, 115
 pumpkin, 120
  frosty, 117
 silhouette parfait, 127
 strawberry snowcap, 139
Imperial cherry cream pie, 97
Individual Danish puffs, 131
Italian
 cheese puffs, 31
 prune pie, fresh, 110

J

Jam tartlets, 136
Jelly gems, 16
Jiffy
 petal tart shells, 146
 tarts, 144

K

Kabobs, cocktail, 30
Key lime pie, 103

L

Lattice top, and variations, 15
Leaves, cream-filled, 135
Leftover pastry snacks, 16
Lemon
 curd tarts, 144
 glaze, 25
 pastry, 17
 roses, 27
 sauce, old-fashioned, 23
 windmills, 27
Lemon pie
 angel, 94
 cake, 105
 chiffon, 83
 creamy, 97
 double-crust, 109

Lemon pie *(cont.)*
  frozen, 97
  lime chiffon, 88
  meringue, 80
  mile high, 85
Lemonade pie, 88
Lime pie
  chiffon, 83
    lemon, 88
  Key lime, 103
  meringue, 81
Liver pâté canapés, 36
Loganberry pie, 57
Low-calorie
  filling, whipped, 94
  pie, 94
  topping, whipped, 25

M

Main dish pie(s)
  beef Burgundy, 50
  Cheddar cheese, 49
  cheeseburger, 42
  chicken dinner, 46
  chicken party, 45
  crab rémoulade, 40
  defrosting, 22
  double meat, 48
  freezing, 22
  ham 'n chicken, plantation, 45
  meat loaf, 42
  meatball, Spanish, 52
  sausage, homespun, 42
  shepherds', 50
  sombrero, 51
  steak and kidney, 49
  tuna, 40
  Yankee Doodle, 41
Main dishes
  Cornish pasties, 48
  ham stacks, 41
  Henny Penny cass-a-rolls, 45
  pizza, 51
    anchovy, 51
    ground beef, 51
    mushroom, 51
    pepperoni, 51
    sausage, 51
    shrimp, 51
    Spanish, 52
  quiche Lorraine, 50
  salmon turnovers, 41
  scrambled eggs in puffy bowl, 46
  shrimp supreme, 40
  Spanish
    meatball pie, 52
    pizza, 52

Mallow
  pie
    candy, 97
    pineapple, 94
  tarts, strawberry, 145
Marlborough pie, 106
Marron-cheese topping, 136
Marshmallow(s)
  pies
    candy-mallow, 97
    pineapple mallow, 94
  strawberry mallow tarts, 145
  toasted treat, 27
Mazarine torte, 138
Meat loaf pie, 42
Meat pies and turnovers. *See also* Main dish pie(s); Main dishes
  beef Burgundy, 50
  cheeseburger, 42
  Cornish pasties, 48
  double meat, 48
  empanaditas, 35
  homespun sausage, 42
  meat loaf, 42
  plantation ham 'n chicken, 45
  shepherds', 50
  sombrero, 51
  Spanish meatball, 52
  steak and kidney, 49
Melba sauce, 66, 147
Meringue (for pie), 82
  brown sugar, 82
Meringue pie
  apple, 71
  lemon, 80
  lime, 81
  orange, 82
  parfait, and variations, 115
  shell, 19
  sour cream raisin, 82
Meringue torte, strawberry, 90
Mexicali puffs, 30
Mile high lemon pie, 85
Mince (meat) pie(s)
  chiffon, 89
  cream cheese, 122
  flaming, 122
  fried, 142
  old-fashioned, 122
  orange, 122
  pear, 61
  pecan, creamy, 125
  Santa Claus, 126
Mincemeat
  Christmas tree, 125
  sauce, tangy, 24
  tarts, 146

Miniature cream puffs, 132
Mint topping, 26
Mock sugar crisps, 153
Molasses apple pandowdy, 106
Mother's Day
  meringue parfait pie, 115
  party petal tarts, 117
Mushroom
  pizza, 51
  sauce, easy, 40

N

Napoleons, 136, 137
Neapolitan pie, 139
Nesselrode pie, 88
  chocolate, 133
New Year's Day pie(s)
  eggnog, 116
  meringue parfait, 115
Nut crust, 18
  butter-crunch, 18
  crunchy, 19
Nut pastry, 17

O

Old-fashioned
  lemon sauce, 23
  mince pie, 122
  pumpkin pie, 119
Olive-cheese balls, 31
Orange
  glacé, 66, 122, 147
  glaze, 25
  fresh, 142
  glazed cherry pie, 58
  hard sauce, 24
  pastry, 17
  pie
    chiffon, 83
    meringue, 82
    mince, 122
  prune tarts, 45
  sauce
    clear, 110
    flaming, 23
    hard sauce, 24
  topping, 120
    spiced cream, 25
  windmills, 27

P

Pandowdy, apple, 106
Pans, 7
Parfait pie(s)
  meringue, and variations, 115
  silhouette, 127

Parsley pinwheels, 45
Partridge-in-a-pear-tree pie, 125
Party petal tarts, 117
Pastries, continental, 136
Pastry. *See also names of pastries*
  blender for, 7
  celery seed, 17
  cheese, 17
  cinnamon, 17
  cloth and stockinet for, 7
  colored, 17
  cornmeal, 17
  crusts. *See* Crust(s)
  defrosting, 20
  dill, 17
  edges, 14
    pastry wheel for, 7
  egg, 18
  egg yolk paint for, 16
  electric mixer method, 9
  fans, flaky, 136
  freezing, 20, 21
  lattice top, 15
  lemon, 17
  mixes, 22
  nut, 17
    butter-crunch, 18
    crunchy, 19
  oil, 13
  one-crust pie, 11, 12, 13
  orange, 17
  poppy seed, 17
  puff
    freezing, 21
    streamlined, 135
  rolling pin for, 7
  sesame seed, 17
  snacks, leftover, 16
  standard, 8–12
    baked pie shell, 11
    condensed method, 12
    cutouts, 16
    electric mixer method, 9
    freezing, 20
    leftover, snacks, 16
    silhouettes, 16
    variations, 17
  topping, 49
  two-crust pie, 11, 12, 13
  variations, 17
  wheel, 7
Peach
  cobbler
    fresh, 151
    quick, 152
  dumplings, 153
  melba tarts, 147

INDEX

Peach pie(s)
　blossom, 67
　blueberry, 66
　brown sugar, 65
　canned, 65
　easy, 78
　fresh, 64
　fried, blushing, 142
　frozen, 65
　glacé, 90
　green apple, 65
　melba, 66
　peaches 'n cream, 67
Peanut butter
　crust, 19
　pudding pie, 78
Pear
　cobbler, quick, 152
　pie, 61
　　canned, 61
　　crumble-topped, 61
　　mincemeat, 61
　　rhubarb, 73
Pecan
　glaze, crunchy, 25
　pie, 100
　　apple, 68
　　apple, upside-down, 72
　　chocolate, 100
　　creamy mince, 125
　　deluxe, 100
　　tarts, 148
　　topping, 61
Penny surprises, 35
Pepperoni pizza, 51
Perfect pineapple pie, 75
Perky pastries, 16
Pie meringue, 82
Pies, dessert. See names of pies
Pies, main dish. See Main dish pie(s)
Pineapple pie
　almond-crunch, 61
　cherry, 62
　fresh, 62
　mallow, 94
　perfect, 75
Pink peppermint pie, 116
Pizza, 51
　anchovy, 51
　bambinos, 36
　ground beef, 51
　mushroom, 51
　pepperoni, 51
　sausage, 51
　shrimp, 51
　Spanish, 52
　topping, 51

Plantation ham 'n chicken pie, 45
Plum pie, 67
Pocketbooks (appetizers), 33
Poppy seed pastry, 17
Prune
　orange tarts, 145
　pie
　　apricot, 67
　　Italian prune, fresh, 110
Pudding pie(s)
　banana sour cream, 79
　cherry-chocolate, 79
　chocolate, 78
　　sour cream, 79
　fruit cream, 79
　peach, easy, 78
　peanut butter, 78
　strawberry glacé cream, 79
　vanilla sour cream, 79
Pudding-filled Napoleons, 136
Puff(s)
　cheese, Italian, 31
　crabmeat, 31
　cream. See Cream puff(s)
　Danish, 131
　　individual, 131
　Italian cheese, 31
　Mexicali, 30
Puff pastry
　appetizers, streamlined cheese, 37
　dough, streamlined, 135
　freezing, 21
Pumpkin pie(s)
　baked Alaska, 131
　cheese, 119
　chiffon, 121
　　surprise, 121
　crumble-topped, 120
　dark and spicy, 120
　freezing, 20
　frosty, 117
　ice-cream, 120
　old-fashioned, 119
　surprise chiffon, 121
　toppings. See Topping(s)
Pumpkins, cheese, 27

Q

Quiche Lorraine, 50
Quick
　cobblers
　　blueberry, 152
　　cherry, 152
　　peach, 152
　　pear, 152
　Lorraine tarts, 36

R

Raisin pie, 105
　frosted apple, 117
　sour cream, meringue, 82
　spicy walnut, 75
Raspberry pie
　chiffon, 87
　glacé, 90
　grape and, 57
　minute, 93
Raspberry sauce, 78
Rhubarb pie
　custard, 109
　fresh, 73
　frozen, 73
　pear, 73
　strawberry, 73
Rolling pins, 7
Roses, lemon, 27
Rum
　flavored whipped cream, 135
　sauce, browned butter, 24

S

St. Patrick's Day pie, 115
Salmon turnovers, 41
Sandwiches (appetizers), 33
Santa Claus pie, 126
Sauce
　butter-rum, browned, 24
　butterscotch, 24
　chocolate, 127
　cinnamon blueberry, 23
　cucumber, 41
　dark sweet cherry, 23
　easy mushroom, 40
　egg, 40
　flaming orange, 23
　fudge, 24
　hard, and variations, 24
　lemon, old-fashioned, 23
　melba, 66, 147
　mincemeat, tangy, 24
　orange
　　clear, 110
　　flaming, 23
　raspberry, 78
　rum, browned butter, 24
　strawberry, 23, 139
　tangy mincemeat, 24
　tomato, 48
Sausage(s)
　cocktail kabobs, 30
　double meat pie, 48
　homespun pie, 42
　pizza, 51

Savory surprises, 31
Schnitz pie, 105
Scrambled eggs in puffy bowl, 46
Seafood
　crab rémoulade pie, 40
　crabmeat puffs, 31
　salmon turnovers, 41
　shrimp
　　dip, 37
　　pizza, 51
　　supreme, 40
　tuna pie, 40
Seasonal chart for fruit, 63
Sesame seed pastry, 17
Shell(s)
　baked
　　pie, 11
　　tart, 146
　defrosting, 20
　freezing, 20
　meringue pie, 19
Shepherds' pie, 50
Shoo-fly pie, 106
Short pie crust, 18
Shortcut Napoleons, 137
Shrimp
　dip, 37
　pizza, 51
　supreme, 40
Silhouette parfait pie, 127
Silhouettes, pastry, 16
Silken sour cream pie, 78
Slip-slide custard pie, 74
Snack(s). See also Appetizers
　leftover pastry, 16
　stacks, 16
Sombrero pie, 51
Sour cream pie(s)
　banana, 79
　cherry-chocolate pudding, 79
　chocolate, 79
　fruit, 79
　raisin meringue, 82
　silken, 78
　strawberry glacé, 79
　vanilla, 79
Sour cream topping, 119
　spicy, 25
　strawberry, 62
Spanish
　meatball pie, 52
　pizza, 52
Spiced orange cream topping, 25
Spicy
　sour cream topping, 25
　walnut raisin pie, 75

Spiral lattice top, 15
Steak and kidney pie, 49
Strawberry
  glacé, 79
    cream pie, 79
    pie, 90
  mallow tarts, 145
  meringue torte, 90
  sauce, 23, 139
  sour cream topping, 62
  torte, Chantilly, 128
  turnover, 148
Strawberry pie, 57
  chiffon, 87
    frozen, 87
  glacé, 90
    cream, 79
  minute, 93
  rhubarb, 73
  snowcap, 139
Streamlined puff pastry
  cheese appetizers, 37
  dough, 135
Sugar
  crisps, mock, 153
  glaze, 135
Summer jewel
  pie, 66
  tarts, 147
Sundae bubble crown, 132
Surprise pumpkin chiffon pie, 121
Sweet potato pie, 100

T

Tangy mincemeat sauce, 24
Tart(s)
  baked Alaska, 147
  chess, 147
  easy foil, 146
  jiffy, 144
  lemon curd, 144
  mincemeat, 146
  party petal, 117

Tart(s) *(cont.)*
  peach melba, 147
  pecan, 148
  prune-orange, 145
  quick Lorraine, 36
  shells
    baked, 146
    jiffy petal, 146
  strawberry mallow, 145
  summer jewel, 147
Tartlets
  fruited cheese, 137
  jam, 136
Thanksgiving Day pies
  meringue parfait, 115
  mince
    cream cheese, 122
    flaming, 122
    old-fashioned, 122
    orange, 122
  pumpkin
    cheese, 119
    chiffon, 121
    crumble-topped, 120
    dark and spicy, 120
    ice cream, 120
    old-fashioned, 119
    surprise chiffon, 121
Thousand leaves torte, 132
Toasted
  coconut crust, 18
  marshmallow treat, 27
Toffee whipped topping, chocolate, 26
Tomato sauce, 48
Topper(s). *See* Topping(s)
Topping(s). *See also* Garnishes; Glaze; Sauce
  cheese, 42
  cheesecake, 96
  cheese-marron, 136
  cherry, 116
  cream cheese, whipped, 25
  crumb, 68
  crumble, 108

Topping(s) *(cont.)*
  Della Robbia wreath, 126
  low-calorie whipped, 25
  orange, 120
  pastry, 49
  pecan, 61
  pizza, 51
  sour cream, 119
    spicy, 25
    strawberry, 62
  spiced orange cream, 25
  spicy sour cream, 25
  strawberry sour cream, 62
  whipped
    cream. *See* Whipped cream
    cream cheese, 25
Torte
  chocolate-mocha pastry, 128
  mazarine, 138
  strawberry
    Chantilly, 128
    meringue, 90
    thousand leaves, 132
Triple-cheese appetizer wheel, 34
Tuna pie, 40
Turnover(s)
  apple, 142
  Cornish pasties, 48
  date, 142
  empanaditas, 35
  salmon, 41
  strawberry, 148
Turn-ups, apricot, 152
Tutti-frutti pie, 84
Twister lattice top, 15
Twists (appetizers), 33

U

Upside-down apple-pecan pie, 72

V

Valentine's Day pies
  cherries on a cloud, 116
  meringue parfait, 115
Vanilla
  cream pie, 77
  glaze, 25
  sour cream pie, 79

W

Wafers, cream, 148
Walnut raisin pie, spicy, 75
Washington pie, 104
Washington's Birthday pie, 115
Whipped cream
  favorites, 26
  frozen, 27
  rum-flavored, 135
  sweetened, 26
  topping(s)
    candy fluff, 26
    caramel fluff, 26
    chocolate toffee whipped, 26
    heavenly, 26
    honey-ginger cream, 26
    mint, 26
    peanut crunch, 26
    pink peppermint fluff, 26
    spiced orange, 25
Whipped cream cheese, 25
Whipped filling, low-calorie, 94
Whipped topping, low-calorie, 25
White Christmas pie, 121
Windmills, orange or lemon, 27

Y

Yankee Doodle pie, 41